Modernity
on Endless Trial

Modernity
on Endless Trial

Leszek Kolakowski

The University of Chicago Press
Chicago and London

The University of Chicago Press, Chicago 60637
The University of Chicago Press, Ltd., London
© 1990 by The University of Chicago
All rights reserved. Published 1990
Paperback edition 1997
Printed in the United States of America
01 00 99 98 97   5 4 3 2

Library of Congress Cataloging-in-Publication Data

Kołakowski, Leszek.
    Modernity on endless trial / Leszek Kolakowski.
        p.   cm.
    ISBN 0–226–45045–7 (cloth)
    ISBN 0–226–45046–5 (paperback)
    1. Civilization, Modern—20th century. 2. Philosophy,
Modern—20th century. 3. Civilization—Philosophy. I. Title.
CB430.K64   1990
909.82—dc20   90–35966
                                                        CIP

Contents

Foreword

The essays selected for this book were written on various occasions and in various languages between 1973 and 1986. They do not purport to offer any "philosophy." They are, rather, semiphilosophical sermons in which I was trying to point out a number of unpleasant and insoluble dilemmas that loom up every time we attempt to be perfectly consistent when we think about our culture, our politics, and our religious life. More often than not we want to have the best from incompatible worlds and, as a result, we get nothing; when we instead pawn our mental resources on one side, we cannot buy them out again and we are trapped in a kind of dogmatic immobility. We might imagine ourselves to be treasure hunters in a forest, but we spend our effort on evading ambushes, and if we succeed, our success is precisely that: evading ambushes. This is a net gain, of course, but not the one we were after.

Therefore these essays are not edifying. They are rather appeals for moderation in consistency—a topic which I have been trying to look at from various angles for many years.

Since these texts were written separately and without any idea of them appearing together in one volume, some remarks might be repeated here and there. This does not worry me much, for who—apart from myself, under duress—would be persistent enough to wade through the whole thing, anyway?

Leszek Kolakowski
3 March 1990

PART ONE

On Modernity, Barbarity, and Intellectuals

Chapter One

Modernity on Endless Trial

If we are to believe Hegel—or Collingwood—no age, no civilization, is capable of conceptually identifying itself. This can only be done after its demise, and even then, as we know too well, such an identification is never certain or universally accepted. Both the general morphology of civilizations and the descriptions of their constitutive characteristics are notoriously controversial and heavily loaded with ideological biases, whether they express a need for self-assertion by comparison with the past or a malaise in one's own cultural environment and the resulting nostalgia for the good times of old. Collingwood suggests that each historical period has a number of basic ("absolute") presuppositions which it is unable clearly to articulate and which provide a latent inspiration for its explicit values and beliefs, its typical reactions and aspirations. If so, we might try to uncover those presuppositions in the lives of our ancient or medieval ancestors and perhaps build on this basis a "history of mentalities" (as opposed to the "history of ideas"); but we are in principle prevented from revealing them in our own age, unless, of course, the owl of Minerva has already flown out, and we are living in the twilight, at the very end of an epoch.

And so, let us accept our incurable ignorance of our own spiritual foundation and be satisfied with the survey of the surface of our "modernity," whatever the word might mean. Whatever it means, it is certain that modernity is as little modern as are the attacks on modernity. The melancholic "Ah, nowadays . . . ," "there is no longer . . . ," "in olden days . . . ," and similar expressions contrasting the corrupted present with the splendor of the past are probably as old as the human race; we find them in the Bible and in the *Odyssey*. I can well imagine paleolithic nomads angrily resisting the foolish idea that it would be better for people to have permanent dwellings or predicting the imminent degeneration of mankind as a result of the nefarious invention of the wheel. Mankind's history conceived as a degra-

Reprinted with revisions by permission of the publisher from *Encounter* (March 1986). Copyright © 1986 by Encounter, Ltd.

dation belongs, as we know, to the most persistent mythological topics in various parts of the world, including both the symbol of the exile and Hesiod's description of the five ages. The frequency of such myths suggests that, apart from other possible social and cognitive functions, they voice a universally human, conservative mistrust of changes, a suspicion that "progress," on second thought, is no progress at all, a reluctance to assimilate transformations, however beneficial in appearance, of the established order of things.

The changes go on, nonetheless, and they usually find a sufficient number of enthusiastic supporters. The clash between the ancient and the modern is probably everlasting and we will never get rid of it, as it expresses the natural tension between structure and evolution, and this tension seems to be biologically rooted; it is, we may believe, an essential characteristic of life. It is obviously necessary for any society to experience the forces both of conservation and of change, and it is doubtful whether any theory will ever provide reliable tools for measuring the relative strength of those opposite energies in any given society, so that we could add and subtract them from each other like quantifiable vectors and build on this basis a general schema of development, endowed with predictive power. We can only guess what gives some societies the ability to assimilate rapid changes without falling apart, what makes others satisfied with a very slow pace of development, and under precisely what conditions development or stagnation lead to violent crises or to self-destruction.

Curiosity, that is, the separate drive to explore the world disinterestedly, without being stimulated by danger or physiological dissatisfaction, is, according to students of evolution, rooted in specific morphological characteristics of our species and thus cannot be eradicated from our minds as long as the species retains its identity. As both Pandora's most deplorable accident and the adventures of our progenitors in Paradise testify, the sin of curiosity has been the main cause of all the calamities and misfortunes that have befallen mankind, and it has unquestionably been the source of all its achievements.

The impulse to explore has never been evenly distributed among the world's civilizations. Generations of scholars have asked why the civilization that emerged from joint Greek, Latin, Judaic, and Christian sources was so uniquely successful in promoting and spreading rapid and accelerating changes in science, technology, art, and social order, whereas many cultures survived for centuries in almost stagnant conditions, affected only by barely noticeable changes or sunk into slumber after short-lived eruptions of creativity?

There is no good answer. Each civilization is a contingent agglutination of various social, demographic, climatic, linguistic and psychological circumstances and any search for one ultimate cause of its emergence or decline seems very unpromising. When we read studies which purport to show, for example, that the Roman empire collapsed because of the widespread use of lead pots, which poisoned and damaged the brains of the upper classes, or that the Reformation can be accounted for by the spread of syphilis in Europe, we cannot keep from strongly doubting their validity. On the other hand, the temptation to look for "causes" is hard to resist, even if we guess that civilizations arise and crumble under the impact of uncountable factors, independent of each other, and that the same may be said about the emergence of new animal or plant species, about the historical locations of cities, the distribution of mountains on the surface of the earth, or the formation of particular ethnic tongues. By trying to identify our civilization, we try to identify ourselves, to grasp the unique, collective ego which we sense is necessary and whose nonexistence would be as inconceivable as my own nonexistence is for me. And so, even though there is no answer to the question "Why is our culture what it is?" it is unlikely that we can delete the question from our minds.

Modernity itself is not modern, but clearly the clashes about modernity are more prominent in some civilizations than in others and never have they been as acute as in our time. At the beginning of the fourth century, Iamblichos stated that the Greeks are by nature lovers of novelty (φύσει γὰρ Ἕλληνές εἰσί νεωτεροποιοί)[1] and disregard tradition—in contrast to the barbarians; yet he did not praise the Greeks for that reason, quite the contrary. Are we still heirs of the Greek spirit in this respect? Is our civilization based on the belief (never expressed in so many words, to be sure) that what is *new* is good by definition? Is this one of our "absolute presuppositions?" This might be suggested by the value judgment usually associated with the adjective *reactionary*. The word is clearly pejorative, and one hardly finds people who would be ready to use it to describe themselves. And yet to be "reactionary" means nothing more than to believe that in some of its aspects, however secondary, the past was better than the present. If to be reactionary automatically means to be wrong—and the adjective is almost

1. Iamblichos, *Egyptian Mysteries* 7.5.

invariably employed with this assumption—it appears that one is always wrong in believing that the past might have been better in whatever respect, which amounts to saying that whatever is newer is better. Still, we hardly ever state our "progressism" in such a bold manner. The same ambiguity haunts the very word *modern*. In German the word means both "modern" and "fashionable," whereas English and other European tongues distinguish the two meanings. And yet the Germans might be right; it is not clear how the distinction should be defined, at least in contexts where both adjectives are usable. To be sure, in some cases those words are not interchangeable; in expressions like *modern technology, modern science,* and *modern industrial management,* the word *fashionable* would not do, but it is hard to explain the difference between *modern ideas* and *fashionable ideas, modern painting* and *fashionable painting* or *modern clothes* and *fashionable clothes.*

In many instances the term *modern* seems to be value-free and neutral, not unlike *fashionable:* modern is what is prevailing in our time, and indeed the word is often used sarcastically (as in Chaplin's *Modern Times*). On the other hand, the expressions *modern science* and *modern technology* strongly suggest, at least in common usage, that what is modern is thereby better. The ambiguity of meaning reflects perhaps the ambiguity, just mentioned, which haunts our attitude toward changes: they are both welcomed and feared, both desirable and cursed. Many companies advertise their products with phrases implying both attitudes: "good old-fashioned furniture" or "soup like Grandma used to make" as well as "an entirely new soap" or "an exciting novelty in the laundry-detergent industry." Both kinds of tricks seem to work; perhaps the sociology of advertising has produced an analysis of how, where, and why those apparently contradictory slogans prove to be successful.

Having no clear idea what *modernity* is, we have recently tried to escape forward from the issue by talking about *postmodernity* (an extension or an imitation of the somewhat older expressions *postindustrial society, postcapitalism,* etc.). I do not know what postmodern is and how it differs from premodern, nor do I feel that I ought to know. And what might come after the postmodern? The post-postmodern, the neo-postmodern, the neo-antimodern? When we leave aside the labels, the real question remains: Why is the malaise associated with the experience of modernity so widely felt, and where are the sources of those aspects of modernity that make this malaise particularly painful?

How far back modernity may be extended depends, of course, on what we believe constitutes the meaning of the notion. If it is big business, rational planning, the welfare state, and the subsequent bureaucratization of social relationships, the extent of modernity is to be measured in decades rather than centuries. If we think, however, that the foundation of modernity is in science, it would be proper to date it from the first half of the seventeenth century, when the basic rules of scientific inquiry were elaborated and codified and scientists realized—thanks mainly to Galileo and his followers—that physics was not to be conceived as a report from experience but rather as an elaboration of abstract models never to be perfectly embodied in experimental conditions. Yet nothing prevents us from probing more deeply into the past: the crucial condition of modern science was the movement toward the emancipation of secular reason from revelation, and the struggle for the independence of the faculties of arts from those of theology in medieval universities was an important part of this process. The very distinction between natural and divinely inspired knowledge, as it was worked out in Christian philosophy from the eleventh century onwards, was, in its turn, the conceptual foundation of this struggle, and it would be difficult to decide which came first: the purely philosophical separation of the two areas of knowledge or the social process whereby the intellectual urban class with its claims to autonomy was established.

Shall we then project our "modernity" onto the eleventh century and make St. Anselm and Abelard its (respectively unwilling and willing) protagonists? There is nothing conceptually wrong with such an extension, but there is nothing very helpful about it either. We can go indefinitely far, of course, in tracing back the roots of our civilization, but the question so many of us have been trying to cope with is not so much when modernity started, but What is the core—whether or not explicitly expressed—of our contemporary widespread *Unbegahen in der Kultur*? Anyway, if the word *modernity* is to be useful, the meaning of the first question has to depend on the answer to the latter. And the first answer that naturally comes to mind is summed up, of course, in the Weberian *Entzauberung*—disenchantment—or in any similar word roughly covering the same phenomenon.

We experience an overwhelming and at the same time humiliating feeling of déjà vu in following and participating in contemporary discussions about the destructive effects of the so-called secularization of Western civilization, the apparently progressive evaporation of our religious legacy, and the sad spectacle of a godless world. It appears as if we suddenly woke up to perceive things which the humble, and not necessarily highly educated, priests have been seeing—and warning us about—for three centuries and which they have repeatedly denounced in their Sunday sermons. They kept telling their flocks that a world that has forgotten God has forgotten the very distinction between good and evil and has made human life meaningless, sunk into nihilism. Now, proudly stuffed with our sociological, historical, anthropological and philosophical knowledge, we discover the same simple wisdom, which we try to express in a slightly more sophisticated idiom.

I admit that by being old and simple, this wisdom does not necessarily cease to be true, and indeed I do believe it to be true (with some qualifications). Was Descartes the first and the main culprit? Probably so, even on the assumption that he codified philosophically a cultural trend that had already paved its way before him. By equating matter with extension and therefore abolishing the real variety in the physical universe, by letting this universe infallibly obey a few simple and all-explanatory laws of mechanics, and by reducing God to its logically necessary creator and support—a support, however, that was constant and thus robbed of its significance in explaining any particular event—he definitively, or so it seemed, did away with the concept of Cosmos, of a purposeful order of nature. The world became soulless, and only on this presupposition could modern science evolve. No miracles and no mysteries, no divine or diabolical interventions in the course of events, were conceivable any longer; all the later and still-continuing efforts to patch up the clash between the Christian wisdom of old and the so-called scientific worldview were bound to be unconvincing for this simple reason.

To be sure, it took time for the consequences of this new universe to unfold. Massive, self-aware secularity is a relatively recent phenomenon. It seems, however, from our current perspective, that the erosion of faith, inexorably advancing in educated classes, was unavoidable. The faith could have survived, ambiguously sheltered from the invasion of rationalism by a number of logical devices and relegated to a corner where it seemed both harmless and insignificant. For generations, many people could live without realizing that they were denizens of two incompatible worlds and, by a thin shell, protect the comfort of faith while trusting progress, scientific truth and modern technology.

The shell was eventually to be broken, and this was ultimately done by Nietzsche's noisy philosophical hammer. His destructive passion brought havoc into the seeming spiritual safety of the middle classes and demolished what he believed was the bad faith of those who refused to be witnesses to the death of God. He was successful in passionately attacking the spurious mental security of people who failed to realize what really had happened, because it was he who said everything to the end: the world generates no meaning and no distinction between good and evil; reality is pointless, and there is no other hidden reality behind it; the world as we see it is the Ultimum; it does not try to convey a message to us; it does not refer to anything else; it is self-exhausting and deaf-mute. All this had to be said, and Nietzsche found a solution or a medicine for the despair: this solution was madness. Not much could have been said after him on the lines he had laid out.

It might have appeared that it was his destiny to become the prophet of modernity. In fact, he was too ambiguous to assume this task. On one hand he affirmed, under duress, the irreversible intellectual and moral consequences of modernity and poured scorn on those who timidly hoped to save something from the old tradition; on the other hand he denounced the horror of modernity, the bitter harvest of progress; he accepted what he knew—and said—was terrifying. He praised the spirit of science against the Christian "lies," but at the same time, he wanted to escape from the misery of democratic leveling and sought refuge in the ideal of a barbarous genius. Yet modernity wants to be satisfied in its superiority and not torn asunder by doubt and despair.

Therefore Nietzsche did not become the explicit orthodoxy of our age. The explicit orthodoxy still consists of patching up. We try to assert our modernity but escape from its effects by various intellectual devices, in order to convince ourselves that meaning can be restored or recovered apart from the traditional religious legacy of mankind and in spite of the destruction brought about by modernity. Some versions of liberal pop-theology contribute to this work. So do some varieties of Marxism. Nobody can foresee for how long and to what extent this work of appeasement may prove successful. But the previously mentioned intellectuals' awakening to the dangers of secularity does not seem to be a promising avenue for getting out of our present predicament, not because such reflections are false, but because we may suspect they are born of an inconsistent, manipulative spirit. There is something alarmingly desperate in intellectuals who have no religious attachment, faith or loyalty proper and who insist on the irreplaceable educational and moral role of religion in our world and deplore its fragility, to which they themselves eminently bear witness. I do not blame them either for being irreligious or for asserting the crucial value of religious experience; I simply cannot persuade myself that their work might produce changes they believe desirable, because to spread faith, faith is needed and not an intellectual assertion of the social utility of faith. And the modern reflection on the place of the sacred in human life does not want to be

manipulative in the sense of Machiavelli or of the seventeenth-century libertines who admitted that while piety was necessary for the simpletons,
skeptical incredulity suited the enlightened. Therefore such an approach,
however understandable, not only leaves us where we were before but is
itself a product of the same modernity it tries to restrict, and it expresses
modernity's melancholic dissatisfaction with itself.

We ought to be cautious, however, when we make judgments about what
in our culture expresses modernity and what expresses the antimodern resistance. We know from historical experience that what is new in cultural
processes often appears disguised as the old, and vice versa—the old may
easily put on fashionable clothes. The Reformation was ostensibly and self-
consciously reactionary: its dream was to reverse the corrupting effects of
the centuries-long developments in theology, in the growth of secular reason, in institutional forms of Christianity, and to recover the pristine purity
of faith of apostolic times; but, by doing away with accumulated tradition
as a source of intellectual and moral authority, it in fact encouraged a movement which was exactly opposed to its intention; it liberated the spirit of
rational inquiry into religious matters because it made reason — otherwise
violently attacked — independent from the Church and tradition. Romantic nationalism often expressed itself as a nostalgic quest for the lost beauty
of the preindustrial world, but by thus praising the *praeteritum,* it contributed greatly to the eminently modern phenomenon which is the idea of the
nation-state; and such a superbly modern product as Nazism was a monstrous revival of those romantic reveries, thereby perhaps disproving the
notion that we can properly measure modernity on the axis "tradition-
rationality." Marxism was a mixture of an unequivocal enthusiasm for modernity, rational organization, and technological progress with the same
yearning after the archaic community, and it culminated in the utopian expectation of the perfect world of the future, in which both sets of values
would be implemented and make a harmonious alloy: modern factory and
the Athenian agora would somehow merge into one. Existential philosophy
might have appeared to be a highly modern phenomenon—which it was,
in its vocabulary and conceptual network—yet from today's perspective it
seems rather a desperate attempt to revindicate the idea of personal responsibility in face of a world in which progress insists that human persons
become, with their assent, no more than the media whereby anonymous
social, bureaucratic, or technical forces express themselves and in which
people are unaware that in letting themselves be reduced to irresponsible

instruments of the impersonal work of the society, they rob themselves of their humanity.

And so the "cunning reason" of history probably has not stopped operating, and nobody can guess, let alone have any certainty about, whether his own contribution to the collective life is to be seen in terms of modernity or of the reactionary resistance to it, nor, for that matter, which of them deserves support.

We might look for comfort in the idea that civilizations are able to take care of themselves and to mobilize self-correcting mechanisms or produce antibodies that fight the perilous effects of their own growth. The experience that led to this idea is not quite reassuring, though: after all, we know that the symptoms of a disease are often the organism's attempts at self-cure; most of us die as a result of self-defense devices which our bodies employ to combat external dangers. Antibodies can kill. So might the unpredictable cost of self-regulation kill a civilization before it regains the sought-after equilibrium. It is true, no doubt, that the criticism of our modernity—the modernity associated with, or perhaps put into movement by, the industrialization process—began as soon as did modernity itself, and that it has continued to spread since. Leaving aside the great eighteenth- and nineteenth-century critics of modernity—Vico, Rousseau, Tocqueville, the romantics—we know in our age a number of outstanding thinkers who have pointed out and deplored the progressive loss of meaning in the manipulation-prone *Massengesellschaft*. Husserl attacked, in philosophical terms, the inability of modern science to identity its own objects meaningfully, its satisfaction with the phenomenalist exactitude that improves our predictive and controlling power over things but is gained at the expense of understanding. Heidegger spotted the root of our descent into impersonality in the oblivion of metaphysical insight. Jaspers associated the moral and mental passivity of seemingly liberated masses with the erosion of historical self-awareness and the subsequent loss of responsible subjectivity and of the ability to base personal relationships on trust. Ortega y Gasset noticed the collapse of high standards in the arts and humanities as a result of intellectuals being compelled to adjust themselves to the low tastes of the masses. So, in spuriously Marxist terms, did the Frankfurt School people.

The critique of modernity, whether literary or philosophical, might be seen, in its immense variety, as a self-defense organ of our civilization, but so far it has failed to prevent modernity from advancing at an unprecedented speed. The lament seems all-pervading; whatever area of life we reflect upon, our natural instinct is to ask, What is wrong with it? And indeed we keep asking, What is wrong with God? With democracy? With socialism? With art? With sex? With the family? With economic growth? It seems as though we live with the feeling of an all-encompassing crisis without being able, however, to identify its causes clearly, unless we escape into easy, one-word pseudosolutions ("capitalism," "God has been forgotten," etc.). The optimists often become very popular and are listened to avidly, but they are met with derision in intellectual circles; we prefer to be gloomy.

It seems to us sometimes that it is less the content of changes and more their dizzy pace which terrifies us and leaves us in a state of never-ending insecurity, feeling that nothing is certain or established any longer and that whatever is new is likely to become obsolete in no time. There are a few people still living among us who were born on earth where there were no cars and no radios, and the electric light was an exciting novelty; during their lifetimes, how many literary and artistic schools have been born and died away, how many philosophical and ideological fashions have arisen and gone, how many states have been built or have perished! We all participate in those changes, and we bemoan them nonetheless, because they seem to deprive our lives of any substance we can safely rely upon.

I was told that near a Nazi extermination camp, where the soil was superbly fertilized with the ashes of uncountable cremated bodies of the victims, the cabbage grew so rapidly that it had no time to form a head and produced instead a stem with separate leaves; apparently it was not edible. This might serve as a parable for thinking about the morbid tempo of progress.

We know, of course, that we must not extrapolate the recent curves of growth—some of them exponential—in various areas of civilization, and that the curves must decline one way or another or perhaps turn into S-curves; we fear, however, that the change might come too late or be caused by catastrophes that will destroy the civilization by healing it.

It would be silly, of course, to be either "for" or "against" modernity *tout court,* not only because it is pointless to try to stop the development of technology, science, and economic rationality, but because both modernity and antimodernity may be expressed in barbarous and antihuman forms. The Iranian theocratic revolution was clearly antimodern, and in Afghanistan it is the invaders who carry in various ways the spirit of modernity against the nationalist and religious resistance of poor tribes. It is trivially true that very often the blessings and the horrors of progress are inseparably tied to each other, as are the enjoyments and the miseries of traditionalism.

When I try, however, to point out the most dangerous characteristic of modernity, I tend to sum up my fear in one phrase: the disappearance of taboos. There is no way to distinguish between "good" and "bad" taboos, artificially to support the former and remove the latter; the abrogation of one, on the pretext of its irrationality, results in a domino effect that brings the withering away of others. Most sexual taboos have been abolished, and the remaining few—like the interdiction of incest and pedophilia—are under attack; groups in various countries openly advocate their right to engage in sexual intercourse with children, that is, their right to rape them, and demand—so far unsuccessfully—the abolition of corresponding legal sanctions. The taboo regarding respect for the bodies of the dead seems to be a candidate for extinction, and although the technique of transplanting organs has saved many lives and will doubtlessly save many more, I find it difficult not to feel sympathy for people who anticipate with horror a world in which dead bodies will be no more than a store of spare parts for the living or raw material for various industrial purposes; perhaps respect for the dead and for the living—and for life itself—are inseparable. Various traditional human bonds which make communal life possible, and without which our existence would be regulated only by greed and fear, are not likely to survive without a taboo system, and it is perhaps better to believe in the validity of even apparently silly taboos than to let them all vanish. To the extent that rationality and rationalization threaten the very presence of taboos of our civilization, they corrode its ability to survive. But it is quite improbable that taboos, which are barriers erected by instinct and not by conscious planning, could be saved, or selectively saved, by a rational technique; in this area we can only rely on the uncertain hope that the social self-preservation drive will prove strong enough to react to their evaporation, and that this reaction will not come in barbarous form.

The point is that in the normal sense of "rationality" there are no more rational grounds for respecting human life and human personal rights than there are, say, for forbidding the consumption of shrimp among Jews, of meat on Friday among Christians, and of wine among Muslims. They are all "irrational" taboos. And a totalitarian system which treats people as exchangeable parts in the state machinery, to be used, discarded, or destroyed according to the state's needs, is in a sense a triumph of rationality. Still, it is compelled, in order to survive, reluctantly to restore some of those irrational values and thus to deny its rationality, thereby proving that perfect rationality is a self-defeating goal.

Chapter Two

Looking for the Barbarians
The Illusions of Cultural Universalism

I do not propose to engage in historical description; nor am I interested in prophesies. I intend, first, to consider a proposition of an epistemological nature, and second, to advance a value judgment, which I shall present as such. The value judgment concerns the defense of an idea which in recent decades has been the subject of such scathing attacks that it has now fallen almost entirely into disuse—the idea of Eurocentrism. The word itself no doubt belongs in that ample category of catchalls for miscellaneous rubbish: words we use lightly, regardless of their definition, and tend to stuff with a mixture of absurdities so blatant as not to be worth refuting; statements of fact, true or false; and value judgments, defensible or not defensible. The crucial point about such words is that in using them we direct attention to the absurdities with which they are vaguely associated while our purpose is to attack ideas which are very much worth defending. Indeed, the defense of such ideas may turn out to be crucial for the fate of civilization.

These words, then, are ideological par excellence, not because they contain normative elements, but because their function is to prevent the separation of issues which are logically distinct by concealing the normative content within statements that are ostensibly straight description. In journalistic jargon the list of such words is a long one, containing, apart from *Eurocentrism,* words like *elitism, liberalism,* and *male chauvinism,* as well as words with positive connotations, like *egalitarianism, social justice, humanism, liberation,* and so forth. The job of the word *Eurocentrism* is to bring into relief a number of absurdities associated with it and, by emphasizing them, discredit the idea as a whole. The following propositions are ex-

Translated from the French by Agnieszka Kolakowska from "Où sont les barbares? Les illusions de l'universalisme culturel," a lecture delivered in Collège de France in March 1980 and published in *Commentaire* (1980). Revised by the author in English.

amples of absurdities of this sort: Europeans have no reason to be interested in the rest of the world; European culture has never borrowed anything from other cultures; Europe owes her successes to the racial purity of the Europeans; it is Europe's destiny to hold eternal sway over the world, and her history is a tale of reason and virtue, triumphant and unsullied. The word should convey indignation at the ideologies of the slave traders of the eighteenth century (white traders, naturally) and of the partisans of the simplistic evolutionism of the nineteenth century. But its real function is different: it selects easy targets like these and lumps them, in one hazy, nebulous mass, with the very idea of European culture in all its specificity. This culture, as a result, becomes vulnerable not merely to outside threats but, perhaps even more dangerously, to that suicidal mentality characterized by indifference to our own distinct tradition, by doubt, indeed by an auto-destructive frenzy, all given verbal expression in the form of a generous universalism.

It is perfectly true that European culture is impossible to define—geographically, chronologically, or with regard to its content—without recourse to certain value judgments. How are we to define the spiritual territory which is Europe in a way that is not arbitrary? Its very name, scholars tell us, is Assyrian in origin; its founding text, the book par excellence, was written for the most part in a language which is not Indo-European; the vast richness displayed in its philosophy, art, and religion has drawn upon and absorbed the knowledge of Asia Minor, Central Asia, the Orient, and the Arab world. And if we ask *when* this culture was born, we shall find many possible replies: with Socrates; with Saint Paul; with Roman law; with Charlemagne; with the spiritual transformations of the twelfth century; with the discovery of the New World. It is not for lack of historical knowledge that we are hard put to deliver a precise verdict on the event; rather, it is because each of these replies is plausible if we agree from the start that such and such an ingredient is essential to or constitutive of the mixture, and *that* decision lies in the sphere of values. Similar problems arise when we come to talk of geographical limits: are we to include Byzantium? Or Russia? Or parts of Latin America? The discussion drags on endlessly unless we slice through to the root of the question, not by an appeal to history—which could bear out both replies—but by concentrating on the elements we believe to be essential constituents of the cultural space that we inhabit. It would, then, be a matter for a vote rather than a question of scientific research, were it not for the fact that the abolition of this culture cannot be voted through by a majority which declares that it no longer wishes to belong to it or that no such culture exists; its existence is assured by a minority which persists in believing in it.

It is, as we know, a matter of dispute at which point the Europeans became conscious of belonging to a cultural entity that was unique; one, at least, which could not be reduced to the unity of Western Christianity. There is no reason to suppose that those who fought at different historical periods against the Saracens in the Iberian peninsula, the Tartars in Silesia, or the Ottoman armies in the Danube basin shared such a consciousness of identity. Yet there is no doubt that it arose out of the unity of faith, and that it began to establish itself at a time when that unity was crumbling, not merely in islands of heresy, but throughout Europe. This was also a time of a swift and extraordinarily creative surge in the arts and sciences, which was developing at an ever-increasing rate and was to culminate in all the grandeur and all the miseries of today's world. And today, since fears and miseries are naturally dominant in our sensibilities, the very idea of European culture is being questioned. The point of contention is perhaps not so much the actual existence of this culture as its unique value and above all its pretensions to superiority, at least in certain fields of primary importance. It is this superiority which must be defined and affirmed.

A few years ago I visited the pre-Columbian monuments in Mexico and was lucky enough, while there, to find myself in the company of a well-known Mexican writer, thoroughly versed in the history of the Indian peoples of the region. Often, in the course of explaining to me the significance of many things I would not have understood without him, he stressed the barbarity of the Spanish soldiers who had ground the Aztec statues into dust and melted down the exquisite gold figurines to strike coins with the image of the emperor. I said to him, "You think these people were barbarians; but were they not, perhaps, true Europeans, indeed the last true Europeans? They took their Christian and Latin civilization seriously; and it is because they took it seriously that they saw no reason to safeguard pagan idols; or to bring the curiosity and aesthetic detachment of archaeologists into their consideration of things imbued with a different, and therefore hostile, religious significance. If we are outraged at their behavior, it is because we are indifferent both to their civilization and to our own."

It was banter, of course, but banter of a not entirely innocent kind. It may prod us into thinking about a question which could well be decisive for the survival of our world: is it possible for us to display tolerance and a benevolent interest toward other civilizations without renouncing a serious interest in our own? In other words, to what extent is it conceivable for us to affirm our exclusive membership in one civilization without wanting to destroy the others? If it is true that one renounces barbarity only with respect to one's own culture, it follows that the only civilizations capable of nonbarbarity are those which cannot survive—not a comforting conclusion, and not, I believe, a true one. I believe, on the contrary, that the development of our civilization contains arguments that bear out its falsity. In what sense is it true to say that the soldiers of Cortés were barbarians? There is no doubt that they were conquerors, rather than conservers of monuments, and they were cruel, greedy, and merciless. Very likely they were also pious, sincerely attached to their faith, and convinced of their spiritual superiority. If they were barbarians, it was either because all conquerors are barbarians by definition or because they showed no respect for people who had different customs and worshipped different gods; in short, because the virtue of tolerance toward other cultures was lacking in them.

But here a difficult question arises: to what extent is respect for other cultures desirable, and at what point does the very desire not to appear barbaric, admirable as it is, itself become indifference to, or indeed approval of, barbarity? The term *barbarian* was initially used of someone who spoke an incomprehensible tongue, but soon the word became charged with a pejorative meaning in the cultural sense. Anyone who has studied philosophy will remember the famous prologue of Diogenes Laertius, in which he attacks the misguided notion that there was philosophy before the Greeks among the barbarians, the Indian gymnosophists, and the Babylonian or Celtic priests: an attack on cultural universalism and the cosmopolitanism of the third century. No, he says, it is here, here among the tombs of Musaios the Athenian and Linos the Theban, son of Hermes and Urania, that philosophy and the human race were born. He cites the bizarre customs of Chaldean magicians and the wild beliefs of the Egyptians; he is outraged that the name of *philosopher* might be applied to Orpheus of Thrace, a man not ashamed to invest the gods with even the basest of human passions. Here, in this defensive self-affirmation, written at a time when the ancient myths had lost their vitality or become sublimated in philosophical speculation, and when the cultural and political order was visibly in a state of decomposition, a kind of doubt has already crept in. Those who would inherit that order were barbarians—to wit, Christians. We sometimes imagine, under the influence of Spenglerian philosophy or some other kind of "historical morphology," that we live in a similar age, the last witnesses of a condemned civilization. But condemned by whom? Not by God, but by some supposed "historical laws." For although we do not know any historical laws, we are in fact capable of inventing them quite freely, and such laws, once invented, can then be realized in the form of self-fulfilling prophecies.

But what we feel about this is ambiguous and possibly contradictory. On one hand, we have managed to assimilate the kind of universalism which refuses to make value judgments about different civilizations, proclaiming their intrinsic equality; on the other hand, by affirming this equality we also affirm the exclusivity and intolerance of every culture—the very things we claim to have risen above in making that same affirmation.

There is nothing paradoxical in this ambiguity, for even in the midst of this confusion we are affirming a distinctive feature of European culture at the peak of its maturity: its capacity to step outside its exclusivity, to question itself, to see itself through the eyes of others. It was at the very beginning of the conquest that Bishop Bartolomé de las Casas launched his violent attack against the invaders in the name of those same Christian principles which they professed. Regardless of the immediate results of his struggle, he was one of the first to turn against his own people in an attempt to defend others and to denounce the destructive effects of European expansionism. It took the Reformation and the beginning of the religious wars to spread a generalized skepticism about Europe's pretensions to spiritual superiority. It began with Montaigne and came to be commonplace among the Libertines and the precursors of the Enlightenment . It was also Montaigne who (following Rosario, whose name was later to gain fame through an article in Bayle's dictionary) compared man to animals only to concede superiority to the latter, and thus initiated the trend, later so popular, of regarding the human race as a whole with contempt. Seeing one's own civilization through the eyes of others in order to attack it became a literary mannerism prevalent in the writings of the Enlightenment, and the "others" could equally well be Chinese, Persians, horses, or visitors from space.

I mention all these well known things only in order to say the following: we may quite plausibly claim that Europe, at the same time as she acquired, perhaps largely thanks to the Turkish threat, a clear consciousness of her own cultural identity, also began to question the superiority of her values, thus setting in motion the process of endless self-criticism which was to become the source not only of her strength but of her various weaknesses and her vulnerability.

This capacity to doubt herself, to abandon—albeit in the face of strong resistance—her self-assurance and self-satisfaction, lies at the heart of Europe's development as a spiritual force. She made the effort to break out of the closed confines of ethnocentricity, and her ability to do so gave definition to the unique value of her culture. Ultimately we may say that Europe's cultural identity is reinforced by her refusal to accept any kind of closed, finite definition, and thus she can only affirm her identity in uncertainty and anxiety. And although it is true that all sciences, social and natural, either were born or reached their maturity (maturity in a relative sense, of course, from the perspective of what they are today) within European culture, there is one among them which, because of its very content, is the European science par excellence: anthropology.

The anthropologist (I have in mind contemporary anthropology, not Frazer's or Morgan's) must suspend his own norms, his judgments, his mental, moral, and aesthetic habits in order to penetrate as far as possible into the viewpoint of another and assimilate his way of perceiving the world. And even though no one, perhaps, would claim to have achieved total success in that effort, even though total success would presuppose an epistemological impossibility—to enter entirely into the mind of the object of inquiry while maintaining the distance and objectivity of a scientist—the effort is not in vain. We cannot completely achieve the position of an observer seeing himself from the outside, but we may do so partially. It seems obvious to us that an anthropologist cannot understand a savage completely unless he himself becomes a savage and thus ceases to be an anthropologist. He may suspend judgment, but the very act of suspending judgment is culturally rooted: it is an act of renunciation, possible only from within a culture which, through learning to question itself, has shown itself capable of the effort of understanding another.

For this reason the anthropologist's stance is not really one of suspended judgment; his attitude arises from the belief that description and analysis, freed from normative prejudices, are worth more than the spirit of superiority or fanaticism. But this, no less than its contrary, is a value judgment. There is no abandoning of judgment; what we call the spirit of research is a cultural attitude, one peculiar to Western civilization and its hierarchy of values. We may proclaim and defend the ideals of tolerance and criticism, but we may not claim that these are neutral ideals, free from normative assumptions. Whether I boast of belonging to a civilization that is absolutely superior or, on the contrary, extol the noble savage, or whether, finally, I say all cultures are equal, I am adopting an attitude and making a judgment, and I cannot avoid doing so. This does not mean that it makes no difference whether I adopt one position rather than another; it means that by adopting one I reject or condemn others. To adopt none, even implicitly, is impossible once I become aware of the existence of other civilizations.

While the first two of the attitudes I have mentioned are sufficiently clear, the third—that all cultures are equal—requires some explanation. If taken in its strong sense, it seems to lead to contradiction and lapses into a paradox analogous to that of consistent skepticism.

The word *culture,* in common parlance, encompasses all forms of behavior particular to humans: techniques and customs, rituals and beliefs, artistic expression, educational systems, laws. The extent to which all these spheres of life may be universalized is, of course, subject to gradation, beginning, on the lowest rung, with language, the least comprehensible and the least universalizable, and ending with mathematics, unquestionably the most universalizable, both actually and potentially. When we say that all cultures are equal, we have in mind the more specific, less universal disciplines; primarily it is art that we mean, and it seems that what we intend by saying this is to deny that there are any supracultural, transcendental norms we might use as a base for aesthetic judgment and comparison, in terms of value, between different forms of artistic expression.

No more can we discern the presence of such universal rules in moral and intellectual life. If there are suprahistorical rules, rules that hold for all known cultures, like the rules of bivalent logic or the prohibition of incest, this is no proof that such rules are valid in the transcendental sense.

Nonetheless, when we apply the principle *all cultures are equal,* we see that there is a difference between artistic expression on the one hand and moral, legal, and intellectual rules on the other. In the sphere of art, tolerance comes easily, either because we are indifferent or because we see nothing logically wrong in the confrontation of different aesthetic criteria. Indeed, universalism tempts us, and we like to imagine ourselves capable of entering into the aesthetic perceptions of all cultures, as if Japanese art, for example, were as accessible to us as the European baroque, as if we were able to participate fully in that perception without an equally full insight into the rituals and language of that civilization (indeed with no knowledge of it at all).

But this is the least dangerous of the illusions of universalism. It is in domains with a direct bearing on our behavior that the confusions universalism engenders become genuinely threatening—in the spheres of religion and morality, law, and intellectual rules. Here we face differences which are indeed contradictory, genuinely conflicting norms which cannot coexist in mutual indifference, to be exhibited side by side like museum pieces from different civilizations. If the phrase *all cultures are equal* is to mean more than that people live and have lived in different traditions and fulfill their aspirations within them, then it must mean one of three things. It may mean that I live in a particular culture, and other cultures do not interest me; or that there are no absolute, ahistorical standards by which to judge any culture; or, finally, it may mean that, on the contrary, such standards do exist, and according to them all mutually conflicting rules are equally valid. While this last attitude, insofar as it assumes approval of mutually exclusive rules, is impossible to maintain, the first may, by contrast, be held with consistency. But in that case the way it has been expressed is misleading; for if that is the meaning with which I use the phrase, I do not really want to say that all cultures are equal, but rather that all other cultures are of no interest to me, and I am satisfied with my own. It is the second version, then, that deserves genuine attention, for it is quite prevalent, and it is probably impossible to maintain coherently.

It is indeed possible to argue that, revealed truth apart, all systems of values are immune from logical and empirical attack as long as they are internally consistent; it is not possible to prove—in the proper sense of the word—that religious tolerance is actually *better* than a regime in which people are sentenced to death for christening their children, that equality in the face of the law is superior to a legal system which confers privileges on certain castes, that freedom is better than despotism, and so on. It is no good saying that these things are obvious, because our sense of what is obvious and what is not is also culturally determined; any appeal to the obvious will therefore lead us into a vicious circle. And yet we cannot avoid having a preference in such matters, whether or not we are able to justify it. A European who says that all cultures are equal does not normally mean that he would like to have his hand cut off if he is caught falsifying his tax forms, or be subjected to a public flogging (or, in the case of a woman, a stoning) if caught making love to a person who does not happen to be his legal wife (or husband). To say, in such a case, "This is the law of the Koran, and we must respect traditions other than our own" essentially amounts to saying, "That would be dreadful if it happened here, but for those savages it's just the right thing." Thus it is not respect but contempt for other traditions that we are expressing, and the phrase *all cultures are equal* is the least suitable to describe such an attitude.

But if we try to persist in our traditions while maintaining respect for others, we shall soon find ourselves up against the antinomy of skepticism mentioned above. We affirm our belonging to European culture by our ability to view ourselves at a distance, critically, through the eyes of others; by the fact that we value tolerance in public life and skepticism in our intellectual work, and recognize the need to confront, in both the scientific and legal spheres, as many opinions as possible; in short, by leaving the field of uncertainty open. And while we concede all this, we also maintain, tacitly or explicitly, that a culture capable of expressing these ideas in a vigorous way, defending them, and introducing them, however imperfectly, into its life, is a superior culture. If we behave fanatically, if we protect our exclusivity to the extent that we will not consider other arguments, if we are incapable of self-questioning, then we think we are behaving barbarically; consequently we must also consider barbaric the fanatics of other traditions, locked, like us, into their own exclusivity. One cannot be skeptical to the extent of failing to notice the difference between skepticism and fanaticism; that would be tantamount to being skeptical to the extent of no longer being skeptical.

Of course, the paradox of skepticism has been recognized since antiquity, and as a way out of it, a radical solution was proposed: that the skeptic should remain silent, and in particular that he could not voice his skepticism without at the same time betraying it.

This solution is no doubt possible, but it is not amenable to discussion; once we begin to discuss it, we fall into the very trap of pragmatic antinomy that we had been trying to avoid. We may plausibly claim that the perfectly consistent skeptic will remain silent, and that for this reason we shall never know the names of the great skeptics, as they never said anything. But as soon as we open our mouths we find ourselves under constraint.

Cultural universalism comes up against exactly the same difficulty. It contradicts itself if its generosity extends to ignoring the differences between universalism and exclusivity, tolerance and intolerance, itself and the barbarity; and it contradicts itself if, in order to avoid the temptations of barbarity, it concedes *to others* their right to be barbarians.

My own claims are thus instances of inconsistent skepticism and inconsistent universalism: skepticism and universalism, in other words, of a kind that avoid this paradox by remaining within certain limits, beyond which the difference between themselves and barbarity becomes blurred.

To say as much in this context is to affirm the superiority of European culture as a culture capable of uncertainty about its own standards and able to preserve that uncertainty. Thus I believe that there is an important reason to preserve the spirit of Eurocentrism in this sense. And this belief presupposes that certain values particular to that culture—to wit, its self-critical faculties—should be not only defended but indeed propagated, and that by definition they cannot be propagated through violence. In other words, universalism brings about its own paralysis if it does not see itself as being universal in just this sense of being suitable for propagation.

This discussion is no mere juggling of concepts. Europe is now under pressure from the barbarity of totalitarianism, which feeds on the West's hesitations regarding its own cultural identity and its lack of will to insist upon its universality.

And yet acknowledging the universality of the European tradition does not by any means entail believing in an ideal world of uniformity, where we all share the same tastes, the same beliefs (or rather the same absence of beliefs), customs, and even language. On the contrary, what is wanted is a selective propagation, as it were, of the values which I have stressed and which have been the source of all of Europe's greatness. Of course this is easy to say; cultural influences act according to their own principles of selection, which are almost impossible to control. The first thing the rest of the world expects from European culture is military technology; civic freedoms, democratic institutions, and intellectual standards come last. Western technological expansion entails the destruction of dozens of small cultural units and languages, a process which really gives no cause for rejoicing.

There is nothing uplifting in the fact that a great family of Indo-European languages, the Celtic branch, is dying out before our very eyes, despite all efforts to halt the process of its extinction. The great old cultures are, of course, resisting, but we cannot predict the extent of their transformation after only a few dozen years of Western influence. Even the languages of old cultures, such as Hindi or Arabic, are giving way to European languages in the teaching of modern science; not, of course, because they are intrinsically incapable of keeping pace with scientific developments, but because they have been outdistanced by the competition. A sorry spectacle, and one we can do almost nothing about. If our destiny were to annihilate cultural variety in the world in the name of a planetary civilization, it could probably be accomplished only at the price of so radical a break in the continuity of tradition that human civilization as a whole, not merely particular civilizations, would be in danger of extinction.

Consider the following quotation:

> Our own descendants are not going to be just Western, like our-
> selves. They are going to be heirs of Confucius and Lao-Tse as
> well as Socrates, Plato, and Plotinus; heirs of Gautama Buddha
> as well as Deutreo-Isaiah and Jesus Christ; heirs of Zarathustra
> and Muhammed as well as Elijah and Elishah and Peter and
> Paul; heirs of Shankara and Ramanujah as well as Clement and
> Origines; heirs of the Cappadocian Fathers of the Orthodox
> Church as well as our African Augustine and our Umbrian Ben-
> edict; heirs of Ibn Khaldun as well as Bossuet; and heirs, if still
> wallowing in the Serbonian Bog of politics, of Lenin and Gan-
> dhi and Sun Yat-Sen as well as Cromwell and George Washing-
> ton and Mazzini.

This optimistic prophecy (optimistic, at least, in its intent) was written in 1947, and its author is Arnold Toynbee.[1] It expresses the ideal of a world made radically uniform, and it gives rise to grave doubts, even if we agree with Toynbee's criticism of Spengler's speculations about historical cycles. For what, in fact, would it mean for us to be "heirs" of all the prophets, philosophers, and statesmen listed here? In a trivial sense we are already the heirs of all these men, in that we live in a world they all helped to shape; but Toynbee clearly has in mind a heritage in a stronger sense, a positive continuity of ideas. But in order that our descendants may be heirs in this sense, we must admit that everything that makes the values and ideals of these people incompatible today will lose its significance; and then, far from having them all as our spiritual ancestors, we shall have no one at all.

The difference between Catholics and Protestants could conceivably vanish, but then Bossuet and Cromwell will not so much become synthesized by our descendants as vanish altogether, losing what was specific and essential to each; and *heritage* will have no discernible meaning. It is, similarly, difficult to imagine how someone who values spiritual liberty might one day consider himself the heir of Lenin or Mohammed. We can imagine the question of liberty losing all significance in some future society that is perfectly totalitarian and accepted as such by its members; but in that case our descendants will indeed be the heirs of Lenin, but not of George Washington. In short, to imagine our grandchildren combining all these conflicting traditions into one harmonious whole, being at once theists, pantheists, and atheists, advocates of liberalism and of totalitarianism, enthusiasts of violence and enemies of violence, is to imagine them inhabiting a world lying not only far beyond the scope of our imagination and prophetic gifts but

1. Arnold Toynbee, *Civilization on Trial* (New York, 1948), 90.

also beyond the possibility of any kind of tradition whatsoever; which means that they will be barbarians in the strictest sense.

Again, it is not a question of wordplay or conceptual juggling. We are all well aware that powerful cultural forces are indeed' pushing us towards unity, a barbarian unity built on the loss, the forgetting of tradition. One such force is the barbarity of totalitarianism of the Soviet type, which attempts, with a considerable (but, fortunately, diminishing) measure of success, to harness all spiritual forces to the service of the State, to nationalize everything, including the human individual, historical memory, moral consciousness, intellectual curiosity, science, and art. It also manipulates tradition, deforming it, ceaselessly mutilating and falsifying it according to the needs of the State. Another such force, of European provenance, is the spirit of technology. Born of the extraordinary successes of science—including its struggle against misery, sickness, and suffering—and rightly proud of its spectacular achievements, it has led us to doubt the value and the validity of any traditions that do not contribute to the progress of science and technology. The gradual reduction of the place and importance accorded to classical languages and historical disciplines as they are taught at secondary-school level throughout the world bears witness to its destructive influence. Needless to say, these forces do not act without encountering resistance; indeed, recent years have seen a certain resurgence of this resistance, as they have seen a partial renaissance of religious tradition—even if this renaissance has, at times, taken some grotesque and macabre forms.

There is no reason to think that these are mortal threats, or that our civilization is stricken with an incurable disease. Despite the defeats it has suffered, despite the mass of indigenous barbarity against which it has had to struggle and must continue to struggle, our civilization has not lost is momentum; the very fact that so many of its major ideas have been verbally assimilated throughout the world, that its institutional forms have been imitated *in name,* that tyrannical régimes insist upon the use of European signs and phraseology—all this is not negligible. Even the most ludicrously inept attempts to assume a European guise, to parade decked out in Western clothes, are proof that if barbarity is far from being defeated, the shame of being a barbarian has spread considerably; and the barbarian who is ashamed of his barbarity is half-defeated already, despite strong resistance from his other half.

It is quite true that the threat hanging over Europe does not reside merely in her own enfeebled will to self-affirmation; some barbaric aspects of Europe are indigenous. The sources of totalitarianism are largely European, and they may be traced, in their various forms, through the whole history of socialist utopias, nationalist ideologies, and theocratic tendencies. It turns out that Europe has not developed an immunity to its barbaric past, a past whose monstrous conquests we have seen with our own eyes; yet she has also shown herself capable of mobilizing powerful resources against it.

If we try to trace the origins of this resistance to barbarity, both foreign and indigenous, and if what we have in mind is a search for the "ultimate source" of Europe, we shall get stuck: all the Greek, Roman, Judaic, Persian, and other influences which mingled to produce this civilization, not to speak of material, demographic, and climactic conditions, whose importance may only be guessed at, are obviously not amenable to presentation in the form of vectors, each with its respective, calculable power. But if what we have in mind is a grasp of what constitutes the core of this spiritual region, and if we describe this core in the way I have suggested, as the spirit of uncertainty, incompleteness, and unestablished identity, we shall come to see more clearly how and why it is that Europe is Christian by birth.

One might suspect—it would be pretentious to call this suspicion a hypothesis—that there is a necessary link, a *vinculum substantiale,* uniting the doctrinal tradition of Western Christianity with the creative momentum that gave birth not only to Europe's scientific and technological achievements, but also to the idea of humanism as faith in the absolute value of the individual, and finally to that spirit of openness and capacity for self-questioning from which modern civilization sprang.

Such a suggestion might (indeed must) seem paradoxical, if we consider some familiar facts: that so many of the social and intellectual triumphs of the West were won in the face of stiff opposition from the Church; that this opposition proved both lengthy and obdurate; and that it encompassed as well crucial points in the evolution of the sciences, the shaping of modern democratic ideas, institutions, and social legislation—many things without which Europe as we know her today would be unthinkable.

The history of this opposition is not negligible; we cannot shrug it away as a series of insignificant accidents or consign it to oblivion as part of a distant and long-forgotten past. But this has no bearing on my question. Rather what I want to ask is whether there are grounds for seeking Christian inspiration in the movement of the Enlightenment, which carved out its path largely in defiance of the Church and often in defiance of Christianity. I have in mind enlightenment in the broadest sense, in accordance with Kant's well-known description of it as "man's emergence from an immaturity of which he himself is guilty": the totality of spiritual effort which urged forward the forces of secular reason and imagination, scientific curiosity, the passion to dominate matter, the courage to explore and the skill to analyze, the skeptical distrust of simple solutions, and the habit of questioning every solution obtained.

Now it seems to me that one may view Christian religiosity, both in its doctrinal aspects and as regards its particular sensitivity, as the seminary of the European spirit, and that one may do so without minimizing the dramatic conflict between the Enlightenment and the Christian tradition or reducing it to a mere misunderstanding. The outline of my speculations is as follows.

In the Christian faith, as in other great religions, an inevitable tension persists between the idea of a finite world through which the Creator is revealed, and the image of that same world as a negation of God; between a vision of nature as displaying the glory and goodness of God and one in which nature, through her corruption and her contingency, is seen as a source of evil; between the biblical *cuncta valde bona* and the earth as a place of exile or even, in the extreme version, almost as the fruit of God's sin. The Christian idea as it has been developed and expressed over the centuries has had to wage an unceasing battle with heretical tendencies which affirmed one of the elements of this tension while neglecting or forgetting about the other. Almost the entire history of heresies, viewed through the theological forms in which it was expressed, may be organized in this way, and the main problems in the history of dogmas and antidogmas will then appear as variations on the same theme: Christ's humanity *as against* his divinity; man's freedom *as against* grace and predestination; the visible Church *as against* the invisible Church; the law *as against* charity; the letter *as against* the spirit; knowledge *as against* faith; salvation through deeds *as against* salvation through faith; the State *as against* the Church; the earth *as against* Heaven; God the Creator *as against* God the Absolute. The balance maintained by these fatally ambiguous formulas could not but be continually disturbed; and what hung in this precarious, ever-swaying balance was not the condemnation of some heresy, nor prison or the stake for some rebellious spirit, but indeed, at times, the fate of civilization.

To succumb excessively to the gnostic temptation of condemning the body and the physical world as the kingdom of the devil, or at least as a region from which nothing worthwhile could be born, is to declare one's indifference to, indeed to condemn, all that takes place within civilization; it is morally to cancel secular history and secular time. It is a temptation that has been very marked throughout the troubled history of Christianity, and one to which Kierkegaard gave eloquent expression. Yet to succumb entirely to the contrary—let us call it, for the sake of simplicity, the Pantheist temptation—to glorify the world as it is and refuse to acknowledge the inevitability, or even the reality, of evil, is also to kill or weaken the will that is needed to triumph over matter.

On the one hand, then, there is the ascetic rejection of the world and its lures; on the other, its deification and the refusal to see evil in it. Christian thought oscillates ceaselessly between these two poles. The main current of Western Christianity has always been to persist in the search for ways to avoid this fatal choice, even though there is no lack of biblical passages one might cite to support either extreme. Europe has groped for and appears to have found, in Christian form, the measure it needed to develop its scientific and technical abilities: to persist in her wariness towards the physical world, not to the extent of condemning it as intrinsically evil in its entirety, but rather perceiving it as an adversary that should be dominated. The question arises whether the moral and metaphysical rejection of nature in Buddhist culture may not have been linked to that culture's relative technical stagnation, and whether an excessively far-reaching affirmation of nature did not go hand in hand with the feeble technological development in the Christian world of the East. These are, of course, no more than speculations, but they are difficult to avoid if one tries to understand the uniqueness of the extraordinary cultural flowering which took place in Europe. The dilemma may be extended to more limited questions, such as the affirmation and limitation of natural reason and the place of free will in salvation. One is tempted to see the whole struggle between humanism and the Reformation in terms of the conflict of these complementary principles, between which Christianity constantly strives to strike a stable balance that can never be achieved.

This is not the place for a discussion of particular dogmas. I want only to express my suspicion that modern humanism, born of the Christian tradition and about to turn against it, seems to have reached the point of turning against the *humanum* itself. The humanism outlined in Pico della Mirandola's famous *Discourse on Human Dignity*, a humanism defined by the idea of man's incompleteness, his inevitable state of hesitation, and the insecurity caused by his freedom of decision, is perfectly compatible with Christian teaching. A humanism that goes beyond this in allowing that man is free, not only in the sense that he can turn toward good or evil, but also in the sense that he can discover no rules of good and evil that he himself has not decreed, that no norms were given him either by God or by nature, and that it is man himself who possesses *legitimate and unlimited* power to shape these norms according to his will—such a humanism is not compatible with any recognizable form of Christianity.

There are grounds for supposing (although no decisive proof exists one way or the other) that in order to develop its potential, humanism had to take a non-Christian, even an anti-Christian, form; that if it had remained within the limits of tradition as defined by the Church and conformed to the spiritual tutelage of established theology, it would not have been capable of creating the climate of intellectual liberation in which Europe was formed. To suppose this is not to deny the Christian origins of humanism; it is possible to see, in the atheistic and violently anti-Christian humanism of the Enlightenment, an extreme form of Pelagianism, an extreme negation of original sin and an unqualified affirmation of the natural goodness of man. We may, in addition, suppose that this humanism, having obliterated all traces of its origins and done away with all limits to our freedom in establishing criteria of good and evil, has finally left us in the moral void that we are now so desperately trying to fill; that it has taken a stand against freedom and provided the pretexts for treating human beings like instruments to be manipulated.

One might venture an analogous argument, on the same dangerously vast scale, regarding the increase of confidence in secular reason during Europe's formation. Skepticism, which of course drew on Greek sources, was also developed largely in a Christian context. The humanist *quod nihil scitur* marked the collapse of scholastic certainty; at the same time it was a dramatic expression of the meeting of reason, searching within itself for its foundations, with the mysteries of faith. But despite the importance of the skeptical themes developed by Charron, Pascal, Huet and Bayle within the Christian conceptual framework, it was the non-Christian form of skepticism, expressed in the epistemological nihilism of David Hume, that proved victorious and effective; and in this form it has survived, almost unaltered, until today. Yet again it seems to have reached an intellectual impasse.

A Christian inspiration may also be seen at the roots of the ideas upon which modern democracy was founded. Locke's God, and the God of the American Declaration of Independence, were not merely rhetorical flourishes: the theory of the inalienable rights of man was developed from the Christian idea of a person as an inexchangeable value. Again, this theory was to establish itself despite resistance from the Church; and later, when its various imperatives proved less than perfectly compatible, and the idea of the State as the distributor of all material and spiritual goods took precedence over the idea of the inviolable rights of persons, it turned against itself. Thus the rights of man became the right of the State to possess man, and a foundation was laid for the idea of totalitarianism.

Everywhere we find the same doubly self-destructive process. The Enlightenment emerges from a reconsidered Christian heritage; in order to take root, it must defeat the crystallized and ossified forms of that heritage. When it does begin to take root, in an ideological humanist or reactionary shape, that is, in the shape of the Reformation, it gradually drifts away from its origins to become non-Christian or anti-Christian. In its final form the Enlightenment turns against itself: humanism becomes a moral nihilism, doubt leads to epistemological nihilism, and the affirmation of the person undergoes a metamorphosis that transforms it into a totalitarian idea. The removal of the barriers erected by Christianity to protect itself against the Enlightenment, which was the fruit of its own development, brought the collapse of the barriers that protected the Enlightenment against its own degeneration, either into a deification of man and nature or into despair.

It is only today that a spiritual movement on both sides is taking shape: Christianity and the Enlightenment, both gripped by a sentiment of helplessness and confusion, are beginning to question their own history and their own significance. From this doubt a vague and uncertain vision is emerging, a vision of new arrangements of which, as yet, we know nothing. But this double movement of self-questioning is itself a continuation of the very principle upon which Europe was founded; in this sense, therefore, Europe has remained true to herself in her state of uncertainty and disarray. If she survives the pressure of the barbarians, it will not be because of any ultimate solution she might one day discover, but rather thanks to a clear consciousness that such solutions do not exist anywhere; and *that* is a Christian consciousness. Christianity has neither found nor promised any lasting solution to man's temporal lot. It has thus provided us with a way out of the pessimism/optimism dilemma, if it is seen as a dilemma between belief in ultimate solutions and despair. The degeneration into despair is common among those who once believed in a perfect and ultimate solution and later lost that certainty. But it is the tradition of Christian teaching to shield us from both these perils: from the wild certainty of our infinite capacity for perfection on the one hand and from suicide on the other. The mainstream of Christianity has always been opposed to the spirit of millenarianism which swelled and proliferated along its outer edges and finally exploded, spectacularly, when it took an anti-Christian form. Christianity said, "The philosopher's stone, the elixir of immortality, these are superstitions of alchemists; nor is there a recipe for a society without evil, without sin or conflict; such ideals are the aberrations of a mind convinced of its omnipotence, they are the fruits of pride." But to admit all this is not to give way to despair. The choice between total perfection and total self-destruction is not ours; cares without end, incompleteness without end, these are our lot. Thus, in the doubt which Europe entertains about herself, European culture can find its spiritual equilibrium and the justification for its pretensions to universality.

Chapter Three

The Intellectuals

The intellectuals: in God's menagerie, are they necessary? For what? Are they mediators or producers? If the latter, what do they produce? The word? It appears, however, that the word is just a tool of mediation. Are they, then, producers of tools of mediation? Since the earliest periods of the division of labor, mediators have probably been useful and necessary: They carried products from one location to another and in return had to be compensated. Thus they were tradesmen, the carriers of goods in a physical sense. Actually, they did not produce anything, but they were indispensable to the spatial distribution of products. It was nevertheless physical work— the transferal of material goods. In the history of trade economy, the division of labor continued to develop: The tradesman did not need to move about any longer; he simply organized business and thus worked with pencil and words. No longer did wealth require a physically visible form, and money separated more and more from material appearances. At one time it was cattle, then gold, then bank notes and bonds; today our wealth consists mostly of electronic impulses in a bank computer, something invisible, almost abstract and incomprehensible.

Electronic impulses may be purchased and sold, they may be traded on, or they may cause one to go bankrupt or become rich—all in the sphere of the immaterial. For centuries there has existed a comparatively numerous category of people who are no longer mediators in the old sense, but who deal with the substance of mediation itself—money, which is today an invisible substance. These people are bankers, usurers, and stock brokers, and the medium of exchange has become a commodity itself.

The same has happened to the word, that is, the medium for exchanging and mediating commodities of mind. Besides people who professionally transmitted information, doctrines, commands, traditions, and so forth—

Translated from the German by Wolfgang Freis from "Die Intellektuellen," a lecture delivered over Bavarian radio, 1982. Revised by the author in English.

thus, besides teachers, prophets, scribes, priests, and messengers—there emerged a class of people early on who utilized the word as working material just as a banker used money. In their hands, the word became autonomous and ceased to be a mere medium of exchange; it was treated as a value by itself. Thereby the invisible substance of the word asserted itself as an independent area of reality, instead of being functionally related to the transmission of information, of truth or lie, of feelings or wishes.

The sphere of power, which perhaps at first emerged from necessary military and organizational functions, had assumed independence even earlier.

These three auxiliary tools of communication and organization established their own domain of existence and their own principles; once they became autonomous, modern civil society was built on the three pillars of money, power, and the word. A process of self-enlargement and self-procreation advances continuously in all areas, and corresponding layers are engaged in processing the three invisible substances; thus the money experts, the power-holders, and the word architects (that is, the intellectuals) are agents of this marvelous process of self-accumulation. Owing to them, money produces more money, power produces more power, and word produces more words.

Naturally, the notion that this is in fact production was repeatedly attacked, mostly by unsuccessful back-to-nature ideologies, which appeared within the last one-and-a-half centuries as various anarchistic utopian ideas. Nothing, they said, is actually produced in the spheres of money, power, and words; the existence of these three entities is only apparent; in reality, they are nothing, and they cannot be more than instruments of communication; their pseudoindependence serves to perpetuate the irrational privileges of unproductive and idle social classes. Money is necessary, if at all, to measure the relative worth of commodities and to facilitate exchange—anything beyond that is usury. In addition, a healthy society does not need a government beyond organizational functions. As far as the intellectuals are concerned, what are they but intellectual profiteers, producers of hollow words, babblers, and parasites who continuously exploit their pretended superiority—which consists only in their skill in manipulating words—to strengthen or improve their privileged status?

The entire history of the anarchistic movement reflects a suspicion, even a hatred, of intellectuals; numerous variants appear in the writings of Proudhon, Bakunin, Sorel, and Russian anarchists. The covert or even explicit presupposition of this aversion was the conviction that only production and whatever is necessary to it were important to human life, as if God had bestowed on man the ability to plow fields and build houses, and the remainder came from the devil.

It is hardly necessary to mention that all these execrations and attacks on intellectuals originated with intellectuals. They have, of course, always been the ones to express all ideologies—including those against intellectuals: that is indeed an important part of their function. Therefore it is tempting to view the act of questioning the usefulness of intellectuals as a practical antinomy: one has to be an intellectual oneself in order to thunder convincingly against intellectuals. There is indeed no other profession with such an innate tendency to question continuously its own legitimacy and right of existence. We don't ask, Why plumbers? or Why physicians? but the question Why intellectuals? has been asked as long as the profession has existed. Certainly, at times we ask, Why generals? or Why government? Why bankers? but these questions are not asked by generals, bankers, or government officials. The question, Why intellectuals? however, is among the most common and most favorite pursuits of intellectuals themselves. Naturally, the question is often put within special communities: the philosophers ask, Why philosophers? the poets, Why poets? Even if they do find good or bad reasons to justify their existence, the frequency of such examination betrays either a bad conscience or, at least, a feeling that their legitimacy is never secure or that the social or moral foundation of their work is not definite. And why? Why do intellectuals in particular feel compelled to defend their right to exist?

The answer is not difficult and seems to be founded in the nature of language, hence, in human existence. Just as it was part of the nature of money that, once created, it would develop into a peculiar autonomous commodity and produce interest rates and usury, so the future autonomy of the word perhaps arose with its nature from the very beginning, assuring that it would exceed its function as an instrument of exchange and reach the level of an independent entity.

Ever since objects, actions, and attributes were named by Adam, reality, which thus far had been perceptible without words, could not remain the same. The word does not operate just as a substitute for an object in certain circumstances, and it may not just represent or replace an object: the object itself is perceived necessarily through mediation of the word, that is, it is provided with meaning in the process of perception. Hence, not only is the word necessary to reproduce reality, it is reality's coproducer. The object is what it is only within an all-embracing linguistic network, only as its particle. The known world corresponds to this network, not on the basis of conventional symbolization, but in reciprocal determination, without either side taking precedence. One cannot decide whether the object or the word comes first without a vicious circle, since the object in the act of asking the question appears already supplied with meaning; it is already known and named. The world is not simply reproduced *in* language, it is appropriated only in the form of language.

Yet, since language is productive, it does not simply encompass the world; it anticipates the possible and examines the unreal, even the impossible; it has future tense, interrogative forms, and *modus irrealis* at its disposal, in past tense as well as present; thus it tends to question everything, including itself. It is a peculiarity of language that it has become not only autonomous but, moreover, self-reflective. Money became autonomous, but it cannot call itself into question. The word, however, can do that. Therefore, the intellectuals—those masters, manipulators, and tamers of the word—are both producers of all possible worlds and all-questioning, all-doubting revolutionaries. Under various circumstances, both money and the word are able to steer the world off its tracks; but money, even though it is self-reproducing, is not self-related, and cannot take objection to itself. But since language embraces all, including language itself, its creative and destructive potential is infinite. "Faciendi plures libros nullus est finis," Ecclesiasticus says: There is no end to the production of books.[1] In other words, the creative—or, if one prefers, the destructive—potential of the word, its ability to alter the perception of the world and thus the world itself, thereby creating new worlds, to consider the possible or even the impossible, and to question what is generally accepted—all that makes intellectuals a fatefully destabilizing element in society.

In saying so, we already presuppose a certain notion of the intellectual that coincides, it appears, with a notion commonly held. Speaking of intellectuals as a class, we do not think of all those whose profession relates to the word, but of those in whose work the word becomes, as it were, creative (as well as destructive); thus, we do not consider those who simply convey the word as mediators, but those who use it to obtrude a particular world perception on others in order to create thereby a new world.

A priest, who certainly works primarily with linguistic means, is not as such an intellectual: it is his task to preserve in ritual the holy word of religious tradition and transmit the inherited wisdom in sermons. Neither

1. Eccl. 12:12.

is a teacher as such an intellectual when he endeavors to convey the accumulated stock of knowledge and the technique of thinking to the young. Indeed, even scholars—linguists, historians, or archaeologists—are not intellectuals as long as they attempt to remain *true* to the material found or discovered in order to describe it and as long as they attempt to minimize their own intervention in the process. The intellectual, on the other hand, is not a researcher or discoverer in a strict sense; he lays claims beyond that: he uses the word to suggest his own world interpretation; he does not wish simply to transmit truth, but to create it. He is not a guardian of the word, but a word manufacturer.

Thus, by definition, is he a liar? No, at least not necessarily. In lying, the word is used legitimately, so to speak. When we are lying, we remain within the borders of the factual: we simply reverse, hide, or disfigure facts as we know them. Lies are a normal component of human behavior in military, public, and private matters, and they do not require creative powers. Lying uses the word in its common basic function as a means of exchange, not as a creator of worlds. In lying we remain true to the nature of the word and to nature itself. It may be argued that lying is embodied in prehuman behavior: mimicry, perhaps, may be seen as a lie of nature.

Intellectuals are not liars, but seducers. Of course, a lie may occasionally aid in their work, but it is not absolutely necessary. Drawing on the resources of the word, they desire to obtrude or suggest a view of the world that facts alone—whether they are presented correctly or falsely—could never produce. A view of the world does not emerge from an accumulation of facts; it also requires words to interpret, judge, and order the facts. Thus, by attempting to uncover, that is, to produce, the meaning of facts, the intellectuals—as philosophers, poets, writers of fiction, and political thinkers—turn out to be ideologists. That is to say that they uphold an idea of the world as it ought to be, and from it they derive a picture of the world as it is—not in the sense that the existing and the desired converge, but rather in the sense that from a world desired or imagined they derive the rules for how the facts of the existing world must be interpreted—or *what* the facts are in their essence.

But the intellectuals are masters and rulers of the word, and not its servants—at least in their own estimation. For that reason, they are destroyers of tradition even if they attempt to preserve it with the best of intentions, because to defend tradition on one's own already means to question it. Plato wished to ban poets from the ideal state. He believed, rightly, that poets destroyed the legacy of morals through their manner of portraying the gods. But one may go further than that: even those who venerate tradition are dangerous when they appear as intellectuals. Had Plato followed his argument, consequently, he would have recognized that he would fall victim to his own rules. The ideological state—that is, Plato's ideal republic as well as the modern totalitarian state—does not need intellectuals in the sense of people who independently question and take a position; it needs those who preserve the word of tradition, which provides legitimacy to established powers, without concessions. The intellectuals, on the other hand, always make themselves natural enemies of stability, either by relying on self-supported reason or by referring to other sources of wisdom independent of the ideological state—whether they are sophists in Socrates' Athens, early medieval dialecticians, or philosophers in the eighteenth century.

All that is sufficiently obvious. Less obvious is the difficulty we encounter in distinguishing clearly between defenders and destroyers of established ideologies in the past and the present. Every established ideology occasionally has to make headway against unexpected circumstances and new dangers. When existing and proven means will not suffice any longer, it takes people with a more imaginative faculty than the common ideological warrior has available to forge new intellectual weapons; it takes intellectuals. They usually attempt to beat the enemy with his own weapons and appropriate to themselves various components of his doctrine in order to render it innocuous within the transmitted ideology. The independent force of the word, however, carries them almost inevitably further than the defense requires and, for all their good intentions, they become destroyers of what they were determined to defend; indeed, they are often unable to avoid that in order to succeed.

Who was a more loyal guardian of Church doctrine than Thomas Aquinas in attacking the Averroists' demands for the full autonomy of secular reason? But in attacking them, he defined specific rules for how secular reason should be separated from faith and established the boundaries of its relative autonomy. With this clear distinction, he exposed Church doctrine to the same danger against which he had sought to defend it: from his adversaries he adopted the conceptually identifiable category, which then solidified its rights against church and Thomism.

Or—at the opposite pole within Christianity—who was a more irreconcilable enemy of secular reason, dialectics, and philosophy than Calvin? But by pitting his profound biblical conservatism against the haughtiness of scholasticism, he destroyed trust in the continuity of the Church as a source of interpretation of the doctrine. For the task of interpretation, he left to future generations only the very secular reason he so vigorously had condemned. In spite of his intentions, he thus created an intellectual environment that soon nurtured the advocates of natural religion and the deists. Descartes, with his irrefutable proofs of God's existence, contributed decisively to the development of European atheism, and the profoundly pious Pierre Bayle became the teacher par excellence of all skeptics of the Enlightenment. We do know, indeed, that the boundaries between great teachers and great heretics, in general, are never quite certain; if someone finally falls within one or the other category, it is mostly due to accidental circumstances.

Or—to take a contemporary example—who was a more loyal bedfellow of communism than Georg Lukács? And yet, despite his efforts and devoutness, all through his life he never managed to get on with the party and repeatedly was stigmatized, with most diverse labels, as a renegade. His intellectual mind was not satisfied with being faithful; he aspired to improve communist doctrine and to defend it even more forcefully than the party chiefs, which led him to various errors. Even though intellectuals are responsible to a large extent for the spread and consolidation of the communist world, it is generally plausible to think that they were contributing enormously to its decline as well. Sooner or later, obedience proved to be unbearable and irreconcilable with intellectual claims, and those among the intellectuals who did not completely renounce obedience and attack the doctrine from the outside, but rather attempted to improve it from the inside, were especially destructive. Today, when there are hardly any communist intellectuals left, and most of the doctrinal work rests in the trusted hands of obtuse party officials, the case of communism seems to be more secure: no more trouble with this pretentious and eternally dissatisfied species. But that is only half the truth: ideological security is important, but so is the ability to react to new ideological circumstances, and relinquishing this ability is the price one has to pay for comfortable safety. Thus, the fact that communism as an intellectual movement and, generally speaking, as an intellectual matter is as good as finished may be advantageous for the time being to the cause of communism on one hand; on the other hand, however, it must be considered as sign of its downfall. To have intellectuals within the pale of an ideological institution certainly causes endless vexation. At the same time, however, it shows that the institution is still alive and willing, to a certain degree, to confront new intellectual situations. In this sense it is possible to say that Christianity is steadily alive; communism, however, is not.

The question of the so-called responsibility of the intellectual has been discussed for decades. For obvious reasons such debates are generally fruitless. Why should intellectuals be specifically responsible, and differently responsible than other people, and for what? Their superiority, one may think, consists in a skill in using words; and if it is right to label them as seducers, they are able to seduce to either good or evil, of course. But as far as the distinction between good and evil is concerned—be it in moral or political matters—are they necessarily more reliable, are they less fallible guides than other people? Hardly. People who know somewhat more than most about the precariousness of all our judgments, who know better the history of many deceitful hopes and the failures of many excellent and well-intended ideas, and who generally are aware of the ambiguities of the human fate, ought to be more reasonable—one would say—in their political decisions and choices. As we all know, this is not always the case. The long history of terrible errors that so many intellectuals in our century have committed in their political choices and of their noisy identification with the most cruel tyrannies is well known and has been described repeatedly; it probably has contributed to the significant decline of their authority as leaders in political matters.

To talk about responsibility in the abstract is simple and unproductive, and in all specific discussions, the intellectuals are hardly less divided, and not necessarily for any better reasons, than everybody else. When they take up the subject, they usually do not have in mind "responsibility" in general—that is, the simple need to take sides in political or moral conflicts; rather, it is a question of supporting a certain matter that somebody is backing at the time. A mere feeling of responsibility is a formal virtue that by itself does not result in a specific obligation: it is possible to feel responsible for a good cause as well as for an evil one. It is certainly true that nobody in our world may declare himself to be unpolitical with good conscience, but from that it does not follow that one is obliged to identify oneself with an existing movement, ideology, or party.

In the case of the intellectuals, the only specific matter they are professionally responsible for is the good use—that is, the upright and least misleading use—of the word. It is less a matter of truth than of the spirit of truth, since nobody can promise that he will never be mistaken; but it is possible to preserve the spirit of truth, which means never to abandon a vigilant mistrust of one's own words and identifications, to know how to retract one's own errors, and to be capable of self-correction. That *is* humanly possible, and one should expect it from intellectuals since, for obvious reasons, the common human qualities of vanity and greed for power among intellectuals may have particularly harmful and dangerous results. If this sounds like trite nagging, so be it. One should consider, however, that no profession (if the term *profession* is appropriate) creates a better opportunity for neurosis; that is, no other profession by its nature creates so many colliding pretensions. Intellectuals often aspire to be prophets and heralds of reason simultaneously, but those roles are of course incompatible. Occasionally boasting of it, they want to be intellectually independent; yet because of this, they experience a need for identification more than other people, and the very matter they boast of generates in them an embarrassing feeling of inferiority. Often they experience their freedom and independence as a desert rendering them useless and isolated. But the tension between intellectual independence and total identification can never be resolved, except when the independence is given up. The need for identification may result in an almost unbelievable loss of critical reasoning, as has been confirmed by all the well-known intellectuals who identified themselves with Stalinism, Nazism, Maoism, and various fanatic sects. Occasionally, when hatred of their own milieu, which makes them outsiders, becomes all-consuming, the result is something of a hysteric blindness of reality, so to say—as once could be observed in Sartre, and is today in Chomsky.

One would expect all intellectuals to be interested in freedom of speech for immediate professional reasons, if not matters of principle. Most often that is indeed the case. On the other hand, they desire something else, too: they want to be heard. But the only *sure* way to be heard is to enjoy a word monopoly. The intellectuals cannot create such a monopoly themselves; it can only be granted to them by a despotic power for the price of being enslaved. There are reasons to believe that the intellectuals in the first phase after the Russian revolution contributed to their own subsequent destruction when various groups attempted to secure privileges or even a monopoly from the rulers. Elements of this tragic history of self-destruction can be found in the memoirs of Nadeschda Mandelshtam, which for various reasons ought to be obligatory reading for intellectuals. In addition, freedom of the word is by no means universally accepted as a matter of course. It is remarkable that Heidegger, in an interview posthumously published by *Der Spiegel*, still confirmed his criticism of academic freedom, which originated during Nazi times; it was, he said, merely a "negative freedom" (as if there were any other freedom than a "negative" one). Marcuse's fierce attacks against the idea and the practice of tolerance also come to mind. Such cases are the result of dreams of gaining for oneself a monopoly on words, guaranteed by governmental powers. This is of course expressed as the claim to a monopoly for truth; nobody may doubt that the authors of such claims themselves are the exclusive owners of truth.

Perhaps some among those intellectuals would be willing—and this is only a suspicion—to accept employment as privileged court philosophers to enlightened despots. Oddly enough, though, there are no enlightened despots in our century and no absolute rulers, as in the sixteenth and seventeenth centuries, who support intellectuals for the price of a flattering dedication or some occasional encomia, but otherwise leave them the freedom of creation. Today's despots need intellectuals inasmuch as they are no longer intellectuals; that is, inasmuch as they can be bought as slaves and devote all their work to their masters. In the century of totalitarianism, the time of enlightened autocrats has passed.

Even more interesting is the cult of power as such, which runs through intellectual history in covert or, at times, articulated form. Nietzsche, who—already half-insane and at the brink of final intellectual deterioration at Turin—voiced his violent attack against Christianity (which he denounced as the glorification of disease and disease itself), is of course a paradigm: he, the sad prophet of health and vigor, was a genius of seduction, no doubt, but he was also a model to those who were never satisfied with their role as powerless word producers.

But are we talking about matters that actually belong to the past? To some extent, perhaps. After so many horrible mistakes and such spectacular discrediting of their predecessors, the intellectuals are on the whole probably more careful in their political commitments. Compared to the once enormous vogue of Stalinism, the attraction of Maoism, for instance—a period that has fortunately passed as well—proved to be much weaker, even at the peak of its popularity. There is much less willingness to offer unconditional support to existing ideologies, and more inclination to keep a distance from political matters, with a consequent tendency to withdraw into more secure and specialized areas. As a result, we probably now have fewer influential lunatics and swindlers, but also fewer intellectual teachers.

Nevertheless, the circumstances that create an incurable uneasiness for intellectuals and nurture their contradictory feelings are omnipresent. On the one hand, there is contempt for ordinary people; on the other hand, there is a desire for solidarity with the oppressed and poor, which often results in a purely cerebral identification with ideologies that have made themselves champions of the demands of the masses. The contempt for ordinary people to a large degree was part of anti-Americanism among European intellectuals, to which the German war emigrants to the United States had contributed. This tendency was expressed frequently by the Frankfurt School. One could almost feel the envy, mixed with abhorrence, of the American culture of the middle classes—people who had proven to be so tremendously successful in technological achievements as well as in shaping democratic institutions and who read no Kant, did not listen to Bach, and moreover did not confer on intellectuals a superhuman status of honor but treated them at best as ordinary workers or, at worst, as useless loafers, even parasites.

A never-ending inner struggle takes place in the souls of intellectuals. They are torn between a feeling of their superiority, their special mission, *and* a secret envy of humans whose work bears visible and verifiable results. Writing about the superiority of criticism compared to literature, Oscar Wilde argued that it is generally easier to make something than to talk about it; it is easier to make a bed than to describe the process of doing it. Mickiewicz, on the other hand, wrote "that it is more difficult to live well through one day than to write a long book." Well, I don't know if Oscar Wilde ever attempted to make a bed, but Mickiewicz's remark appears to be inhumanly exaggerated. Nevertheless, intellectuals perhaps have the "right" to feel insecure about their status and the value of their work. What tangible results does the work of an intellectual yield? There are, of course, several examples of intellectuals who exerted an enormous influence on their eras and thus on the entire course of world history. But we note that, first, such examples only represent the "tip of the iceberg," the small number of the relatively large population of intellectuals; second, a long time must usually pass before such influence is measurable; and third—this is the most embarrassing aspect—the real results are forever contestable and uncertain. If we look back to the sixteenth century, the era in which the class of independent word-workers emerged, we may notice several types who reappear in subsequent history: withdrawn scholars, militant freethinkers, militant defenders of the establishment, skeptics, failed politicians, curious seekers of novelties and polyhistorians. The original model of an intellectual in modern history certainly was Erasmus of Rotterdam: a peace-loving incendiary, philologist, and moralist, often vacillating; deeply engaged in the major conflicts of his time, but also withdrawn and careful, unwilling to go to extremes; one of the greatest promoters of the reform movement in religious life, yet one who never joined the Reformation; a gentle warrior, scholar, and satirist. Even today, his historic role as a whole is controversial: was he ultimately a restorer or destroyer of Christianity? Too many more or less arbitrary criteria must be considered to answer such questions unequivocally. Similar questions may be asked about almost all great intellectuals who have contributed to Europe's intellectual and political history, also without reaching definite answers. Tensions between a typical intellectual like Melanchthon and a popular tribune like Luther could hardly be avoided, and if intellectuals attempted to be popular leaders or professional politicians themselves, the results were usually far from encouraging: the marketplace of words with all its dangers is, in the end, a more appropriate place for them than a king's court.

Chapter Four

Why Do We Need Kant?

My subject could also be called, "Why do we need Kant in the Struggle against Slavery?" or even "Against the Jargon of 'the concrete human being.'" I am not a Kant expert and no Kantian but, I should say, a Kant sympathizer—especially where conflicts between Kantian and so-called historicist thinking are concerned, both in epistemology and in ethics.

I do not claim to offer a special and original interpretation of Kant in any respect. My question is: Is Kant's philosophical anthropology significant to the main questions and fears of our times? Is it indispensable to continue from there when we set out to examine the tensions of our civilization? It is not a question of Kant's political or social opinions. That he was a radical democrat; that he perhaps—as Vorländer and other social-democratic Kantians have argued—in some points anticipated socialist thought; how he reacted to the French Revolution; whether he was really a philosophical Robespierre (following Heinrich Heine's famous parable)—all that is immaterial to the present context. Naturally, Kant's political attitudes are interesting to historians; but it is obvious that we cannot expect from them answers to specific challenges of the present. Rather, we should keep to what was fundamental in Kant's theories of knowledge and ethics, and what has made his criticism into an event of radical change in the history of European culture. We should ask whether there are incipient traces and guideposts, from which we certainly should not expect to derive conclusive answers directly, but which may hold good as necessary conditions for the survival of our culture. My answer is yes, and I like to defend it.

Kant's teachings of the conditions of theoretical and practical knowledge are really transcendental, not anthropological. That is, all forms and categories that we apply to perceive—and hence also to shape—objects are not

Translated from the German by Wolfgang Freis from "Warum brauchen wir Kant?" *Merkur* 9/10 (1981). Copyright © 1981 by Klett-Cotta Verlag, Stuttgart. Revised by the author in English.

to be defined as characteristics of human psychology or as fortuitous peculiarities of our zoological species, but as the necessary condition of all possible experience. Thus they are valid for all beings endowed with reason, since they identify reason as such, not in a particular species. The same holds in the area of practical reason: moral principles, even if—formulated abstractly—they define only the necessary formal requirements of any norm, apply to all beings provided with free will. This means mankind is not an object born or given by nature, and being human is not a zoological but a moral concept; the advocates of ethical socialism, among others, have emphasized that repeatedly. Being human is not determined by specific characteristics that distinguish our species from others, but by participation both in the area of rational necessities, which are expressed epistemologically in synthetic a priori judgments, and in the sphere of moral imperatives, which cannot be deduced empirically.

From there it follows that one must not derive standards for what people ought to be doing from what they actually are doing. If this tenet is so generally formulated, Kant naturally shares it with the tradition of both positivism and radical empiricism; but the substantiation of the tenet as well as its sense and its results differ significantly from each other in both cases. Kant's point is not that one may not deduce value judgments from descriptive ones, and that therefore the whole sphere of values and moral norms is left to arbitrary decisions of each individual, because—as empiricists argued—in the realm of purposes and duties, there is no "objective" validity. On the contrary, the question is, if observation of human action may not result in distinction of good and evil, and no rules of moral obligation may be derived from it, how, then, can such distinctions and rules—as norms that are unconditionally binding and independent of simple experience—be found and detected in the autonomous sphere of practical reason? Did Kant succeed in discovering this area of the morally obligatory? Is it actually possible to lay claim to such discovery without relying on sources of religious certitude?

Here I have to leave aside the last question, as important as it may be. I am concerned with a question that is logically independent: can our civilization actually survive without the belief that the distinction between good and evil, between the prohibited and the mandatory, does not depend on our respective decisions and thus that it does not coincide with the distinction between the advantageous and the disadvantageous? Since something that may be beneficial to one human being or group may obviously be unfavorable to others (and by the same token, something that is disadvantageous to a person or group at some point in time may turn out to be advantageous to that same person or group in the long run); in short, since there is after all no concept of what is advantageous or disadvantageous *tout court*, the notion that moral precepts coincide with utilitarian criteria evidently amounts to nothing but the tenet that moral precepts do not exist. Kant knew that, of course; thus by turning against the popular utilitarianism of the Enlightenment, he also knew exactly that what was at stake was not of any particular moral code, but rather a question of the existence or nonexistence of the distinction between good and evil and, consequently, a question of the fate of mankind.

Kant has frequently been accused of being a naive preacher who was a stranger to the realities of life, and who expected that people would do good purely from their sense of duty, not from any other motives. Nothing was further from his mind. On the contrary, the naïveté in the judgment of real human motivations and behavior occurred on the side of the optimistic utilitarians of the Enlightenment, who believed—certainly not without exceptions—that the natural instincts of solidarity and friendship would return after faulty political institutions and religious superstition had been abolished, and humanity would be blessed with lasting harmony and conflict-free order. Kant did not believe that. The professor at the boring provincial city had a better understanding of human nature than the intellectual dandies of Paris. He did not expect that the actual behavior of mankind could meet the imperatives his moral theory had established. His theory of radical evil, which was clearly directed at utopian thinking, was not an accidental addition to his anthropology; it was related to his doctrine of free will. Freedom fatefully does include not only the capacity of doing evil; it implies that evil cannot be eradicated. Thus, in *Grundlegung zur Metaphysik der Sitten* he wrote,

> . . . even if there never were actions springing from such pure sources our concern is not whether this or that was done but that reason of itself and independently of all appearances commands what ought to be done. Our concern is with actions of which perhaps the world has never had an example, with actions whose feasibility might be seriously doubted by those who base everything on experience, and yet with actions inexorably commanded by reason. (trans. by L. W. Beck)

From an empirical point of view, the questions of the validity of value judgments and the criteria of good and evil are naturally meaningless; experience does not know good and evil, unless we substitute such terms for psychological or social facts. It is much worse, however, if we contend that both distinctions as well as the norms of moral obligation may indeed be determined to be valid or invalid on the basis of what we can ascertain by investigating either our biological mechanisms or historic processes. To say it more plainly, in the first case, this contention means that we do not simply follow our natural inclinations but that we are justified by following them; in the second case, it means that everything that has proven to be historically successful is automatically morally justified. The followers of neo-Kantianism have repeatedly called attention to the absurdity of the latter idea, which is especially popular among Marxists.

It is less a question of the so-called naturalistic fallacy, whose logical insufficiency always has been stressed by empiricist philosophy, than a matter of its cultural significance. If one adopts this pseudo-Hegelian perspective, it becomes apparent that only one guidepost is available for our conduct: we shall participate in what is successful or what promises to have success. I call it *pseudo-Hegelian* since Hegel's retrospective orientation prohibited him from extending historically determined value judgments to the future and thus sanctifying something that perhaps promises success in the future. With their futuristic attitude, the young Hegelians—Marx among them— have disposed of this safeguard and so authorized us to trace tendencies in the process of history that have a good chance for victory, and to join their cause for that reason.

This is crucial for civilization. If we do indeed renounce the notion of a ready-made distinction between good and evil, one that is independent of our own decision (whether this distinction originated in religious tradition or was accepted as a postulate of Kant's practical reason), then no moral boundary prevents us from engaging in any action for no better reason than that it promotes the success of a tendency which, by definition, will be legitimate if it succeeds, even if it carries the name of Hitler or Stalin. To respond by saying that people have historically failed to provide many impressive examples of action that conformed to the decalog would be to commit exactly the fallacy Kant has pointed out. It is not only a logical fallacy, but also an anthropological one; anthropologically, there is an immense difference between a society in which traditional criteria of good and evil remain valid, no matter how often they have been violated, and one in which these criteria have been abrogated and have fallen into oblivion. Kant's assertion that rules of moral obligation cannot be derived from what we are actually doing and that it is extremely important to be aware of these rules even if we often violate them remains a prerequisite of any society not destined to fall into ruin. The belief that good and evil are not determined in the context by historic accidents but precede all contingent facts is a precondition of any living culture. This point of Kant's philosophical heritage is so important both because he knew how to construe it so clearly and forcefully and because he proved that it can maintain validity only by its link to a principle he shared with Hume, namely, that moral obligation can never be rationally derived from the facts of experience.

To search for criteria of moral obligation that are produced by or remain hidden in a factual historical process is never a means of identifying such criteria in unqualified form. But to criticize empiricism because it does not permit one to gather such criteria from historic experience and thus leaves undecided the matter of good and evil is not only to criticize the best and the most irresistible of empiricism; it is also morally bad criticism. Since it is impossible to discover what is unconditionally obligatory in what is historically conditional, any attempt to ascertain the good and the right in philosophical speculation on history is not only a logical failure but morally hypocritical as well: these are attempts to legitimize moral opportunism. They are a trait steadfastly common among Marxists: the intention is to justify anything that is politically profitable at a given moment and to maintain at the same time that it is moral in itself, not simply through an arbitrary decision. It amounts to recasting opportunism into iron moral law.

In short, without the belief that the distinction between good and evil depends neither on the arbitrary decision of the individual nor on the political conditions of the moment, and that this distinction cannot be traced back to the distinction between the helpful and the harmful, our civilization will be lost. And Kant made the most important and forceful attempt to substantiate the irreducibility of this distinction as a matter of reason, not as a matter of revelation.

All this applies, however, only to the general framework of Kant's moral philosophy: the simple fact of the distinctions between the "is" and the "ought to" and between good and evil. But since this distinction is rooted in the empirically unprovable free will of the rational being and is thus obligatory to all, Kant came to the natural conclusion that all human beings—as morally acting individuals and as objects of moral judgment (therefore, as free beings)—are in the same position regarding all more specific rules. This means that their reciprocal duties and rights are identical inasmuch as they are human beings.

I am touching upon the key question of the significance today of the

Kantian heritage: the question of the so-called abstract human being, against which the jargon of historicism—conservative as well as revolutionary—tends to set the *concrete human being*. And it is my cause to defend Kant's heritage against the jargon of the concrete human being.

Kant indeed believed in the essential equality of human beings with respect to their dignity as free beings endowed with reason. In this point, he certainly continued the seventeenth-century doctrine of natural law—he was an heir of Puffendorf and Grotius—even if he based his doctrine on different anthropological presuppositions. He believed, therefore, that all norms, as far as they are moral, must be applied unconditionally to each individual and that there are claims which every human being may make, since all people should be considered as ends in themselves, not as means for other people.

It is exactly this point of Kant's doctrine—and of the entire doctrine of natural right as well—that has been attacked since the beginning of the nineteenth century. "Man as such does not exist" is the usual phrase; "there are only the concrete human beings." Yet what does that mean, the *concrete human being*? De Maistre is credited with the famous remark that he had seen Frenchmen, Germans, and Russians, but never a man. We may ask, has he really ever seen a Frenchman, German, or Russian? No, he could see only Mr. Dupont, Mr. Müller, and Mr. Ivanov, never anyone who was nothing but a Frenchman, a German, or a Russian. For all that, his remark reveals the point in question: the so-called concrete human being is not a concrete human being; that is, he is not an individual. He is a being determined by his nationality, contrasted with the "human being as such," that is, with the human being who is equal in his dignity to all others.

Based on general human nature, the doctrine of natural right, Kant's included, asserts that each human being is entitled to fundamental rights. Kant's insistence on considering people as ends in themselves, and thus on considering each person separately, postulates that no human being may be the property of another and that slavery contradicts the concept of being human. If we deny, however, the presence of common humanity in the name of the concrete human being, we thereby also deny the single foundation of the principle of human rights. This principle is valid only under the precondition that rights exist to which every individual may lay claim simply by being human, under the precondition of everyone's equal participation in human nature or, in other words, on the basis of the "abstract human being." The concrete human being, on the other hand—as the word is commonly used—is concrete only in the sense that he is determined, not by his human nature, but by a more specific category. From this point of view, it does not matter how we choose this more specific category—it may be a race, a class, or a nation. In any case, the ideological intention, on which the jargon of the concrete human being is based, is to weaken or even to invalidate the general principle of human rights and to permit some sections of humanity to deem others as natural objects. And this means in fact, though not necessarily in ideological declarations, to legitimize slavery.

In this context, the so-called French New Right presents an interesting example. The movement should be taken seriously, I believe. It is distinguished by a certain openness, resolution, and willingness to speak out without excuses. These people are often denounced as racists, even Nazis. Their answer is, "We have never justified any theory that speaks of higher or lower races, of anti-Semitism, or of race hatred." It is true that they have not disseminated such doctrines. They do not seem to have taken their inspiration from Nazism; rather, they present a continuation of the old anti-Enlightenment tradition, which originated with de Bonald, de Maistre, Savigny and was later found in Nietzsche and finally in Sorel. Their ideology expresses a reaction against the abstract human being in the name of historically determined man. A volume of their journal *Eléments* of January/March 1981 is devoted entirely to the struggle against the theory of human rights; it is entitled "Droits de l'homme: Le piège" (Human rights: A trap). They do not claim that there are better races, master nations, and so on. First, they state that the theory of human rights, however it is defined in modern philosophy, is of Judeo-Christian and biblical origin—which is true. Then they claim that this theory may not be derived from historical material, and that humanity represents an entity only as a biological concept; otherwise, in a cultural sense, humanity does not actually exist. Various "organic" crystallizations of cultures have produced their own norms and value systems; in contrast, the theory of human rights expresses cultural imperialism, which endeavors to force our specific Judeo-Christian doctrine upon other civilizations and thus attempts to destroy any diversity. The ideologists of the New Right are heathens and represent themselves as such. They wish to return to a prebiblical, supposedly Greek, conception of humanity and to adopt actual, historically grown cultures (instead of philosophically distilled abstractions of the human being) as the basis of any possible anthropology.

It is certainly true—and both Kant and the new Kantians were fully aware of this—that the concept of humanity in a cultural sense is not based on any empirical description; it can be derived legitimately from neither anthropological nor historical research. It must be substantiated morally. Whether such substantiation is conceivable through postulating absolutely autonomous principles of practical reason and hence without reliance on religious tradition is, I repeat, another question. In both cases one must admit, however, that the concept of humanity in a cultural sense—a concept presupposed in every recognition of human rights—may be constructed morally, but not empirically or historically.

Disposing of such a concept, and consequently the principle of universal human rights (as in the given example), creates the prerequisites for legitimizing slavery and genocide—of course without necessarily encouraging them in one or the other case. It suffices that people living in a particular civilization may consider the members of another civilization as natural objects. In order to eat shrimp or apples, for instance, we do not need a special theory to convince us of their inferiority in comparison to human beings; they are natural objects, and that will do for us. The same result may be obtained with human beings, regardless of whether other parts of our species are defined biologically in the category of race or historically, through association with a nation or culture—if only the despised abstract human being is forgotten.

The same holds true for the description of concreteness in class categories; the jargon of the concrete human being appears frequently in some variants of Marxist ideology. Marx's heritage in this point, as is well known, is ambiguous, as it is in many others. Marx believed, on the one hand, that people in communism would return to their true individuality, of which the capitalist commodity economy had robbed them, once they were freed of the necessity of selling themselves as a labor force. On the other hand, he expected this individual of the future to identify completely and spontaneously with the society and that social techniques would exist to establish this identification, namely, abolition of private property and centralization of production processes in the hands of the State. From this perspective, the matter of so-called negative freedom, as it had been proclaimed by the French Revolution, seemed meaningless to him, since it assumed conflicts of interest among individuals and thus specifically exhibited conditions of bourgeois society. In contrast, in Marx's imagined society of the future, the interests and aspirations of the individual are by no means limited by the needs of others but are supported thereby.

From the very beginning, not just after the political victory of slightly altered Marxism as the official ideology of the police state, this notion was denounced, especially by anarchists, as the anticipation of state slavery—

and, I believe, deservedly so. Overall nationalization means the nationalization of people. The Marxist doctrine contained no secure barrier, in the form of recognition of inalienable rights of the individual, against state-ownership of people—because bourgeois society was divided into hostile classes. Recognition of universal rights, it appeared, would breach the principle of class struggle, whereas in the perfect community the individual would be able to identify freely and without coercion with the "totality."

Social democratic neo-Kantians, like Cohen and Vorländer, have realized that. Kant's principle, they asked, according to which the human beings ought to be regarded as ends in themselves and never as a means—that is, each one as an individual, not as a member of a nation, class, race, state, or civilization—did it not concur with the central ideal of socialism, since this idea aims at liberating people from the conditions in which they function as objects or commodities, not as moral individuals? Thus, the socialist idea can only be viable inasmuch as it adopts Kant's tenet. Marx's philosophy of history does not itself, to be sure, provide us with this principle, but it may be compatible with Kant's moral philosophy without contradiction, if it were to renounce hopeless and morally dangerous claims of having conquered the dichotomy of facts and values, of historic realities and normative ideals. Such an endeavor became the laughing stock of the orthodox, who believed that the socialist idea did not need an ethical foundation—either because it represented (in the opinion of many German Marxists) only a value-free analysis of historic development, or (as Lenin and Trotsky maintained later) because no ethic exists or ever could exist apart from the techniques of class struggle.

The significance of this confrontation manifests itself even more today than it did then. Kant's ridiculed abstract human being, who ought to be considered as end in himself, is each one of us, whose freedom, life, civil rights, and rights of self-determination are threatened by the expansion of totalitarianism. It is of course possible to say that one should not interpret Kant's principles in such a utopian and far-reaching manner, as if it were possible to replace the so-called thing-like interrelations between human beings with purely personal ones. Surely, there are areas of existence in which people interact as representatives of institutions and not as persons. Bureaucratic and technical levels of communication do exist in life, and it would be naive to believe that they could be eliminated. Neither can we gather from our principle, in Kant's sense, clear indications of whether or to what degree it is applicable to struggles, conflicts, and wars. But even if we reduce the principle to its minimal content, it signifies that no human being may be the property of another; thus it prohibits any form of slavery.

In the old days of slavery, some people were subject to being bought and sold, just like any other commodity. In a market economy, the neo-Kantian socialists argued, human beings continue to appear as commodities; even though they are personally free, they are forced to sell their work, their personal strengths and talents, in the marketplace. But one must add that to replace these conditions with those under which people become the property of the state—and that is the principal idea of communism—means to replace something very imperfect with something infinitely worse. State slavery, the inevitable result of total nationalization, theoretically has no boundaries once the principle of the unexchangeable value of the individual is surrendered. Without it, the socialist idea unavoidably degenerates into slave socialism, into a society in which the individual is reduced to an elementary particle in the productive process.

I repeat, it is important, but secondary in the present context, in what manner the individual loses the status of an autonomous being and becomes an object: be it that we claim the right to consider people of other races, nations, or cultures as natural objects; that we consider the nation to be of highest value, in which individuals appear only as components of a larger organism; or, finally, that the right to treat human beings as its instruments is conferred upon an almighty state. Hence, no matter whether the corresponding principle is construed in biological, historical, or cultural categories, in all cases the jargon of the concrete human being serves as the basis of enslavement. From this point of view, explicitly racist doctrines as well as philosophies preaching the mutual incommunicability of cultures, and thus the impossibility of adopting a common notion of humanity, are no less antagonistic to humanity than communist-totalitarian ideologies. Their negative common ground consists exactly in the denial of *being human* as a universal category, applicable to each individual human being, confirmed by the inviolability, irreplaceability, and unexchangeability of the person. They are all anti-Kantian, as well as anti-Christian and antihuman.

Politically compelled, reluctant, and (naturally) merely verbal recognition of the principle of human rights by some communist states changes the facts no more than the reluctance of racist and radical nationalistic movements to deny the same principle. The rulers of communist states know very well (and they are correct) that this contradicts their ideology—although there are few today who dare to say so. Mao Tse-tung was a rare and commendable exception who explicitly condemned the theory of human rights as a bourgeois invention.

In short, even though the idea of human dignity, conferring the same equality on every human being, is older than Kant and actually of biblical origin, we owe Kant not only the attempt to establish it independently of revealed religion, but also the clear distinction of this idea from everything that may ever be discovered in anthropological, historical, and psychological research. Thanks to him, we know that neither our understanding of history and ethnology nor our knowledge of physiology will enable us to recognize the validity of this idea, and that failing to recognize it is most dangerous. If one attempts to derive human rights from historical or anthropological material, the result will always be only the exclusive rights of some groups, races, classes, or nations, which confer permission on themselves to subordinate, destroy, or enslave others. Humanity is a moral concept. Unless we recognize that, we have no good reason to challenge the ideology of slavery.

Chapter Five

In Praise of Exile

The familiar twentieth-century figure of the "intellectual in exile" can boast an impressive spiritual pedigree, from Anaxagoras, Empedocles, and Ovid, through Dante, Occam, and Hobbes, down to Chopin, Mickiewicz, Herzen, and Victor Hugo. More often than not, however, modern expatriates have been refugees, rather than exiles in the strict sense; usually they were not physically deported from their countries or banished by law; they escaped from political persecution, prison, death, or simply censorship.

This distinction is important insofar as it has had a psychological effect. Many voluntary exiles from tyrannical régimes cannot rid themselves of a feeling of discomfort. They are no longer exposed to the dangers and deprivations that are the daily lot of their friends—or of the entire country with which they identify themselves. A certain ambiguity is therefore unavoidable, and it is impossible to draw up any hard-and-fast rules to distinguish justifiable from unjustifiable self-exile. It is easy to see that nothing would have been gained had Einstein or Thomas Mann remained in Hitler's Germany or had Chagall not left Soviet-ruled Vitebsk. There are, on the other hand, many people living in the Soviet Union or in Poland whom the rulers would love to ship off to a foreign land but who doggedly refuse to move, choosing instead prison, persecution, and misery. Who would dare to say that they are wrong? Solzhenitsyn and Bukovsky had to be handcuffed and kicked out of their country, thus following the sad route of a couple of hundred prominent Russian intellectuals whom the Soviet rulers banished shortly after the Revolution. Many Solidarity leaders were offered freedom at the price of emigration and they refused; some are in jail again; others probably will be soon. Milan Kundera left Czechoslovakia, and Czeslaw Milosz left Poland, and they made of their experiences major works of modern literature; Havel has stayed in his land, and so has Herbert; and we owe a lot to all of them. *Doktor Faustus* and Nabokov's novels are fruits of emi-

Reprinted by permission from *The Times Literary Supplement*, 11 October 1985, with revisions by the author. Copyright © 1985 by *The Times of London*.

gration, as are the works of Conrad, Ionesco, and Koestler, yet *Gulag Archipelago* could not have been produced by an exile. No universal standards can be devised to decide in what condition self-exile, if practicable at all, is preferable.

When we speak of an "intellectual in exile" we almost automatically think of an escapee from such or another form of tyranny and thus assume that exile—even a forcible one—is in some important respects preferable to or better than the alternative. Russia's speciality (arising from her sheer size) is internal exile, which gives people the worst of both worlds: emigration from their homeland together with the same repressive régime as before (here, as everywhere, there are degrees of misery, of course: just compare the exile of Pushkin in Crimea and Odessa with that of Sakharov in Gorky). Leaving this aside, the advantages of exile (freedom) as well as its miseries (uprootedness, intractable difficulties with foreign tongues, etc.) are obvious. Not so obvious is the answer to the question whether exile is merely a lesser evil, or whether it offers privileges unknown to those who are securely settled on their native soil.

We can look for an answer in the vicissitudes of the most experienced exiles, exiles par excellence, the Jews. As long as they lived in ghettos, protecting their identity by an impenetrable shell of highly complicated rituals and taboos (perhaps the very complexity of their law made their survival possible: a pious man could not live among the Gentiles and observe all his customs, the very number of which compelled Jews to live together and prevented them from dissolving in the Christian environment), they might have produced outstanding Talmudists and commentators, but their cultural life was necessarily self-contained. Geographically they lived for generations as expatriates, but they were by no means aliens in ghettos; they kept sheltering tenaciously in heart and mind the lost imaginary fatherland, more or less indifferent to the Gentile cultural world; to a pious Hassid it did not matter much, in cultural terms, whether he lived in Warsaw, Shanghai, or Buenos Aires; he carried the deposit of faith, and to be a guardian of this deposit was enough to sustain his mental life. Once the walls of ghettos began to crumble with the so-called emancipation (one needs to be aware of dubious aspects of this value-loaded word), the Jews invaded the spiritual space of Europe in an astonishingly rapid and powerful march. Some of them, like Marx, Freud, and Einstein, were to become real world-conquerors; thousands found their places in the élites of all realms of civilization—the sciences, arts, humanities, and politics. It was only by, as it were, exiling themselves from their collective exile that they became exiles in the modern sense. However hard they might have tried, they failed (at least most of them) to lose entirely their identity of old and to be unreservedly assimilated; they were looked upon as alien bodies by the indigenous tribes, and it was probably this uncertain status, the lack of a well-defined identity, which enabled them to see more and to question more than those who were satisfied with their inherited and natural sense of belonging. One is even tempted to say that it was the anti-Semites (as long as they did not express their ideas in terms of gas chambers) who were to a large extent responsible for the extraordinary achievements of the Jews, precisely because by barring to them the path to the moral and intellectual safety of the tribal life—whether French, Polish, Russian or German—they left them in the privileged position of outsiders.

That the position of an outsider offers a cognitive privilege is well known and unquestionable. A tourist often sees things which a native does not notice, as they have become a natural part of his life (one thinks of a tourist in America named Alexis de Tocqueville). For the peoples of the Book, both Jews and Christians, exile is, of course, the normal and inescapable lot of mankind on earth. One can go further and say that the myth of exile, in one form or another, lies at the core of all religions, of any genuine religious experience. The fundamental message embedded in religious worship is: our home is elsewhere. We know, however, at least two radically different practical interpretations of this message. There is the contempt of earthly realities and eventually of life itself, which can offer nothing but misery and suffering—this is the conclusion which Buddhist wisdom often endorses. And there is also the notion that exile provides the human race with a great opportunity to be exploited on its way back to the Father—this interpretation prevails in the mainstream of Judaeo-Christian civilization. A global scorn for matter, for the body, for terrestrial values, was a marginal phenomenon in Christian history. The kernel of the concept of Christian life may be summed up thus: we live in exile and we must never forget it; therefore all the temporal goods and goals have to be seen as relative and subordinate; they are real all the same, and our natural duty is to use them; Nature is an adversary to be conquered, not to be denied.

Suppose that the theologians are right and that our progenitors in Eden would have acquired the knowledge of carnal love and produced offspring even if they had resisted temptation and remained blissfully unaware of Good and Evil. They would nonetheless never have originated mankind as we know it—a race capable of creating. It was the *felix culpa* and the subsequent exile, including its miseries and risks, that tore them out of their celestial safety, exposed them to evil, danger, struggles, and suffering and thus laid the necessary condition of human existence. Creativity arose from insecurity, from an exile of a sort, from the experience of homelessness.

Philosophy can simply deny the fact of exile or rather, as Christians would contend, conceal it from us—this is what the adherents of empiricism, naturalism, materialism, and scientism used to do. It can accept the fact and try to show a path of return to an ultimate reconciliation of man with Being—this is the Hegelian approach. Or it can accept the fact but deny that our condition is curable, thereby condemning us to a never-ending nostalgia for the nonexistent paradise; the existential philosophy of our century was most successful in expressing this gloomy insight, thus exposing the bitter harvest of the Enlightenment.

The Christian notion of the first exile can be enlarged and applied to the second one—that is, the exile from exile—and the third, and the fourth. (It is arguable, for instance, that Spinoza was a quadruple exile, being excommunicated from the Jewish community which established itself in Amsterdam after the expulsion from Portugal, where they had lived as exiles from the Eretz given them by God as a place of exile from Eden.) Any exile can be seen either as a misfortune or as a challenge; it can become no more than a reason for despondency and sorrow or a source of a painful encouragement. We can use a foreign tongue simply because we have to, or try to discover in it linguistic treasures which are unique to it, untranslatable, and which therefore enrich our mind, not only our technical ability to communicate. We can confront the perspective of an alien with that of a native and thus sow an alarming mental discomfort which frequently turns out to be productive and mutually beneficial. The examples abound throughout modern history. I am not aware of any study specifically examining the cultural role of various forms of exile, individual and collective, in the history of Europe. There is no doubt, however, that without so many religiously or politically motivated expulsions and self-expulsions, without all those wanderers and refugees, European intellectual and artistic life would be much different from what it is. One thinks of Huguenots in England and Holland; of Italian Christian radicals and Unitarians looking for shelter in the (then very tolerant) Poland of the second half of the sixteenth century; of Polish Unitarians in Western Europe in the second half of the seventeenth century, promoters of the early Enlightenment; of Jews expelled from Iberic countries; of refugees from communist-ruled Central and Eastern Europe. All of them contributed, sometimes dramatically, to the civilizations of the host lands, much as they might have been occasionally less than welcome and greeted with suspicion. Emigrés from the Third Reich made an enormous impact on American intellectual life (some say it was a nefarious impact, but who knows the ultimate balance?).

We have to accept, however reluctantly, the simple fact that we live in an age of refugees, of migrants, vagrants, nomads roaming about the continents and warming their souls with the memory of their—spiritual or ethnic, divine or geographical, real or imaginary—homes. A total homelessness is unbearable; it would amount to a complete break with human existence. Is a perfect cosmopolitanism possible? Diogenes Laertius reports that Anaxagoras, when asked if he did not care about his motherland, replied that he did care very much indeed and pointed at the sky. Some people today make similar claims, denying any partial interest in, or special loyalty to, their original tribal community; to what extent this claim may be made in good faith is debatable.

Aside from individuals who have either escaped tyranny or been driven away from their land, there are entire nations whose people, without moving from native soil, have been robbed of their right to be citizens of their motherland, while being citizens of the State, because their country itself is under foreign rule; this is the destiny—temporary, let us hope—of Central and East European nations. The split between the State, which people feel is not theirs, though it claims to be their owner, and the motherland, of which they are guardians, has reduced them to an ambiguous status of half-exiles. The ambition of the unsovereign State is to rob its subjects of their historical memory by distorting and falsifying it according to actual political requirements. And the collective memory is ultimately the motherland. One half of Europe having been thus uprooted, what can the other half expect? Is the entire world going to be driven into an internal half-exile? Does God try to remind us, somewhat brutally, that exile is the permanent human condition? A ruthless reminder, indeed, even if deserved.

PART TWO

On the Dilemmas of the Christian Legacy

Chapter Six

The Revenge of the Sacred in Secular Culture

The statistics are, or seem, indisputable: wherever urbanization and general education have spread, they have almost always been accompanied by a decline in religiosity and an increase of religious indifference. Statistical analysis evaluates the degree of religiosity by the degree of participation in religious rites (churchgoing, baptisms, confirmations, religious marriages, funerals, etc.) and by the distribution of responses to surveys concerning certain traditional beliefs. It is also the only method of quantifying religiosity by reducing it to its outward manifestations. Nevertheless, it is not surprising that we wish to know more—more, in particular, about the cultural significance of such calculatons and their predictive value. But in this domain our judgments must be arbitrary, as in all cases where we try to grasp the significance and predict the future of global processes in human society. However modest the number of infallible principles we have at our disposal when dealing with global predictions, one thing is certain: the most fallible method is that of unlimited extrapolation from a curve that has begun to take shape, for here, as in all other spheres of life, every curve breaks off at some unpredictable point. About fifteen years ago, at the height of the boom in university teaching, it was a simple matter to calculate in which year the number of scholars would exceed that of human beings. An easy counterexample, I admit. In the same way, one may easily predict that the current curve of population growth will not attain the point at which there will be one person per every square centimeter of the earth's surface—a point simply obtained by extrapolation from a curve.

Other less simplistic (albeit less readily calculable) examples abound. In the nineteenth century everything seemed to point to the truth of the rational conviction that national sentiment was rapidly becoming extinct and

Translated from the French by Agnieszka Kolakowska from "La revanche du sacré dans la culture profane," in *Le besoin religieux* (Neuchâtel, Switzerland: Editions des Baconnière, 1973). Copyright © 1973 by Editions des Baconnière. Revised by the author in English.

would soon be supplanted by forces tending inexorably to reduce human culture to a definitive state of uniformity and universality. Naturally, when stark reality flies in the face of these rational predictions and we find ourselves contemplating an astonishing growth of nationalism throughout the world, little effort is needed to explain the phenomenon with arguments as convincing and convictions as rational as those which had accompanied the previous, exactly contrary, prophecies.

Indeed, nothing could be simpler than adducing historical necessity to explain events after they have happened; but the contingency of history mocks our predictions. The vicissitudes of religious life also have their place among the testimonies, if any more were needed, to our inadequacy in the sphere of prophecy and prediction. They, too, have in great measure persuaded us that the course of events is determined, not by any supposed laws, but by mutations, which are by definition unpredictable but easily rationalized once they have occurred. When we amass statistics dealing with church attendance over a period of thirty or forty years and proceed, on that basis, to forge a historical law, are we applying a scientific method?

We are not. What we are in fact doing is paying tribute to the philosophical prejudices of evolutionism by applying them to the study of religion. They are prejudices which we have inherited directly from the progressivism of the Enlightenment. It is true that this evolutionism has been almost entirely abandoned in contemporary studies of religion, but it continues to influence those who consider themselves enlightened and who, in large measure, also shape public education. One often reads in newspapers that politics has replaced religion, that the psychiatrist has taken the place of the priest, and that technological utopias have supplanted eschatological dreams. At first sight all this is plausible. It is also borne out in the observation of everyday life, which shows intellectuals that intellectuals resort more often to the psychiatrist than to the confessional for spiritual assistance, that they prefer national weeklies to parish magazines, or that television viewers on the whole prefer to watch the launching of Apollo rather than Sunday mass.

Elevating such observations to the status of historical laws, however, involves admitting much more than they can imply by themselves. It involves accepting the evolutionist theory whereby religion has been and continues to be no more effective than magic as a technique for covering the gaps in our knowledge and practical abilities. But nothing is less certain than that this is the case. If magic were no more than a clumsy and ineffective technique based on contingent associations and links that do not exist in nature, its persistence in spite of its lack of success would be astonishing and inexplicable; it would serve as proof that our nervous system, regulated by laws of conditioned reflexes, is inferior to that of all other animals, in that it is unable to rid itself of reflexes based on nonexistent links. If such an explanation were true, the very survival of the human species, not to speak of its extraordinary technological achievements, would be an incomprehensible miracle.

The same may be said of the theory whereby religious beliefs proper are reducible to practical instruments, applied to spheres that are subject to chance and not susceptible to human influence: a means of imposing order where control is not possible. If religious belief is simply the result of our wish to control the world, it is hard to see how and why so purely technical an attitude could have involved the human imagination in such aberrations as the search for hidden and technically useless meanings in empirical phenomena, or how and why the idea of the sacred was formed.

I do not want to construct a general theory of the meaning of religion; I merely wish to point out that predictions regarding the disappearance of religious phenomena in our culture are based not so much on simple statistics as on a certain interpretation of those statistics, an interpretation drawn, in turn, from an arbitrary metaphysics of human nature. The same applies to any theory that considers religion a technique applied to natural phenomena, or that regards it as a means of adapting to social institutions; the situation remains the same, in other words, whether the interpretation is drawn from Durkheim or from Marx.

It hardly needs pointing out that, at a time not too far removed from our own, religious categories almost entirely absorbed all others; that almost all forms of culture, all human ties, conflicts, and aspirations had some religious significance; and that much of this universality of religion's function has been lost. We no longer feel the need to look to religious tradition for a causal explanation of natural phenomena, nor do we seek in it ideological inspiration at times of social conflict. The time is past when religious sanctions and categories enjoyed universal applicability. But the fact that religious sentiment, ideas, images, and values lent themselves to all spheres of life, that they were able to function as instruments in all forms of communication, not only fails to corroborate the instrumental theory of the sacred but lends support to the contrary view.

Religious values, if they are to be attributed to secular interests and aspirations, must previously have been recognized as such, independently of those interests and aspirations. If the words *God is on my side* are to serve as a defense of any cause, God's authority must already be recognized, not invented ad hoc for that particular defense. The sacred must exist before it may be exploited. It is therefore absurd to claim that the sacred is no more than the instrument of the various interests that have pressed it into service. The instrumentalist interpretation of the sacred conceals an intellectualist illusion: the cultural meaning of a hoe may be grasped entirely in its use by the gardener (or in its secondary use for bashing someone over the head); but to say that ideologies and religious or moral values may be understood in the same way is not only to ignore all that distinguishes human culture from the mere effort at biological adaptation: it is to render that culture incomprehensible. If at some point we passed from the stage of expressing our needs directly to the stage of invoking the sanction of the sacred, or seeking support in "ideological reversal" in order to express them, the passage from one stage to the other is not explained by the content of those needs alone. It remains as mysterious as ever.

I set down these general considerations not in order to question the evidence for the phenomenon commonly known as *secularization,* but simply in order to point out that the meaning of this phenomenon is far from being immediately obvious, and that the term *secularization,* embracing as it does a number of processes which do not normally go hand in hand, tends to confuse the issue.

If, in the traditionally Christian world, secularization means a drop in participation in the activities of traditional Christian organizations, it is clearly visible, although it would be an exaggeration to say that its causes are equally so. If it invariably accompanies the process of industrialization, it does not follow the same patterns and cannot be explained by any perceptible laws. The two do not go hand in hand. Societies which are industrially the most advanced are by no means the most secularized in this sense. If, on the other hand, we mean by secularization the disappearance of religious needs, the matter becomes more doubtful still. If we assume that all religious functions are gradually and irreversibly being taken over by secular institutions, all the symptoms of religious renaissance that we know so well suddenly become quite incomprehensible. I have in mind not only the signs of a renaissance that is visible outside Christianity or on its periphery, such as the extraordinary surge of interest in the occult, magic, and the hermetic arts; the invasion of oriental cults and beliefs in the Christian world; the blossoming of little sects or groups, more or less ephemeral, sometimes bizarre, sometimes grotesque or extravagant. I have in mind also the re-markable number of conversions within Christianity itself. If belonging to a religious community, even participating in the life of that community, can be due entirely to the inertia of tradition, and may be explained in social rather than religious terms, then conversions, in whatever direction, tend to confirm the vitality of religious consciousness in the proper sense of the term.

However convincing the sociological studies that correlate religious be-havior and a large number of social variables such as age, sex, profession, social class, and so forth, there are no infallible methods for penetrating the concealed, underground layers of culture, which reveal themselves at times of social crisis and are hard to discern in normal conditions. The distribu-tion of the forces of tradition, entrenched over thousands of years of history, cannot be grasped in any quantifiable way. As a result, great historical erup-tions and their effects are as unpredictable as the behavior of people when faced with violent crises.

The history of religious belief is no exception to this, either on the indi-vidual or on the collective level. In concentration camps there were believers who lost their faith and atheists who found it. Intuitively we understand both reactions: we can see both how one might say, "If such atrocities are possible, then there can be no God," and how one might be led to say the opposite: "In the face of such atrocities, only God can preserve the sense of life." The rich and satisfied may become devout or indifferent to religion because they are rich and satisfied; the poor and humbled may become devout or indifferent to religion because they are poor and humbled; all this is easily explained. Those who know Russia well have good reason to sup-pose that a minimum of religious freedom in that country would lead to a religious explosion on a large scale; but it would be vain to speculate, on the basis of the information we have, as to what form that explosion might take. Despair may presage the death as well as the resurrection of religious faith; great misery, war, and oppression may strengthen religious feeling or weaken it. The circumstances which push us towards one or the other of these reactions are many: we may guess at their influence, but we cannot anticipate their cumulative effects.

Of course we do not want to stop there: the correlations established be-tween religious and secular behavior are not enough. We want to know more. There is one question in particular that we must ask: alongside all the secular functions of religion, the innumerable ties which, in binding it to all forms of social conflict and activity, made its fate dependent on that of secular society, is there some indestructible residue of the religious phenomenon that persists as such? Is it an inalienable part of culture? Is it the case that religious need can be neither suppressed nor replaced by other satisfactions, nor yet dissolved in them?

No answers to these questions can be found by scientifically approved methods, for the questions themselves belong rather to the realm of philosophical speculation. However, if we consider some of the effects on the decline which the phenomenon of the sacred has suffered in our societies, some answers, tentative and in no way definitive, may suggest themselves.

The quality of being sacred has been attributed to all those things which, on pain of punishment, were not to be meddled with; it thus extended to government, property, law, and human life. The sacredness of government was abolished with the fading of monarchical charisma: that of property, with the coming of socialist movements. These are forms of the sacred whose passing we do not, on the whole, tend to regret. The question arises, however, whether society can survive and provide a tolerable life for its members if the feeling for the sacred and, indeed, the phenomenon of the sacred itself vanish entirely. What we want to know, therefore, is whether certain values whose vigor is vital to culture can survive without being rooted in the realm of the sacred in the proper sense of the word.

Note, first of all, that there is yet another sense—a third—in which the term *secularization* is used. In this sense, secularization does not imply the decline of organized religion, and it may be seen in churches as well as in religious doctrines. It takes the form of a blurring of the differences between the sacred and the secular and a denial of their separation; it is the tendency to attribute to everything a sacred sense. But to universalize the sacred is to destroy it: to say that everything is sacred is tantamount to saying that nothing is, for the two qualities, sacred and profane, can be understood only in contrast to one another; every description is a form of negation; the attributes of a totality are inapprehensible.

The secularization of the Christian world does not necessarily take the form of a direct denial of the sacred; it comes about indirectly, through a universalization of the sacred. This, by abolishing the distinction between the sacred and the secular, gives the same result. This is a Christianity which hastens to sanctify in advance all forms of secular life because it considers them to be crystallizations of divine energy: a Christianity without evil, the Christianity of Teilhard de Chardin. It is faith in the universal salvation of everyone and everything, a faith which promises that, whatever we do, we will be participating in the work of the Creator, in the splendid work of building a future harmony. It is the Church of *aggiornomento,* that peculiar term which manages to combine two ideas that are not only different but, in some interpretations, mutually contradictory. According to one, to be a Christian is to be not only outside the world but also in the world; according to the other, to be a Christian is never to be against the world. One says that the Church must embrace as its own the cause of the poor and the oppressed; the other implies that the Church may not oppose the dominant forms of culture and must support the fashions and values recognized in secular society: that it must, in other words, be on the side of the strong and the victorious. Fearful lest it become relegated to the position of an isolated sect, Christianity seems to be making frenzied efforts at mimicry in order to escape being devoured by its enemies—a reaction that seems defensive, but is in fact self-destructive. In the hope of saving itself, it seems to be assuming the colors of its environment, but the result is that it loses its identity, which depends on just that distinction between the sacred and the profane, and on the conflict that can and often must exist between them.

But where is the cause for complaint? Why not say, "If the imaginary order of the sacred evaporates from our consciousness, we shall have that much more energy to put into the practical effort of bettering our lives"? That is where the crux of the problem really lies. Leaving aside the insoluble (or rather, badly put) question of the truth or falsity of religious faith, let us ask whether the necessity of the sacred and our need for it are defensible from the point of view of a philosophy of culture. Such a point of view seems to be legitimate and important.

I want to try to express what is, for me, a suspicion rather than a certainty: the existence of a close link between the dissolution of the sacred, a dissolution encouraged, in our societies, no less by enemies of the Church than by powerful trends within it, and the spiritual phenomena which threaten culture and herald, in my view, its degeneration if not its suicide. I have in mind phenomena which might loosely be described as the love of the amorphous, the desire for homogeneity, the illusion that there are no limits to the perfectibility of which human society is capable, immanentist eschatologies, and the instrumental attitude toward life.

One of the functions of the sacred in our society was to lend an additional significance, impossible to justify by empirical observation alone, to all the basic divisions of human life and all the main areas of human activity. Birth and death, marriage and the sexes, disparities of age and generation, work and art, war and peace, crime and punishment, vocations and professions—all these things had a sacred aspect. There is no point, now, in speculating as to the origins of that additional meaning with which the fundamentals of secular life were imbued. Whatever its origins, the sacred provided society with a system of signs, which served not only to identify these things but also to confer upon each of them a specific value, to fix each within a particular order, imperceptible by direct observation. The signs of the sacred added a weight of the ineffable, as it were, to every given form of social life.

There is no doubt that thereby the role of the sacred has been a conservative one. The sacred order, which encompassed the realities of the secular world, never ceased, implicitly or explicitly, to proclaim the message, "This is how things are, and they cannot be otherwise." It simply reaffirmed and stabilized the structure of society—its forms and its system of divisions, and also its injustices, its privileges, and its institutionalized instruments of oppression. There is no sense in asking how the sacred order imposed on secular life can be maintained without maintaining its conservative force; that force can never be detached from it. Rather, the question to ask is how human society can survive in the absence of conservative forces; in other words, without the constant tension between structure and development. This tension is proper to life; its dissolution would result in death, either by stagnation (if only conservative forces remained) or by explosion (if only the forces of transformation remained, in a structural void).

That is the most abstract way of putting the question. We live in a world in which all our inherited forms and distinctions have come under violent attack; they are attacked in the name of homogeneity, which is held up as an ideal with the aid of vague equations purporting to show that all difference means hierarchy, and all hierarchy oppression—the exact opposite and symmetrical corollary of the old conservative equations, which reduced oppression to hierarchy and hierarchy to difference. Sometimes it seems as if all the words and signs that make up our conceptual framework and provide us with our basic system of distinctions are dissolving before our eyes; as if all the barriers between opposing concepts are gradually being torn down. There is no longer any clear distinction, in political life, between war and peace, sovereignty and servitude, invasion and liberation, equality and despotism. Nor is there a clear-cut dividing line between executioner and victim, between man and woman, between the generations, between crime and heroism, law and arbitrary violence, victory and defeat, right and left, reason and madness, doctor and patient, teacher and pupil, art and buffoonery, knowledge and ignorance. From a world in which all these words picked out and identified certain objects, certain well-defined qualities and situations, arranged in opposing pairs, we have entered another world, in which our system of opposition and classification, even its most vital and most basic elements, has ceased to apply.

It is not difficult to provide specific examples of this peculiar collapse of our concepts; there are plenty of them, and they are well known. One might mention, as random examples, the grotesque attempt, in certain trends of psychiatry, to portray the very idea of mental illness as an instrument of horrific repression, practiced by doctors on alleged patients; the attempt to question the idea of the medical profession itself as the expression of an intolerable hierarchy; the desperate attempts, observed in teen-age fashions and certain trends among feminists, to suppress the differences between men and women; the ideologies which, while trumpeting educational reform, aim to abolish education entirely, since the difference between teacher and pupil is nothing more than a form of deception invented by an oppressive society; or the movements which claim (falsely) to be Marxist while preaching common thuggery and robbery as a remedy for social inequalities. Finally, there are those who claim (with more reason) to be Marxist only to conclude that, since war is merely a continuation of politics, the difference between a politics of war and a politics of peace is no more than a difference between two techniques, to which it would be absurd to attribute additional moral values; and there are those who pursue this line of argument by saying that, since the law is nothing more than an instrument of class oppression, there is no real difference, except in technique, between the rule of law and brute force.

I do not wish to maintain that the political domain is the main source of this conceptual collapse. There is good reason to suppose that the trend expressed in political ideologies is a more general one. The obsession with destroying forms and blurring divisions has been visible in art, music, and literature, without betraying any distinct political inspiration or any links with analogous tendencies that are making themselves felt in philosophy, sexual behavior, the Church, theology, and fashions of dress. I would not, of course, want to exaggerate the importance of these movements: some of them were no more than fleeting outbursts of extravagance. Nevertheless, they deserve our attention, owing not so much to their size as to their number, their convergent tendencies, and the feeble resistance with which they are met.

To say all this is, I admit, to speak in defense of the conservative spirit.

However, it is a conditional conservative spirit, conscious not only of its own necessity but also of the necessity of the spirit that opposes it. As a result, it can see that the tension between rigidity and structure and the forces of change, between tradition and criticism, is a condition of human life—a thing its enemies are seldom prepared to admit. And this in no way implies that we now possess, or shall ever possess, a scale that would permit us to weigh and measure out opposing forces so that we might, in the end, bring about harmony and dissipate the tension between them; these forces can only act in opposition to each other, in conflict, not in complement.

The conservative spirit would be a vain and empty satisfaction were it not constantly wary of itself and mindful of the extent to which it was, is, and may continue to be used in defense of irrational privilege; and that it may be used in this way is the result, not of contingent circumstances, nor of occasional abuse, but of the very nature of the conservative spirit. This conservative spirit knows the difference between the conservatism of great bureaucrats and that of peasants, just as it knows the difference between the revolt of a people who are starving or enslaved and the purely cerebral revolutionism that reflects an emotional void.

But the function of the sacred is not confined to making fast the fundamental distinctions of culture by endowing them with an additional sense that may be drawn only from the authority of tradition. To distinguish between the sacred and the profane is already to deny total autonomy to the profane order and to admit that there are limits to the degree of perfection it can attain. Since the profane is defined in opposition to the sacred, its imperfection must be intrinsic and in some measure incurable. Culture, when it loses its sacred sense, loses all sense. With the disappearance of the sacred, which imposed limits to the perfection that could be attained by the profane, arises one of the most dangerous illusions of our civilization— the illusion that there are no limits to the changes that human life can undergo, that society is "in principle" an endlessly flexible thing, and that to deny this flexibility and this perfectability is to deny man's total autonomy and thus to deny man himself.

Not only is this illusion demented, but it sows a disastrous despair. The omnipresent Nietzschian or Sartrian chimera which proclaims that man can liberate himself totally, from everything, can free himself of tradition and of all pre-existing sense, and that all sense can be decreed by arbitrary whim, far from unfurling before us the prospect of divine self-creation, leaves us suspended in darkness. And in this darkness, where all things are equally good, all things are also equally indifferent. Once I believe that I am the all-powerful creator of all possible sense, I also believe that I have no reason to create anything whatsoever. But this is a belief that cannot be accepted in good faith and can only give rise to a desperate flight from nothingness to nothingness. To be totally free with respect to sense, free of all pressure from tradition, is to situate oneself in a void and thus, quite simply, to disintegrate. And sense can come only from the sacred; it cannot be produced by empirical research. The utopia of man's perfect autonomy and the hope of unlimited perfection may be the most efficient instruments of suicide ever to have been invented by human culture.

To reject the sacred is to reject our own limits. It is also to reject the idea of evil, for the sacred reveals itself through sin, imperfection, and evil; and evil, in turn, can be identified only through the sacred. To say that evil is contingent is to say that there is no evil, and therefore that we have no need of a sense that is already there, fixed and imposed on us whether we will it or not. But to say this is also to say that our only means of decreeing sense is our innate impulse; and this means that we must either share the childlike faith of old anarchists in our natural goodness or admit that we can affirm our identity only when we revert to our precultural state; in other words, that we can affirm it only as undomesticated animals. Thus the bottom line, as it were, of the ideal of total liberation is the sanctioning of force and violence and thereby, finally, of despotism and the destruction of culture.

If it is true that in order to make society more tolerable, we must believe that it can be improved, it is also true that there must always be people who think of the price paid for every step of what we call progress. The order of the sacred is also a sensitivity to evil—the only system of reference that allows us to contemplate that price and forces us to ask whether it is not exorbitant.

Religion is man's way of accepting life as an inevitable defeat. That it is not an inevitable defeat is a claim that cannot be defended in good faith. One can, of course, disperse one's life over the contingencies of every day, but even then it is only a ceaseless and desperate desire to live, and finally a regret that one has not lived. One can accept life, and accept it, at the same time, as a defeat only if one accepts that there is sense beyond that which is inherent in human history—if, in other words, one accepts the order of the sacred. A hypothetical world from which the sacred had been swept away would admit of only two possibilities: vain fantasy that recognizes itself as such, or immediate satisfaction which exhausts itself. It would leave only the choice proposed by Baudelaire, between lovers of prostitutes and lovers of clouds: those who know only the satisfactions of the moment and are therefore contemptible, and those who lose themselves in otiose imaginings, and are therefore contemptible. Everything is then contemptible, and there is no more to be said. The conscience liberated from the sacred knows this, even if it conceals it from itself.

Chapter Seven

Can the Devil Be Saved?

My purpose in taking up this theme, which I have borrowed from Giovanni Papini's book on the devil, is to use it as the symbol of a fundamental question, one that has recurred throughout the religious and philosophical history of our culture. Can the cosmic and historical drama be interpreted as a movement towards the ultimate reconciliation of all things? Will the evils of the human condition, our sufferings and our failures, reveal their redemptive meaning when seen from the vantage point of ultimate salvation?

Posing the question in such a general form immediately reveals that it is neither a specifically Christian nor even a specifically religious problem but is useful in distinguishing different trends both in Christianity and in secular theories of salvation (including Marxism). The question is more formidable than the traditional theodicies would have it. We ask not only whether evil, envisaged in the broadest soteriological perspective, will turn out to form part of the necessarily good Providential blueprint, *i.e.,* have an instrumental role as a portion of the raw material of the divine construction of history; but we must also ask whether it will prove not to be evil at all, whether at the end nothing will be omitted from universal salvation, nothing rejected, nothing extraneous.

☐

Certainly, early Christian teaching was articulated partially in the struggle against Manichaeism and its derivative Christological heresies such as Monophysitism, though the struggle against the Pelagian heresy was probably far more important in shaping the doctrinal corpus of Christianity. What Christianity attacked in the Manichaean theology was the eternal, unavoidable dilemma put forward by the Epicureans: since evil exists in the world, then God himself must be evil, or impotent—or both. The basic question here was, of course, the limitation of divine omnipotence, a con-

Reprinted by permission of the publisher from *Encounter* (July 1974), with revisions by the author. Copyright © 1974 by Encounter, Ltd.

sequence which seemed inescapable once evil was admitted as a positive reality. The Augustinian theory of the privative character of evil had to cope with this difficulty and come up with a salutary formula which would retain untouched the essential goodness of being, the idea of God as the unique Creator. In denying its ontological foundation, this formula did not, of course, affect the reality of evil, the fact that there is a diabolical will directed towards it. St. Augustine stressed most emphatically that each act that emanates from human will alone is turned against God and is by definition evil and diabolic. Certain consequences of this theory of evil *privatio* are difficult to understand, and in particular the idea that even Satan must be good, in so far as he *exists,* and if one takes being and goodness to be coextensive. Thus, the conventional Christian philosophy of evil avoids the dangers of limiting (and thereby abolishing) divine omnipotence. Certain Christian writers stretch this interpretation so far that they seem to imply that, although human will naturally tends towards the good, because of ignorance, people perceive good where it does not in fact exist—which would seem to run counter to both the idea of original sin and the principle which states that grace is a necessary condition of good will.

The rejection of Pelagianism seems to me to have been crucial in molding Christian teaching. Perhaps I could speak not of Pelagianism in the strict historical sense but rather of a larger tendency which reinforces, implies, renders plausible, or furnishes arguments for the claim that *evil is in principle eradicable*—that evil is contingent, not inherent in the nature of the world.

In Christian thought, the damnation of the devil and the concept of original sin are the most precise forms in which the contingent character of evil is denied. I believe that this denial is of the utmost importance to our culture but that one can also discern in the Christian world a strong temptation to abandon this position and yield to that optimistic Enlightenment tradition which believed in the final reconciliation of all things in ultimate universal harmony. Whether it is expressed in Teilhard de Chardin's pantheist teachings or in Bishop John Robinson's denial of a difference between the sacred and the profane, whether based on certain of Paul Tillich's ideas or on an attempt to assimilate Feuerbach's anthropology to Christianity, this belief in universal reconciliation is not only contrary to the Christian tradition but runs counter to what we gather from the scientists to be the enduring patterns of human life. Eventually it endangers important values in our culture. I do not, however, deny the justness of much of the criticism of the Church for its harmful use of the doctrine of original sin.

The two complementary ideas at the very core of Christian culture—that humanity was basically saved by Christ's coming, and that since the exile from paradise, every human being is basically condemned if we consider his natural status alone and set grace aside—should be considered jointly solely in order to counteract the jaunty optimism or the despair that could result if they were dealt with separately.

Certainly the Church has specifically declared that many people had been saved and has never specifically declared that any one was condemned. There is nothing in the Church's teaching that clearly excludes the possibility that hell is empty, but there is nothing to permit the assumption that hell does not exist. The devil's presence confirms unambiguously that evil is an everlasting part of the world that can never be completely eradicated, and that universal reconciliation cannot be hoped for. One of the basic principles of the Catholic Church is that Christ died for everyone, not merely for the elect, but that man is free only to accept grace or to reject it, without thereby positively reinforcing its energy (denial of irresistible grace); this was a basic idea of the Council of Trent and seems to follow naturally from the doctrine of original sin.

The belief in the eventual synthesis of all values and energies in the universe, which will prove to be differentiated outflowings or ramifications of the same divine root of being, reappears in the "Neoplatonic peripheries" of Christian history. It can be found in Scotus Eriugena's *De Divisione Naturae* and in Teilhard's *Phénomène humain,* and a Christian must view Hegel's *Phenomenology of Mind* as a bastard offspring of the same theodicy. The implication of this belief is that cosmic history leaves no rubbish behind; everything is finally digested, everything incorporated, in the triumphal progress of the spirit. In the ultimate balance, all is justified, each element and event, struggle and contradiction will appear as an individual contribution to the same work of salvation.

This belief in a universal synthesis to be consummated in the Omega point is rooted in the very concept of a unique Creator. Once we know that essence, existence, and love perfectly converge in the primordial divine being, how can we escape the conclusion that whatever occurs in the world is ultimately reducible to that same unique source of energy and conveys the same message of original love? How could this energy be diverted from its natural channel and turned against God Himself? How could any damage be irreparable, any corruption eternal? In fact, how can one believe in the devil? The traditional answer was that evil is pure negativity, *carentia,* absence of good, that it is simply a hole in the compact mass of Being. But this is hardly satisfactory, since a negative energy is still needed to drill this hole. Where does this energy come from? The only answer suggested by the idea of the unique Creator is that this energy must spring from the same source, that an eye which spies on the world from the viewpoint of totality can discover the all-encompassing divine love even in apparent monstrosities, can perceive charity in cruelty, harmony in struggle, hope in despair, order in corruption, ascent in descent.

□

But another danger awaits those who hoped to discover a salutary quibble in their denial of the reality of evil (and not only of its ontological autonomy). They have to reveal a meaning in this self-abolishing movement of evil, and this meaning must obviously be related to God Himself, since only in God may a reason be found for the creation of the world and all its miseries.

This leads them easily to the suggestion—typical of all Neoplatonic theodicies—that God brought the Universe into being so that He might grow in its body; that He needs His alienated creatures to complete His perfection. The growth of the universe, and in particular the development of the human spirit which leads all things toward perfection, involves God Himself in the historical process. Consequently God Himself becomes historical. At the culmination of cosmic evolution He is not what He was "in the beginning." He creates the world and in reabsorbing it enriches Himself. And so long as the odyssey of the spirit is not consummated, God cannot be considered a self-sufficient and timeless perfection. What was supposed to be a theodicy is transformed into a theogony: a history of the growing God. This is what happened to Eriugena and Teilhard, for in attempting to avoid the trap of abolishing God's omnipotence, they abolish His perfection, His timelessness, His self-sufficiency.

□

Needless to say, I am in no position to clarify these difficulties or to propose any new solution to questions that have tormented the most eminent philosophical and religious thinkers for centuries. I am merely trying to say that there is a cultural danger inherent in any utopia of perfect reconciliation and—what is another facet of the same problem—that the concept of original sin gives us a penetrating insight into human destiny.

It is hardly surprising that the optimistic philosophy of universal reconciliation should tempt contemporary Christianity so strongly. After the many failures it suffered through its inability to cope with a secular civilization and its mistrust of intellectual and social changes beyond its control, after its spurious success in overcoming the Modernist crisis at the beginning of this century, a Great Fear seems to have pervaded the Christian world—the fear of being trapped in an alien enclave within a basically un-Christian society. This Great Fear of being out-distanced and isolated now impels Christian thinking towards the idea that the most important task of Christianity is not only to be "within the world," not only to participate in the efforts of secular culture, not only to modify the language of its teachings so that they are intelligible to all men, but to sanctify in advance almost any movement that arises spontaneously from natural human impulses. Universal suspicion seems to have been supplanted by universal approval, the dread of a forced retreat to the Christian culture of the Syllabus seems to inspire a push forward to the Christian culture of Münster, and the threat of being scratched from the competition appears to be stronger than that of losing one's identity. Not surprisingly, this fear finds expression in the shifts of Christian teaching, from which the concepts of the devil and of original sin seem almost to have vanished. Belief in our unlimited natural perfectibility in the *Parousia* that we will ourselves prepare, is gradually prevailing in the minds of Christians.

Even non-Christians are entitled to speculate anxiously about the form of Christianity and about its fate. Christianity is part of our common spiritual heritage, and to be entirely non-Christian would mean exclusion from this culture. Clearly Christianity is an important factor in moral education; spiritual changes in Christianity correspond to changes that occur outside it, and both must be interpreted together. The world needs Christianity, not only in the subjective sense, but also because it is probable that certain important tasks cannot be undertaken without it, and Christianity must assume its responsibility for the world that it has helped for centuries to shape.

No one can deny that the idea of original sin and the incurable corruption of human nature may be (and has been) used as an effective ideological instrument of conservative resistance to social change and attempts to undermine existing systems of privilege. It is tempting to vindicate any kind of injustice simply by saying: "Our destiny is to suffer; our sins are great; no essential improvement of the human condition can be expected on earth." In both the nineteenth and the twentieth centuries, many more or less official pronouncements and much of the Catholic literature on social problems run true to the typical patterns of conservative Catholic mentality and justify even the crude, traditional criticisms by socialist writers.

It would, however, be too easy to shrug off this question simply by saying that the notion of original sin does not entail this type of conclusion, that it was "abused" for an improper purpose, or "misinterpreted." The connection between an awareness of original sin and an attitude of passive resignation in the face of human misery cannot be reduced to a trivial error in logic; it is both stronger and more important. To say that we are infected with original corruption and that the devil cannot be converted does in fact mean that there is a great deal of evil that cannot be eradicated, and that there is something incurable in our misery. It does not mean that all kinds of evil are eternal, all forms of misery unavoidable. But in our human condition we have no means of discovering beyond any doubt what does and what does not depend on us; we are unable to draw the line between the temporary and the lasting aspects of our spiritual and physical poverty. We do not even know how to define these aspects. Many specific misfortunes are reversible, and many burdens can be alleviated, but we can never know in advance what price we must pay for our achievements, since the values we gain are paid for in a coin that is nonconvertible. Each fragment of what we call progress has to be paid for, and we can make no comparisons between the expenditure and the rewards. Our inability to balance the books is itself part of our incurable disablement. Since an increase in our satisfactions is always accompanied by a multiplication of our needs, we cannot know whether the gap between what we subjectively need and what we are capable of satisfying is decreasing or, if it is, how to measure that decrease. We feel it our duty to struggle against all sources of affliction, but we do so without hope of ever being certain that there is fruit on the tree of progress.

The possible disastrous effects of the concept of original sin on our psychological condition and our cultural life are undeniable; and so are the disastrous effects of the opposing doctrine, with its implication that our perfectibility is limitless, and that our predictions of ultimate synthesis or total reconciliation can be realized. However, the fact that both affirmation and rejection of the concept of original sin have emerged as powerful destructive forces in our history is one of many that testify in favor of the reality of original sin. In other words, we face a peculiar situation in which the disastrous consequences of assenting to either of two incompatible theories confirm one of them and testify against its rival.

□

This rival theory—the denial of the ontological meaning of evil, or at least the denial of our inherent inability to dispose of evil completely— is disastrous for other reasons. If everything is ultimately to be justified, everything to receive a meaning in the definitive salvation, then not only will past history be judged innocent, but contemporary history as well—

and contemporary history is precisely what we are doing here and now. Thus we will necessarily be acquitted when the last judgment is delivered, either because our motives were good or because we were merely unconscious agents of the wisdom of Providence. Hope for the full eradication of evil in the future carries with it the testimony of present innocence. Let us rejoice! After Armageddon even the vanquished army will arise from death to glory.

□

The prospect of that final unity, which—thanks to human efforts—will benignly absorb and enoble the painful march of past history, is present both in the Christian world and in the history of socialist movements. The words *thanks to human efforts* should be emphasized. Even the hope of an individual paradise, attainable on earth—as with the mystics— can be disastrous as if it is based on the idea that the mystical *annihilatio* can occur as a result of, or as a reward for, the individual's contemplative training. Indifference to others' needs and sufferings and neglect of one's own moral standards easily follow such hopes (one may see this in the Quietists), since a single undifferentiated act of faith is supposed to absorb (and thereby abolish) all partial and more modest merits. But even in those mystics who awaited the union of love with God as a gratuitous gift of grace, the frontier between exclusive absorption with God and indifference to others is dangerously blurred, not unlike the frontier between contempt for the flesh and idolatry of the physical world as an emanation from the Creator. The dangers are still more patent if we nourish the hope for a collective paradise, as in the Chiliastic movements. This explosive hope is strongly rooted in the tradition of socialist thought. We find it in Marx (rather less in Engels) in the shape of a belief that the communist future will encompass the perfect reconciliation of man's empirical existence with his genuine essence and with Great Nature as well. This return of man to himself—the complete reappropriation of all human forces and faculties—is exactly what the paradisiac state is supposed to be; the perfect unity of human beings on both an individual and a social scale. The spectacle of man perfectly united with himself and with his social and natural environments is as incomprehensible as the concept of heaven. The inconsistency is basically the same: an earthly paradise must combine satisfaction with creativity, a heavenly paradise must combine satisfaction with love. Both combinations are inconceivable, since without dissatisfaction—without some form of suffering— there can be no creativity, no love. Complete satisfaction is death; partial dissatisfaction entails pain.

This seems a most trivial platitude, but somehow in the promise of paradise and the perfect unity of man it goes unnoticed. The inconsistency is perhaps most flagrant in the case of earthly paradise, since the confrontation of empirical realities is in this case possible, whereas no one claims to know the laws by which heaven is ruled. That the very idea of the unity of man is inconceivable again bears witness to the reality of original sin.

And there is further testimony, so extensive and so powerful that it seems unpardonable to ignore it. Our corruptibility is not contingent. We pretend to know this but rarely examine the relevance of this knowledge to our hopes. We pretend to know that nothing is evergreen, that each source of life is eventually exhausted and each concentration of energy eventually dispersed. We pretend to know that the biological process of life itself is the source of anxiety, conflict, aggression, uncertainty, concern. We pretend to know that no consistent system of values is possible and that at every step values that we consider important become mutually exclusive when we attempt their practical application to individual cases; tragedy, the *moral* victory of evil, is always possible. We pretend to know that reason often hampers our ability to liberate our energies, that moments of joy are more often than not wrested from intellectual lucidity. We pretend to know that creation is a struggle of man against himself and, more often than not, against others also, that the bliss of love lies in hopeful dissatisfaction, that in our world, death is the only total unity. We pretend to know why our noble motives slide into evil results, why our will toward good emerges from pride, hatred, vanity, envy, personal ambition. We pretend to know that most of life consists in taking flight from reality and concealing this reality from ourselves. We pretend to know that our efforts to improve the world are constrained by the narrow limits defined by our biological structure and by the pressures of the past which have molded us and which we cannot leave very far behind. All these things, which we pretend to be aware of, compose the reality of original sin—and yet it is this reality that we attempt to deny.

□

Certainly, our denial is not without grounds, and arguments can be put forward to justify it. One can argue that sometimes the truth can poison, and a lie may well be a blessing. One can argue that the truth about original sin entails the conclusion that this truth must not be revealed, since we may be so utterly discouraged by the awareness of the narrow limits within which our efforts are successful that paralysis prevents us from achieving even the modest successes of which we are capable. One can argue that only an infinite hope can set in motion the energy needed to achieve finite results, that although we can never get rid of suffering, we can alleviate or limit it, and in order to do so efficiently we must accept the erroneous belief that eventually suffering will be totally abolished. In short, it is arguable that we can do what we can only because we believe that we can do something we cannot.

There is a good deal of truth in such arguments. It seems probable that we could not endure life if we knew from the beginning all that we have learned from decades of experience. An ingenious device exists in our inability to convince young people of the deceptiveness of their great hopes; if these hopes do result in anything of value, it can only be because they were deceptive. Probably little improvement would have been achieved in human life had people known in advance the price they would have to pay. Perhaps the most usual form in which one perceives the concept of original sin is the conviction that every individual is eventually defeated in his struggle with life, that we have lost before we begin the battle. In most cases, to hold this conviction would deprive us of the will to fight—there is good reason why we prefer to reject the ontological meaning of evil.

But there is also good reason for stating that we ought to face up to its reality, and not only because we admit the primacy of truth over efficiency, since this primacy cannot rationally be demonstrated. The promise of total salvation, the hope of a beneficent Apocalypse which will restore man to his innocence, flies in the face of reason and our right to remain individuals. The connection is obvious.

Our imperfection is revealed by—among other things—our ability to doubt, but this very ability maintains the precarious equilibrium of our social and individual life. Doubt has played an essential role in our attainment of the status of rational beings; we must protect our ability and our right to doubt in order to preserve our intellectual and moral balance. The fact of our imperfection is not alone a sufficient basis to enable us to doubt; we need an awareness of that imperfection. Doubt may be considered one of the consequences of original sin, but it also protects us against its more deleterious effects. It is important for us to be uncertain about the deep motives for our own deeds and the grounds of our convictions, since this is the only device that protects us against an all-justifying fanaticism and intolerance. We should remember that the perfect unity of man is impossible, otherwise we would try to impose this unity by any means available, and our foolish visions of perfection would evaporate in violence and end in a theocratic or totalitarian caricature of unity which claimed to make the Great Impossible an actuality. The greater our hopes for humanity, the more we are ready to sacrifice, and this too seems very rational. As Anatole France once remarked, never have so many been murdered in the name of a doctrine as in the name of the principle that human beings are naturally good.

Nobody wants to doubt, but to destroy doubt is to subvert reason. According to the ancient Persian mythology, which was the main source of the Manichaean philosophy, the God of Evil and the God of Goodness were twin brothers; both were born, and not just one, because a doubt had slipped into the mind of the primordial God. Consequently doubt is the original source of evil, and not its result—not surprisingly, since to the divine mind, doubt is destruction. To our minds, doubt bears witness to our imperfection rather than producing it, but at the same time prevents the evil in us from realizing its full potential. That which makes us painfully imperfect helps us to be less imperfect than we might have been, and this again attests to the reality of original sin.

□

Having abandoned the myth of Prometheus, perhaps we need not portray our condition in terms of the static myth of Sisyphus, despite Albert Camus's pessimism. The biblical legend of Nebuchadnezzar, who was degraded to the condition of a beast when he tried to exalt himself to the dignity of God, would perhaps serve us better.

We know all too well that there is no achievement of mind, no act of human genius, that cannot be turned against man or in some way used as an instrument of the devil. Our inventiveness will never be sufficiently powerful to outwit the devil and prevent him from turning our noblest creations against us. Doubt is one of the natural resources we can employ against him, since doubt may weaken our Promethean self-confidence and mediate between the incompatible demands that life imposes on us. Needless to say, the devil can also harness doubt to his service and make it the pretext for inaction and immobility when we need resolution and a readiness to dare the uncertainties of struggle. Our natural forces can find no safe shelter against evil; all we can do is practice the art of balancing opposing dangers. And this is precisely what the Christian tradition affirms in its statement that certain results of original sin are inescapable, and that if salvation is possible, it can only be through grace.

There are reasons why we need Christianity, but not just any kind of Christianity. We do not need a Christianity that makes political revolution, that rushes to cooperate with so-called sexual liberation, that approves our concupiscence or praises our violence. There are enough forces in the world to do all these things without the aid of Christianity. We need a Christianity that will help us to move beyond the immediate pressures of life, that gives us insight into the basic limits of the human condition and the capacity to accept them, a Christianity that teaches us the simple truth that there is not only a tomorrow but a day after tomorrow as well, and that the difference between success and failure is rarely distinguishable. We need a Christianity that is not gold, or purple, or red, but grey.

□

Yet we need more than Christianity, not for the sake of an abstract pleasure in variety, but because the truth of Christianity is as one-sided as any other truth. We need the living tradition of socialist thought, which appeals to human forces solely by promoting the traditional values of social justice and freedom. And here again we need not just any kind of socialist idea. We do not need foolish fantasies about a society from which any temptation to evil has been removed; or about a total revolution that will secure for us at one stroke the blessings of ultimate salvation and a world without strife. We need a socialism that helps us to understand the complexity of the brutal forces acting in human history and reinforces our readiness to fight against social oppression and human misery. We need a socialist tradition that is aware of its own limitations, since the dream of ultimate salvation on earth is despair disguised as hope—the will to power disguised as a craving for justice.

We cannot, however, expect a grand synthesis of the different and incompatible traditions that we need. We may attempt to reconcile in an abstract generality the values that we really need, but in the majority of actual cases we will find them in opposition to each other. The Eden of human universality is a paradise lost.

Chapter Eight

On the So-Called Crisis of Christianity

The word *crisis* has become one of the most fashionable of the last few decades; it is used in the most varied senses, often only very distantly related to the original. Sometimes it means little more than "shortage" (as in *food crisis,* or *oil crisis*). At other times in speaking of crises we mean to say that some form of social life is weakening or losing vitality (*crisis of the family, crisis of Christianity, crisis of Marxism, crisis of democracy,* and so on). At still other times, we mean that something has changed suddenly (*revolutionary crisis*) or even gradually (*crisis of confidence in government*). *Demographic crisis* can mean that in some country the population is growing rapidly or, on the contrary, that it is declining. *Crisis in science* can mean that in some branch of knowledge there are insoluble problems or, on the contrary, that there are no interesting problems. The economic crises of the nineteenth and first half of the twentieth centuries had mechanisms and appearances so different from the upheavals and catastrophes of the contemporary economy that using the same word for both of them can be justified only by the word's vagueness. *Crisis* loosely means all forms of negativity: collapse, decline, shortage, pathology.

The very word *krino,* as can easily be discovered from any dictionary, primarily meant "to separate" or, derivatively, "to differentiate," hence also "to judge," whence *crisis* subsequently meant not any kind of negative change, but a sudden breach of continuity (regardless of whether it is judged negatively or positively); in this sense events such as religious conversion, political revolution, war, divorce, or death can be termed crises. However, the universalization of the word is not perhaps the result of our linguistic carelessness, but betrays a vague feeling that all forms of life, social

Translated from the Polish by Stefan Czerniawski from "O Tak Zwanym Kryzysie Chrzescijanstwa." First published in German in *Frankfurter Allgemeine Zeitung,* 17 April 1976; later published in Polish in *Aneks,* no. 12, 1976; reprinted in German in a collection of Kolakowski's essays under the title *Leben trotz Geschichte.* Copyright © 1977 by Piper Verlag. Revised by the author in English.

organization, thought, and feeling, all components of our civilization, are afflicted with a sickness for which nobody knows the cure—a feeling that uncertainty about the fate of humanity has become universal, although masked by aggressive platitudes.

When we talk about the "crisis of Christianity" we usually have in mind, first and foremost, that during the last few decades, an ever-increasing percentage of people in traditionally Christian countries either do not think of themselves as Christian any more, or hardly ever take part in church services, or simply do not show that beliefs and moral norms deriving from Christian traditions have any perceptible influence on their behavior. However, the extent to which these known phenomena, normally associated with the growth of urbanization, are symptoms of a crisis of Christianity depends, obviously, on the meaning with which we endow not only the word *crisis* but also the word *Christianity*—and here, as is generally recognized, there has never been agreement.

In the sixteenth and seventeenth centuries, when dozens of greater and lesser sects multiplied in Europe, each of which had a monopoly on the uniquely correct interpretation of the content of Christianity and condemned all the others for their misconceptions about the Holy Trinity, the eucharist, the divinity of Jesus, irresistible grace, the role of the Church, and so on, many writers, tired and despairing of the sectarian squabbles, suggested an irenic program. Let us at least agree, they said, on a common minimum about which all Christians must definitely agree, and in fact do agree, and let us accept that anyone who holds to this minimum is a Christian; but in all other questions "unnecessary for salvation," let us proclaim reciprocal tolerance.

Such suggestions could not, it is clear, lead to the hoped-for religious peace: first, because there was complete disagreement about the content of the minimum and the criteria by which it should be determined; second, because the minimum could never be unambiguous, and every attempt at a more detailed interpretation immediately revived all the disputes that they hoped to avoid; and third, because if all questions lying beyond the projected minimum were acknowledged to be unimportant, no existing church or sect would have a raison d'être as a separate Christian grouping, and this was obviously the crucial point.

These ecumenical programs were inspired to a significant extent by the ideas of evangelical Christianity that originated before the great reformation, of which Erasmus and his followers were the most ardent proponents. These programs could not in fact disturb the rigid exclusivity of the quarreling communities or lead to reconciliation. Despite this, they were not entirely ineffective. They brought certain ideas into play which did not die out in Christianity and are revived on various occasions. They created a model of Christianity not defined by detailed theological doctrines, nor by organizational criteria, but by "faith" in the original sense of the word: that is, trust in divine mercy and in the effectiveness of the act of redemption and of moral observance. In one sense, however, the Catholic Church and the major Protestant congregations had in practice to accept a "minimum" as well as a "maximum" definition of their faith, a limited as well as a complete model. They all had to assume that salvation does not depend on theological erudition, that the faith of simpletons is in no way worse than the faith of doctors and bishops, that a simple, illiterate peasant is by no means a worse Christian or any less deserving of God's attention because he is illiterate—for how many Catholics know all the decrees of all the councils by heart and can expound without error the entire dogma which is theoretically binding for them? On the other hand, even the simple catechism, knowledge of which was demanded of all believers, has for all sects always included not only such a minimal dogma, such as the Nicene Creed, and a minimum of morality, but also a certain number of shibboleths that satisfactorily distinguished a given sect or church from all the remainder and worked against the temptation of ecumenicism. Rituals, even hymns and carols, also included these shibboleths. So even the factually recognized minimum was not an instrument of unity, but rather consolidated organizational fragmentation.

In any case, if we assume that the church is, as it were, on the boundary of heaven and earth, that it is the depository of grace and also the guardian of the law, and that it dispenses invisible goods in a visible world, then it could not have been otherwise. Some radicals of the Reformation wanted to cleanse Christianity of all earthly forms, to make it independent of all connections with the profane. They asserted that everything that Christianity is about takes place in the soul of each individual Christian; that there alone the drama of the fall and reconciliation is played out; there the old man struggles with the new, satan with God; that to place Christian values "outside" conscience—and thus in the Church, in dogmas, in rituals—is simply to throw them away; that these values are attached solely to the individual subject and do not add up to any "objective" whole. They believed that they had restored the real content to Christ's message when they stripped connections with visible earthly realities from it.

This purified Christianity, however, was ceasing to be a message at all.

And yet Christianity was meant to be the gospel, good news proclaimed to the world. It was meant to be the transmitter of grace on earth and accordingly had to have earthly means of communication: congregations, catechisms, and rituals. Reduced to the invisible individual conscience, it would transmit nothing to anyone. Should the apostles have wandered the earth to no purpose, or should they have escaped to the desert and awaited the second coming outside the world? Jesus said that His kingdom is not of this world, but at the same time He sent His disciples to proclaim His teachings to the people of the world. But teachings proclaimed to the world must be expressed and codified in words, and the apostles needed to know that they were teaching with one voice, and that they were therefore a church, not individual believers who communicated separately with God.

Thus Christianity cannot free itself from the tensions that arise from the very nature of its tasks; from the fact that it has to disseminate unworldly values in the visible world and by worldly means. It can abolish this tension only by arbitrarily removing one of its components. This is precisely what the radicals of the Reformation tried to do when they stripped Christianity of its links with the material, the body, the temporal and social life (thus effectively denying the act of incarnation), just as many contemporary "progressives" do in reducing Christianity to a political program and simply chopping off its religious roots (thus also denying the act of incarnation). Christianity, though, is the belief that God became man, not sometime, somewhere, in the indefinable darkness of a prehistoric age, but at a time and place that are precisely designated. Thereby it was established that corporality could not simply be evil, that invisible values may take on a visible form, that secular history may be a medium through which sacred history, the history of salvation, can express itself.

Let us then attempt on our own account to follow the example of the irenists of old and determine a certain minimum of Christianity; not, however, simply to extract the common elements of the various quarreling Christian sects known to history, but to extract the constitutive points from the content of the original message, even if this can be done only with a certain arbitrariness.

There should nevertheless be no dispute that the belief that God became flesh for the redemption of mankind is such a constitutive point, without which the word *Christianity* loses all perceptible sense. The story of the redemption was always most susceptible to the derision of rationalists and freethinkers. It can, in fact, be described in a version that makes it seem absurd and contradictory to elementary moral feeling. Thus the people offended God, after which God agreed to forgive them, but only on condition that his own beloved and entirely innocent son should be tortured to death by these same people. The history of Christianity is a greater miracle in this grotesque version, however, than that which results from its own self-interpretation: since millions of people over hundreds of years have believed in this absurdity, which is quite obviously contrary to the principles that they have otherwise professed, there is no explaining this success by natural circumstances.

In reality, the story of the redemption appears in a different light if it is treated as an expression of two independent beliefs (or perhaps feelings), deeply rooted in people's consciousness, though obviously not amenable to scientific discussion. One of these is the belief in the law of a cosmic clearance of accounts, that is, the belief that there is no absolute "unpunishability," that every moral evil must be redeemed by an appropriate amount of suffering (perhaps the very concept of punishment and justice in the traditional popular sense embodies this belief). The punishment of the innocent for the crimes of others is contradictory to universal moral feeling; it is not, however, contradictory to it that people by their own free will take on suffering in order to spare others. If the Son of God took on Himself this burden—and the Son of God could suffer only in the body—then people are free to believe that the chain of evil had been broken and cosmic justice followed by the fact of external intervention.

Thereby, however—and this is the second branch of belief in the story of redemption—people recognize that they are too weak to break the chain themselves, that salvation cannot be entirely their own doing, that God Himself had to make Himself a part of earthly history in order to complete the act of redemption there. Faith in Jesus the redeemer thus attests that we do not have enough strength to liberate ourselves from evil, that the mark of original sin weighs on us inescapably, that we cannot deliver ourselves from it without external help.

Christianity is thus the awareness of our weakness and misery, and it is useless to argue that there exists or could exist a "Promethean Christianity," that is, that Christian faith could be reconciled with hope for self-salvation. Two great ideas of the nineteenth century which, despite all that separates them, perfectly embodied this Promethean expectation—those of Marx and of Nietzsche—were anti-Christian in their roots, and not as a result of accidental historical circumstances. Nietzsche's hatred of Christianity and of Jesus was a natural consequence of his belief in the unlimited possibility of mankind's self-creation. Nietzsche knew that Christianity is the awareness of our weakness, and he was right. Marx knew this too, and from the young Hegelians, he took over and transformed the philosophy (more Fichtean than Hegelian) of self-creation and futuristic orientation. He came to believe that the collective Prometheus of the future would reach a state in which his thought and action would be indistinguishable and in which even "atheism" would lose its reason for existence, since people's self-affirmation would be entirely "positive," not negatively dependent on the negation of God.

The vitality of the Christian idea has certainly weakened in proportion to the universalization of the Promethean hope and in proportion to the growth of people's belief that their ability to perfect themselves and society knows no limit and that they will produce ever-more-splendid monuments to the greatness of mankind, or even that in the end they will bring about a life from which evil, suffering, aggression, conflict, poverty, anxiety, and sadness have been eliminated once and for all. We have witnessed the gradual growth of this hope, and the two versions of it mentioned—Nietzsche's and Marx's—produced the ideological cover that served to justify the two most malignant tyrannies that our century has seen. Are we witnessing the further growth of this same hope? We may doubt it. It seems rather that it has passed its zenith. We cannot be at all certain that its weakening will mean the renewed growth of Christianity in its traditional forms, but it will mean the renewed fertilization of the soil from which Christianity has always grown.

But the same visible phenomena in which we discern a "crisis" or even the collapse of Christianity are by no means unequivocal. Christianity has been unsuccessfully condemned to death so many times and has so often regenerated itself from unexpected sources that, at the very least, considerable caution is necessary in prophesying its fall, since the prophecies are based mainly on extrapolations from statistics concerning the frequency of participation in church ceremonies. Was Europe more Christian in the eleventh century than today? The answer again depends on the interpretation of the word. If the triumph of Christianity depends on all aspects of culture having a Christian form, then the "crisis of Christianity" has lasted at least since the fourteenth century. Europe in fact went through a period in which Christianity simply had a monopoly on providing the form for all areas of people's lives. It was not only philosophy, painting, architecture, the calendar, and the family that were organized in Christian forms, but wars, invasions, torture, courts, and the organization of government were also all "Christian." All conflicting human interests and all aspirations were expressed in Christian symbols.

According to the interpretation being suggested here (which admittedly is arbitrary, though not capriciously so, and is historically justifiable), the strength of Christianity does not reveal itself in a theocracy or in a monopoly on the creation of rules for all areas of civilization. Its strength in this interpretation is manifested in its ability to build a barrier against hatred in the consciousness of individuals. Indeed, the very belief in Jesus the redeemer would be empty and lifeless if it did not entail the renunciation of hatred as a motive, independently of the circumstances—if, after the words "forgive us our trespasses," Christians did not have to repeat the words "as we forgive those who trespass against us." The requirement of the renunciation of hatred was a challenge thrown down by Christianity to human nature, and it has remained so. If Christians are to be found only among those who know how to meet this challenge, who are disciples of Jesus in the sense that they do not escape from the struggle, but are free from hatred—how many have there been, and how many are there now in the world? I do not know. I do not know whether there were more in the middle ages than there are now. However many there are, they are the salt of the earth, and European civilization would be a desert without them.

If we reduce Christianity to the following minimum—the belief that Jesus the redeemer appeared on earth in historic time in order to free us from evil, from which we could not free ourselves, and the ability to remove hatred which follows from this belief—we notice that, strictly speaking, there is no such thing as a Christian political program or a Christian system of government. In this matter, as in all others, the history of Christianity is full of disputes in which extremely opposed positions were expressed. Communist sects of the middle ages, revolutionary Anabaptists, and various nineteenth-century socialists (such as Weitling) extracted everything from the New Testament that could be turned against the rich, tyrants, and usurers. They argued that a society constructed on Christian principles will proclaim equality as its main slogan, that it is the duty of a Christian, as such, to fight actively against social injustice, and that Jesus was a prophet of revolutionary Communism. On the other hand, the Catholic hierarchy repeated for centuries, until the end of the nineteenth century, that the obligation of a Christian is humbly to bear poverty and suffering on earth, that rebellion is against the law of God, and that social inequality was instituted by God.

It seems, however, that both these interpretations (leaving aside their obvious social bases) were, and are, remnants of medieval culture, in which Christianity was treated as a universal source of norms and standards that were obligatory in all areas of life. In its original form, Christianity did not have, and cannot have, such aspirations. Jesus threw the moneychangers out of the temple not because he opposed trade but because the traders profaned the holy sanctuary. Jesus condemned the greedy and the oppressors, not because he proclaimed a better social order, but because it is morally evil to be oppressive and greedy. Christianity is about moral evil, *malum culpae,* and moral evil inheres only in individuals, because only the individual is responsible. It is wrong to inflict suffering on others with hatred, which means that a torturer who inflicts it is evil (which is certainly completely independent of the cause for which he tortures and how he performs his craft). Suffering itself, however, is not evil in this sense. It is a moral evil to be an owner of slaves, but it is not a moral evil to be a slave. The very idea of a "morally evil" or "morally good" social system makes no sense in the world of Christian belief.

It does not follow from this at all that Christians, because they are Christians, have no right to rebel against social injustice, to struggle against oppressors and tyranny, or that it would be contrary to Christian doctrine to want to correct what can be corrected in society. To be motivated by hatred, vindictiveness, greed, or lust for power is to be opposed to Christianity. We cannot calculate what kind of social relations result in greater or lesser moral evil, that is, in the Christian sense, whether they create greater or lesser reasons for hatred and greed. For Christianity, greed is as evil in a rich man as in a poor man, hatred is as evil in the oppressor as in the oppressed. It is in this that the difficulty of being a Christian consists. Vengeance from this point of view cannot break the chain of evil. Even states which oppress and persecute Christianity can be called anti-Christian only in a figurative sense, namely, that those who govern in them are tyrants and thus not Christians; but tyrants are also not Christians when they do not persecute organized Christianity, but oppress others in its name. In Christianity, however, the principle always remains in force that evil, in its original and proper sense, is in us, not in social relationships. There are rules of Christian life that cover all situations, and are clearly equally obligatory in all political situations and conflicts; there are, however, no Christian politics, that is, specifically Christian political goals.

For the same reason, there is no universally obligatory way of life or way of participating in earthly matters that would be specifically Christian if separated from purely moral motivations. There is also, unfortunately, no indication of how we can entirely avoid evil acts while living in the world (and escape from the world by no means deserves the label of a universal Christian recommendation). Christianity itself cannot resolve the sorry dilemmas that arise at every step of life and make it impossible to avoid evil. Absolute pacifists, referring to Christian principles, should learn unhypocritically to consider whether they do not simply prefer that other people take their part if war should break out. Volunteers in a revolutionary war would be wise unhypocritically to answer the question of why their indignation at social injustice is so outstandingly selective (as notoriously is the case) and on what principle they claim that specifically Christian values (that is, the removal of hatred) have a better chance of flourishing in one system than in another. In reality, however, Christian justifications are of extremely doubtful value in both cases. Jesus' message is not about a just social system or any social system at all. He instructed us to destroy evil starting with ourselves, not with the murder of others whom we consider—rightly or not—to be evil.

To be a Christian, therefore, is and always has been a difficult task, for Christianity demands the ability radically to expose our own evil to ourselves. Great teachers of Christianity have not concealed that in this sense there are not many Christians and never have been many. That there are few of them, however, is not a symptom of any "crisis" of Christianity, but confirmation of something it says about itself: that it is difficult to measure up to its demands. If there is a crisis, it is a permanent one; it is an indispensable way of being for Christianity, or perhaps an expression of the more general and universal "crisis" in which we all find ourselves, having been driven out of paradise.

Those for whom the question of Christianity is unequivocally connected with the question of some political interest must obviously assess its situation as favorable or unfavorable, depending on how they assess the perspectives of their political interest. Those who take Christianity seriously have no reason to forecast its fall.

Chapter Nine

The Illusion of Demythologization

It is not credible that the erosion of the mythological legacy in the traditionally or nominally Christian civilization and the decline (or apparent decline) of religious sensibility can be explained by the progress of science, by the popularization of scientific achievements, and by the growth of the so-called scientific spirit, the latter being coextensive or even identical with the increasing level of general education. This belief is widespread, to be sure. Most people who consider themselves areligious are ready to explain their disbelief in those terms: incompatibility of religious tradition with what science teaches. Such assertions, however, need not be taken at their face value.

Certainly, it would be foolish to deny that the two phenomena—the apparent erosion of the ability to live within and experience the numinosum on one hand, and the trust in science as a means of understanding the world on the other—are linked up with each other. This does not imply that the former is causally determined by the latter. Both phenomena rather appear to be fruits of the centuries-long process of so-called modernization. This process, we may assume, started in the eleventh century with the increasingly powerful advance of the distinction between secular reason and faith. The need for this distinction was growing *pari passu* with the emergence of cities and urban civilization, including its inevitable result: the emancipation of intellectuals. St. Thomas Aquinas himself participated in this development, unintentionally of course, and unaware of its future effects. He reacted to the Averroists' attempts at the total separation of faith and reason, and to do that successfully, he had to make the distinction clear and precise. He established fairly exact rules that were to assure to revealed truth the right to control and supervise profane knowledge, so that the former was not supposed to replace the latter but only to censure it in case of a conflict and to provide it with the ultimate criteria of meaning. He used the

Written in English; previously published only in Dutch as a pamphlet in 1985.

same rules to define the relationships between secular authorities and the Church: the Church's task was not to replace civil authorities but to control their activities and laws as to their conformity with the divine commandments. Making no claims to theocracy—either in the realm of politics or in the realm of knowledge—he opposed the idea of separating the sacred from the profane, such a separation amounting, of course, to giving to the profane life, both intellectual and political, the right to disregard the norms that God and the Church infallibly fixed.

The next step was made by the fourteenth century nominalists who, while separating these two areas, *deprived* secular reasons of any right to venture into theological speculation, to examine not only deep divine mysteries (which St. Thomas naturally accepted as well) but the very question of God's existence. All the ultimate questions were to be left to the authority of revelation. The Occamists opposed the realm of faith, which was by definition irrational, to the kingdom of reason, which was governed by empirical and logical norms; they in fact established the principles of modern empiricism in exactly the same spirit as Hume was to do four centuries later.

It might have appeared that this separation amounted to the degradation of secular reason by limiting its scope of legitimate interest and robbing it of access to the entire area of metaphysical and theological inquiry. In some instances this was indeed the case. Christian mystics who often used similar formulae were indifferent, if not hostile, to any use of reason in divine matters; so, for the most part, were the great thinkers of the Reformation. Their attacks on the profanation of Christianity by the curiosity of mundane scholars often coincided, in their form of expression, with the nominalists' strictures, yet the latter's intention was in fact the opposite: the point was to separate the realms of reason and faith in order to proclaim reason's autonomy and to state that it does not need the support of faith or of revelation. This implicitly entailed that, to our understanding of the physical world, not only faith but the very presence of God is irrelevant; in other words, that physical reality for all practical purposes is self-sufficient, and so is our knowledge of this reality. To say this, one did not need to deny either God or revelation; it was enough to push them both into a corner where they were soon to become useless for secular life and secular science.

This process culminated in the philosophy of Descartes. In the world he depicted, God became an element in the universal machinery, a source of energy that was, no doubt, logically necessary for the ultimate explanation of nature but dispensable in the interpretation of any particular event. It might be argued that Descartes was not a deist in the strict sense since, according to his physics, the same amount of force is needed to keep the world in existence as to create it, and thus God keeps providing a permanently necessary support for the continuing being of the universe; however, in understanding the created world, His presence became indifferent; this world is ruled by the infallibly working laws of mechanics, and when we investigate it, we do not need to remember God at all. In this sense, what Pascal said about Descartes' *chiquenaude* is true (even though not literally true), and it is undoubtedly true that modern deism has emerged and developed from the Cartesian legacy. The fact that there is an immaterial soul has hardly any significance in the examination of the human body, which is a complicated mechanism, not unlike animal bodies, and is governed entirely by the same laws that operate in the movement of inert matter. The path from *bête-machine* to *l'homme-machine* was easy. In the deists' world, God, even if verbally admitted, was signally useless, since there are no miracles and no revelation (the latter being miracle in the order of cognition); therefore—and this is the main point—God is imperceptible in nature.

This process was certainly a necessary condition of the advancement of modern science. This science could not have arisen if God and miracles had not been previously removed from nature, if the rules of the scientific method, as they were codified in the seventeenth century by Bacon, Descartes, Gassendi, and others, had not ruled out any traces of religious beliefs, if science had not been freed from any attachment to tradition, to authority, to the Church, and to anything that had been declared incurably mysterious and inaccessible to the human intellect.

This does not imply that science as such was the efficient cause of the erosion of faith; what contributed to this erosion was not science but scientism or scientistic rationalism. In contrast to science itself, rationalism is a philosophical doctrine or an ideology which includes a normative definition of knowledge; what may be properly called knowledge is what can be efficiently employed in predicting and controlling natural phenomena. The cognitive content of a religious faith (and it must be noted that, to the rationalist credo, religion is a set of statements) is in this respect demonstrably useless or dubiously useful; therefore religion cannot be knowledge in any recognizable sense. The drive to dominate nature—which Descartes and the Enlightenment provided with a philosophical foundation—was in itself neither rational nor irrational; it reflected human passions, not human knowledge. Once this domination, including its obvious beneficial results, became the supreme value, it naturally made the entire religious legacy of mankind dubious and eventually pointless. The perception of religious sensibility as meaningless resulted neither from science nor from the possible conflict between scientific truth and the content of revelation, but from human preferences and from the priority given, on our scale of values, to those kinds of mental activities that were likely to increase the scope of our domination of nature; science was something to be trusted in terms of verifiable effects; religion could not be trusted in the same sense.

Certainly, the idea itself of the domination of nature is of biblical origin, but it turned against the Bible and against the revelation once it ceased to function within a divinely established moral and cosmic order and became a supreme and unconditionally valid objective. Christianity itself was by no means innocent in sharpening the conflict and thus in turning the growth of the Enlightenment against itself. First, it asserted and supported the scholastic rationality of its doctrine longer than was culturally possible, and therefore it put itself in a defenseless position: by claiming that the basic beliefs of Christian tradition could be presented as rationally justifiable in the same sense as scientific truths are, it inevitably displayed the gap between both, but a gap on the same scale of cognitive values; and so instead of being what it had always been—a divine message translated into the human tongue—it tried to be a second-class knowledge of basically the same sort as profane science. Second, Christian education often supported the magical elements or magical expectations attached to religious rites and sacraments by suggesting, or least not opposing, the notion that rituals and prayers, even though they involve the operation of divine energy, have a kind of technical efficiency, as if, for instance, a prayer were a sort of manipulation which, if only it is correctly carried out, will infallibly bring the desired results. If it fails to do that, then either the operation has not been properly executed, or there is something fundamentally wrong with the very idea of prayer: the machinery does not work according to the expectation; consequently there are no good reasons to believe that God exists at all. It was soon to become clear that, if this is how religious worship is interpreted, it could never win in the competition with technology; the latter, if properly applied, does indeed deliver the goods it promises (not to speak of by-products it does not promise and which are not necessarily beneficial). The confusion of faith with knowledge, a confusion for which Christianity to some extent is to blame, inevitably reduced faith to a poor relative of science; the confusion of worship with technique inevitably reduced worship to an inefficient or dubiously efficient technique; insofar as both kinds of confusion were encouraged by Christian churches, Christianity itself contributed to the spread of atheism. The main reason, however, for the erosion of faith lay in moral rather than intellectual changes—in the preference given to those areas of activity which deliver measurable goods.

The conflict of theology with science in the Middle Ages affected only a few. Even later, in the seventeenth and eighteenth centuries, the path from scientific research to technical applications—at least to applications affecting the daily lives of many people—was long and slow, indeed almost unnoticeable to most people. This path was becoming shorter and shorter in the nineteenth century, and in our time it is almost instantaneous; it has become obvious to everybody that science can efficiently change daily life and make it more comfortable.

Briefly, the real conflict is not between science, on the one side, conceived of in each of its particular phases as an absolute standard whereby all spiritual life is to be measured and, on the other side, religion as a set of statements about God, Providence, immortality, the devil, and so forth—statements whose truth must be assessed by scientific criteria. The conflict is cultural, and it is about our hierarchy of preferences: our *libido dominandi* against our need to find meaning in the universe and in our lives. Both desires, *libido dominandi* and the search for meaning, are rooted inalienably in the very act of being human, but they limit each other instead of coexisting peacefully.

It is against this background that the question of the so-called demythologization is to be examined. In the broadest sense the 'demythologization' trend has lasted as long as the entire process of modernity, including seventeenth-century deism. In its early version this was only an attempt to leave for religious life an enclave from which it would not interfere with our intellectual and political affairs. The deeper movement aiming at the complete restructuring of the meaning of religion developed at the end of the nineteenth century, and Catholic modernism (next to the less radical German liberal theology) was at its most salient expression. Without actually using the word *demythologization* it anticipated all the major tenets of Bultmann.

Bultmann stressed that his idea of demythologization made up a part of his hermeneutic work on the New Testament and that it owed a lot to difficulties he had had to cope with in his pastoral work. Since a historian or an exegete is unable to eliminate from his analysis of texts the "existential" relationships between himself and the author as well as with the persons spoken of in the text, he necessarily interprets the text through his own experiences, emotions, and aspirations, in the context of his life and historical milieu. Therefore both the questions asked and comprehension of the answers change with our accumulation not only of historical but also of personal experience. In the sources we investigate—like the New Testament—we often find unexpected answers to personal questions and grasp the word as if it was addressed personally to ourselves.

Up to this point Bultmann remains within the traditional German philosophy of Verstehen, even though, as a Heideggerian, he does not talk about empathy or imitative reproduction but about the "existential" exchange between the test and the reader, this exchange being referred to the reader's actual experience. As a theologian, Bultmann goes beyond Dilthey and Heidegger, of course. In order to understand what it means that a text conveys a divine message, we must previously have had an experience—in the form of a concern, rather than a notion—of God and His word. And we have it, indeed, even if we deny it conceptually. This knowledge makes up an aspect of existential concern we all share; therefore the real understanding, going beyond a philological and historical exegesis, includes the reader's will to face his or her own existence. This is why no definitive understanding is possible; existence is only *hic et nunc,* and so is the understanding.

The impossibility of an immutable sense of revelation was one of the important topics of the Modernists. Since the perception of a text changes with transformations in our sensibility and knowledge, the meaning of the text, they argued, evolves as well. Should we, on this assumption, say that the truth changes as well, that something can be true in one historical period and cease being true in the next? That the Scriptures are inexhaustible and can reveal new aspects any orthodox theologian will admit; this may be true of all texts, not necessarily those which are supposed to be of divine inspiration. This, however, does not prevent one from believing that there is a persistent core in the divine word. And if there is nothing immutable, can Christianity survive? Is it more than a temporary expression of a historically relative sensibility, with no privileged position, no better than any other religion or nonreligion or antireligion? On the assumption that the majority of our society has no need of Christianity any longer, should we admit that Christianity has become false after having been true in a past epoch? And by saying so, would we not destroy the very concept of truth?

The Modernists replied that what is fundamentally true in Christianity remains true, but this truth never arrives at a definitive formulation. Formulae, dogmas, and symbols are historically relative; they can lose their vitality and become obsolete. The core of faith, which is revealed to each of us in personal experience, does not perish, but the way it is articulated is incurably provisional and as contingent as the tongue in which it is expressed; it cannot be grasped in eternally valid propositions.

Bultmann's standpoint is the same. We should ask how far this evolution can go. Why should it be impossible that the genuine Christianity (of which sequential verbalizations are relative) be expressed one day in statements like, "God does not exist, there is no salvation, no redemption, no forgiveness, no original sin, no eternal life, no love"? This seems quite possible on the premise that nothing in the Christian message resists cultural changes. New formulae would be equally provisional and as "true" as the old ones, to be sure, but their provisional character can be perceived only when they are culturally dead.

The language of theology changes, of course; so do the categories people use to reforge the Bible into a metaphysical "system"; new human problems and new forms of sensibility can reveal new meanings in the text; but is the text in all its aspects at the mercy of a reader?

Bultmann does not say so in so many words. He wants to make the Christian message accessible to the contemporary mentality by purifying it from the "mythology," that is, from the habit of expressing the divine things and divine acts in empirical categories that we borrow from earthly realities and human actions.

"Modern man" according to Bultmann cannot, for example, think in terms of the spatial structure of the universe that ancient people accepted: the abode of angels and God "above" in the sky and hell under the surface of earth. And, above all, he cannot imagine that natural causality might be interrupted or canceled by miraculous interventions from the other world, by God, the devil, or the angels; nor can he expect the breaks in causality that our prayers or magical performances produce; he cannot believe that a divine being has sacrificed himself for human sins, that sacramental acts like baptism or eucharist communicate a spiritual power to the faithful, that God is a Father in an intelligible sense, that He created the world *ex nihilo*, and that Jesus was a man and God simultaneously. While those beliefs are inadmissible to people educated in modern science, the "objective" or "existential" meaning of Christianity is not lost; "modern man" can believe that the world he lives in is not a definitive reality and that God encompasses the empirical universe. Faith is an encounter of an existence with the Word and not the acceptance of a number of propositions; and faith, conformably to Lutheran doctrine, cannot be produced by exegetic work; it is an experience, and thus it has no reified essence in the form of dogmas. The divine word is open to me but its meaning is an aspect of my experience here and now. No proofs of Jesus' divinity are conceivable, but in the way He changes my life, He reveals himself as God's word. I find God in Jesus by making a decision to follow His appeal, and by taking it I no longer fear the future because the meaning of the future is defined in the actual presence of Jesus.

What remains of Christianity after this cleaning? Faith in the Lutheran sense, Bultmann says: trust in God revealed in Jesus. It is, so it seems, *fiducia* which has no intellectual foundation and of which it would probably be improper to say that it includes the truth "God exists," as such a truth has no meaning apart from being a possible aspect of personal experience.

The famous discussion on demythologization between Bultmann and Jaspers took place over thirty years ago. According to Jaspers, philosophy can never encompass religion; the latter resists all conceptual explanation. Bultmann's attempt to make religion scientifically respectable is doomed to failure at the outset. First, what he assumes to be a "modern" worldview is not modern at all: the resurrection was as impossible to Jesus' contemporaries as it is to us; on the other hand, contemporary people believe in absurdities no less than ancient people did. Modern science does not pretend to offer a global understanding of reality, nor is Heideggerian ontology capable of doing that.

It is, according to Jaspers, preposterous to think that myths are theories in disguise and that they can be translated into a metaphysical idiom. They are untranslatable in a nonmythical language and we try in vain to interpret them rationally. Although the code of myth is *sui generis,* we should know that there is no devil, no magic causality, and no sorcery. Individuals may deny myth for themselves, but not for other people. Through life in a myth people become aware of transcendence, and in this encounter the objective and the subjective are inseparable; thus it is as impossible to find scientific truth in a myth as to reduce a myth to its personal, existential content. Faith does not arise from the exegetic work; it is conveyed by priests, and it is efficacious to the extent that the priests themselves live in faith. While he tries to assimilate the critique of the Enlightenment in order to save faith, Bultmann takes the Enlightenment in its false and dogmatic version. The liberal attitude does not fight against a simple and naive devotion, but it wants to free God from the "objectified" form. It accepts the idea of a "hidden God"; the transcendence can be accessible only through ciphers, and it becomes real only for a human existence, thus not necessarily in historical Christianity, not necessarily codified in a credo. Bultmann, however, when he tries to save a nonmythological minimum of Christianity, finds it in the

Lutheran dogma of justification by faith, thus falling again into a rigid orthodoxy.

Bultmann's rejoinder to this criticism shows, perhaps better than his theory, the practical problem he had to cope with as a Protestant priest. He denies that he simply tried to save what could be saved from faith after the attacks of science; rather, he wanted to clarify to "modern man" what Christian faith really is. He does admit, like Jasper, that a corpse cannot rise from a tomb and that there are no devils or magic, but he challenges Jaspers to explain to believers the meaning of St. Paul's letter to the Romans on original sin and the redemption. Mythical thinking is as "reified" as scientific thinking when it tries to explain the divine transcendence in empirical categories or to personify evil as Satan. Jaspers, however, says nothing about how the biblical myth can be expressed in a way that would be acceptable to "modern man." To be sure, one cannot prove the reality of revelation without previously accepting it as revelation; after this acceptance I listen to its voice as a word directly addressed to myself. After demythologization, the doctrine of the Incarnation says that God reveals himself not only as an idea, but as my God who speaks to me here and now; the doctrine of Jesus as an "eschatological phenomenon" says that Jesus is "God's Word," always present.

Briefly, Jaspers believes that it would be disastrous to destroy mythological language and that this language has no "objectified" meaning, no reference to empirical realities; it provides us only with ciphers that help us to grasp transcendence and existence, both inseparably tied to each other and both eternally inscrutable. We ought to renounce dogmas, fixed truth, given in a historically identifiable revelation, but we must not reduce myth to an abstract doctrine. Bultmann, on the other hand, wants to save from traditional "objective" faith only what is acceptable to the "modern man"— which means in effect the historically reliable information, having no religious content—and to retain the living faith in form of an "existential" encounter, a realm of a personal "decision."

Here we have the difference between the interests and the worries of a philosopher and of a predicant. Jaspers wants to save the myth in its original expression, both because no better expression is available and because myth is an indispensable part of culture. Yet he refuses to endow it with any empirical significance: there is no resurrection in a real sense, no devils or angels, no revelation in the biblical sense, that is, no God who really speaks to Moses or to Abraham. Still, Jaspers knows that to believers, unlike philosophers, the resurrection and the devils are real things, not ciphers. The final result of his defense of myth does not differ ultimately from the doctrine of the seventeenth-century French libertines: let the *vulgus* live in its superstitions; the simpletons need myths as stories they take literally; as for the enlightened, they can accept myth only as a set of ciphers that vaguely connect us with the inexpressible ultimate reality. Thus we seem to go back to the same division into two cultures that we know from Spinoza and, most explicitly, from Machiavelli's *Discorsi* (even though the need of myth is explained in cultural and anthropological, rather than political, terms). Philosophers who allow simple people to believe in legends they cannot take seriously seem to commit the same *pia fraus* as Numa Pompilius or the Roman generals described by Machiavelli.

Bultmann rejects this solution because he has to speak either to the ministers of the Church or to simple believers who, without being philosophers, have breathed the omnipresent air of science, who are "modern men" and think it impermissible to accept the resurrection or the devil in a literal sense.

Jaspers, I believe, is quite right in saying that it is vain to translate myth into philosophical categories and that an attempt to adjust Christianity to what is permissible or digestible to contemporary science is hopeless. He is right as well when he casts doubt on Bultmann's idea of "modern man," as if millions of "modern men" who believed or believe, say, in the doctrine of Nazism or of Communism proved thereby that they are "rational" beings immune to superstition.

Bultmann's concern cannot be lightly dismissed, to be sure: as a priest he must have often been asked by people how Christian beliefs can coexist with the modern scientific world outlook and, unable to cope with the task, he escaped into his "existential" solution. Many priests, no doubt, have to face similar questions. I remember having a talk with a Catholic priest to whom I said that I was very happy about Pope Paul VI's statement confirming the Church's traditional teaching on the devil; to which this priest replied somewhat bitterly, "Oh, yes, for you it is easy to talk like that because you do not need to go to people and explain this." He was certainly a good believing Christian, and still he seemed to be unable to reconcile himself to the traditional notion of the devil. Why? Why, in our educated classes, does the belief in God still enjoy a kind of respectability, whereas to believe in the devil or the angels passes for a medieval superstition? Why should the latter belief be more "irrational" than the belief in God? It appears that the opposite should be the case: devils and angels are disincarnated but finite intelligent creatures, in many ways not unlike ourselves, and it is easier to describe their nature and to expect that we might meet them one day than it is to do the same with regard to God.

The possible answer is this: to the extent that God is still respectable, it is not a Christian God but a deists' or pantheists' God; a vague notion of a great mind, or a giant computer, that is responsible for the complicated equations according to which our universe moves. The Christian God, providential wisdom, a God who is a person in a recognizable sense, who cares about human creatures and intervenes in their lives, is not respectable at all. Is this because He is unacceptable to science? I do not think so. He is unacceptable to scientistic rationalism which, I should repeat, is a philosophical doctrine and not science itself. This ideology banned from our lives everything that is beyond science, not because of the "irrationality" of such beliefs, but because they do not "deliver the goods" as science does. And our worship of science, as Jaspers rightly says, does not make us "rational" in any other sense; we are not less superstitious than our ancestors of two millenia ago.

There is one more reason why Bultmann's project is hopeless: whatever he wishes to save from Christianity in order to please the "modern man" is as mythological as the ingredients he is ready to do away with. Why should it be less mythological to say that Jesus is "God's Word" than to say He is God's son? No, there is no way for Christianity to "demythologize" itself and save anything of its meaning. It is either-or: demythologized Christianity is not Christianity. Of course one does not need to be a Christian to accept that there was a man called Jesus who preached love, forgiveness, and the coming Kingdom of God and who was crucified in Jerusalem; few people doubt that this is historically true, and any sworn foe of Christianity can believe that; such historical descriptions simply have no specifically religious content. But to say that Jesus was "God's Word" is entirely "mythological" in Bultmann's own sense. And even a purely personal encounter with God, an experience that is in principle inexpressible in a rational discourse, if it is considered real by the believer, must be "mythological" as well.

There is no escape from the dilemma: either "mythological" acceptance of the Christian God, or the scientistic rationalism that dispenses with God altogether. And even if we, conforming to Bultmann's recipe, retain a Christianity that has been reduced to the personal acts of every Christian separately, Christianity cannot be saved as a common faith, a community, a place of encounter for the believers and worshippers. If we have only a historical

Jesus who is not specifically Christian and, next to him, a Jesus who is the purely personal property of a believer and cannot be the focus of a Christian community, these two entities have nothing in common; we are left with a combination of two areas completely closed to each other: "objective" historic knowledge and a monadic experience that people cannot convey to each other.

If it is true, as Jaspers says, that the language of myth is untranslatable into metaphysical categories—and to say so is to make all theologians unemployed—this does not mean that it is unintelligible to believers. For centuries, Christians have believed in the meaning of Jesus Christ's sacrifice as it was explained by St. Paul, and they seem to have understood it. Should we say that the same meaning has become unintelligible to us? And would that mean that we have become stupid? No, what we mean is rather that St. Paul's story is unacceptable according to criteria of contemporary rationality. And why should we accept those criteria as an absolute standard? Because it is according to those criteria that science operates, and science is efficient. We thus come back to the starting point.

And yet Jaspers's strictures, however justified, leave us, as I have just said, with the "two cultures" doctrine, which Christianity has always tried to avoid: myth in its literal sense for the simpletons, and inexpressible "ciphers" for the enlightened. Jaspers knows that philosophy cannot take up the tasks of faith and that mankind cannot survive without myth, but his distinction between revealed and philosophical faith sanctions a split that Christian civilization has as little chance of surviving as it would have of surviving Bultmann's reduction of Christianity to an incommunicable *Erlebnis*. Christianity as we know it cannot live after having lost all vitality in the "higher culture," and the question we are left with after Jaspers's critique is, Is the faith of the enlightened possible at all? It is possible psychologically, no doubt, as there are still many real Christians among the enlightened. It is possible logically as well: there is no contradiction between the tenets of science and the Christian myth, unless *science* means rationalist philosophy; historical information about Jesus does not contradict the belief that Jesus was God's son, even though, of course, it cannot support this belief. We are incapable of proving immortality in accordance with the scientific standard of proof, but we have no reason to think that this belief is logically irreconcilable with our knowledge. Whether the faith of the enlightened will remain possible in terms of the cultural developments of the future we do not know.

After centuries of the growth of the Enlightenment, we suddenly woke up in a mental and cultural disarray; we are more and more frightened in the face of a world that is losing its religious legacy, and our fear is well justified. The lost myths seem to be replaced less by enlightened rationality and more by terrifying secular caricatures or substitutes. We notice with a kind of relief various symptoms of religious renaissance, and the "return of the sacred" has become a fashionable topic. And yet we—and by *we* I mean philosophers, sociologists, psychologists, anthropologists or historians—cannot contribute to this process; we can describe it—with hope or with dread—but we are not priests, and only through priesthood, prophecy, and acts of living faith can human participation in the sacred be maintained or reinforced. Intellectuals are helpless, and least of all can they contribute to the vitality of myth by explaining that myths are indispensable for such or another cultural, moral, psychological, or social reason. And the attempt to endear oneself to the rationalist ideology by "demythologizing" Christianity is the least reliable prescription. Let us leave it at that.

Chapter Ten

Philosophical Faith in the Face of Revelation

In the English-speaking world, Karl Jaspers is a recognized name, certainly, but scarcely more. Several of his works have been translated into English, and there are some works analyzing his philosophy as well; but it is fair to say that he is considered only a marginal phenomenon. Imperceptible in university curricula, absent in philosophical discussions, Jaspers has not entered—or, perhaps, not yet entered—the circulation of ideas in the Anglo-Saxon world. This is especially striking if we compare his position to Heidegger's. And yet, even though they are not easy and popular reading, Jaspers's works are more digestible and on first sight much more lucid than Heidegger's, whose work remained at the farthest distance imaginable from the language and tradition of British philosophy. Why that is, I do not know. Perhaps—and this is only an impression—the reason for it rests less in the content of his philosophy than in his style and manner of self-representation. Heidegger's lexical aggressiveness and prophetic inflexibility made him a highly successful ravisher of minds: irritating and fascinating at the same time, like Nietzsche, he appeared to be a true pioneer, a bearer of the great promise, with whose help we might expect to open by force the door to lost Being. Compared to him, Jaspers appeared to be cautious, moralizing, and much more bound to the conventional language of European philosophy—in spite of his easily recognizable, characteristic and very personal style and vocabulary—fitting better into the mainstream of Western thinking and thus less visible in his uniqueness. Ultimately, the difference between them was perhaps that between a prophet and a teacher.

Jaspers was not the only outstanding philosopher who adapted the entire tradition of philosophy to his own personal manner and translated the thoughts of others into his own language. This assimilation was accom-

Translated from the German by Wolfgang Freis from "Der philosophische Glaube angesichts der Offenbarung," in *Karl Jaspers: Philosoph, Arzt, politischer Denker* (München: Piper Verlag, 1986). Copyright © 1986 by Piper Verlag. Revised by the author in English.

plished conspicuously *modo recipientis.* The entire philosophical past was "Jaspersized," so to say. Occasionally he was accused of having tailored the philosophical heritage arbitrarily to his own philosophical needs (for instance, in Cassirer's critique of his interpretation of Descartes). But Jaspers was not a historian in a strict sense, despite his immense historical knowledge. His historical reflections were intentionally conceived as a neverending dialogue with the great minds of the past rather than a pursuit of historical facts. His historical studies ought to be considered as expressions of his philosophy, not as textbooks. He did not practice the history of ideas. Instead, he sought instances where the continuity of culture was broken by the unpredicatable invasion of a great mind, and where the absolutely new, the unexplainable (therefore what was of permanent and great significance to the world) emerged. Jaspers believed in capitalizing the indestructible wealth of the mind. Hence, historicism—a doctrine that qualifies all cultural phenomena as results of accidental historic circumstances and considers them dependent on their times—was bound to be foreign to him. In *Weltgeschichte der Philosophie,* edited by Hans Sauer from Jaspers's manuscript, we read, "Higher rank is not only what is more valuable, it is what is essentially more real. It represents a reaching beyond biological, existence-bound humanity to a higher reality. . . . Greatness itself is the final measure; and it does not become valuable through historic relation, effect, locality, or origin, or particular and accountable accuracies."[1] Thus, greatness in history ought to be something like an everlasting repository of the mind, where its growing resources will be deposited eternally. Hence it is apparent that Jaspers's notion of the history of philosophy is connected inseparably with this doctrine of transcendence.

Yet, how is transcendence conceivable? On first sight, it may appear that for a philosopher, whose orientation of thinking is defined by the unattainable whole, the question of God is inevitable and that he must feel obliged to give it an unambiguous answer. But it is remarkable that a number of great philosophers did remain ambiguous, at least in the sense that they appeared as plain atheists at times, and at times, as believers, and they suggested such extremely contrary ways of understanding to their readers. This was the case with Spinoza, Hegel, Giordano Bruno, and even Descartes. It was the case with Jaspers, too. As ambiguous and variously interpreted as philosophers may be, this key question—one would presume—they should not leave in suspense.

1. Karl Jaspers, *Weltgeschichte der Philosophie,* Einleitung, ed. Hans Saner (München/Zürich: Piper Verlag, 1982), 155.

But perhaps Jaspers's thinking in particular may acquaint us with the insight that the question, "Do you believe in God or not?" posed as a philosophical question—or within what Jaspers calls *philosophical faith*—is put incorrectly and thus cannot be answered clearly. Since the point in time when the God of Christians, loving Father and Lord, blended with the neo-Platonic Absolute (and this was undoubtedly one of the most decisive events in cultural history), the "question of God" had to be recast significantly, for we have no reliable conceptual tools at our disposal with which to compose a coherent whole from the characteristics of a person and the attributes of an absolute. The mystics were aware of that and repeatedly emphasized that God, revealed to them as a fact of experience, cannot be caught in our conceptual net; therefore, they remained largely indifferent to natural theology.

Jaspers, of course, was no mystic; at least, he does not refer to any particular personal experience that had raised him in a privileged manner to transcendence. He intends to remain within the everyday experience in which everybody participates, and he does not wish to be counted among those chosen by God. In one important sense, however, his literary work is similar to the message of the mystics: he does not attempt to prove what cannot be proven within the conceptual frame of thinking that he described as "the elucidation of existence"; he leaves no room for the question, "Why should I suppose that?" Rather, he wants to appeal to what we all are carrying within ourselves semiconsciously, covertly, or inarticulately, as he believes. He means to touch a string that firmly belongs to our existential constitution; nothing can be done if the string is dead or motionless. Like the mystic writings, his message is also indisputable and hence must appear meaningless to philosophers of the rationalist cast of mind. He seems to expect, however, that his words may evoke spontaneous understanding, since they are aimed at clarifying the meaning of what is within universal experience and daily perception.

But how to clarify it? Clarification as brought about by scientific thinking is, of course, out of the question. The Ultimum is unspeakable; the word is captured within our empirical existence. We are related to Transcendence, Jaspers repeats. That is not a historical, psychological, social, or biological fact; we do not have to be conscious of this relation, either.

Transcendence is not an object; it cannot be objectified, says Jaspers. What does that actually mean? Is there more involved than the fact that we are incapable of expressing it in concepts and words? How is Transcendence accessible to us?

Jaspers confesses to St. Augustine's "Deum et animam scire cupio." In his interpretation, however, the soul is not the soul, and God is not God in a recognizable sense. Existence and transcendence, which replace the two ultimate realities of soul and God, respectively, are extraworldly aspects of the "Encompassing," which we never encounter in a reflection on the world or an experience of the world. They become present to us by a leap that hurls us out of this world, out of our empirical thinking, yes, even out of our spirit. They are entities taken from Christian tradition, yet deprived of all substantiality.

Those two ultimate realities, however, between which our life and that of the world extends, are by no means to be considered as symmetrically ascertained poles or as, in the same sense, incomprehensible *alia*, both similarly located beyond the borders of knowledge. To be sure, existence cannot be objectified, because it is, as Jaspers says, "not being-such (*Sosein*), but possibly being," or because it is *der je Einzelne*. "This means: I am not an existence but a possible Existence."[2] Existence is what I am, if I succeed in considering myself no longer as an object present in the world and determined by this belonging, but if I succeed in placing myself into the negativity of my freedom. It would probably be foreign to Jaspers's language to say that I was a free being, but acceptable to say that I was the movement of freedom itself; and this movement essentially cannot be observed from the outside. For each observation and each analysis, freedom may count only as wanting knowledge of determination in the world, as a cognitive lacuna, but not as reality. By its nature, every objective insight—even a psychological one—must deny freedom, since it aims at explanation, and therefore it must reject in advance anything that is in principle inexplicable.

But although freedom is not tangible or imaginable as an object, and although it can never be expressed in universally valid language, it is yet part of the "subjective side" of the All-Encompassing. Since it is what I am, and since it reveals itself to me as myself, the "leap" toward it must signify something entirely different from the leap toward the border of the All-Encompassing, that is, toward transcendence. To be sure, in this sense it is possible to affirm the negativity of freedom, and to deny transcendence. Nietzsche and Sartre already confirmed this. How, then, is the second leap possible? No existence without transcendence, Jaspers maintained. One may conclude therefrom that those individuals who experience irreducible

2. Karl Jaspers, *Der philosophische Glaube angesichts der Offenbarung* (München: Piper Verlag, 1962), 118.

freedom actually do not experience it, or that they live *mala fide* by remaining insensitive to the attractive power of transcendence.

Believers are in a different position. God is accessible to them in two ways: first, through mystic or quasi-mystic experience, which of course cannot be made manifest, but which confers unshakable certainty upon those who experience it; second, through preservation and continuous mediation of the original revelation, through habituated tradition. In both ways, God reveals Himself—at least in the spiritual space of Christianity—as love and thus as a person. Both ways, however, remain outside of philosophical faith as Jaspers conceives of it. Transcendence does not reveal itself as love.

This is not exactly what Christian theologians used to call *via negationis*. *Via negationis* is certainly an admission of the weakness of human reason and language in the face of infinity, which can only be described as a negation of finite attributes known to us in the world. To say that God is accessible to us only in a negative way does not exclude our grasping Him as love or as a person. Even the Biblical expression "Deus absconditus," used by Jaspers, is perhaps not quite adequate, because in the Christian understanding of faith, God's concealment invalidates neither revelation nor mystical approach. Naturally, the same expression in Jaspers's use can be understood just as little in a skeptical sense, whereupon God's complete inaccessibility leaves us declaring His possible presence to be of no relevance to us.

The passage in *Der philosophische Glaube,* in which Jaspers considers the "leap from Immanence to Transcendence," is surprisingly short, and the meaning of the leap is hardly explained. But it appears to confirm the necessary two-sided connection of existence to transcendence. "If Transcendence subsists, however, only for Existence, that is, if it is only the objective side of which the subjective side is called Existence, then Transcendence is not valid for consciousness-in-general, nor does it subsist as a real object in [empirical] existence."[3] That transcendence "subsists only for Existence" is a disturbing statement. It certainly does not mean that transcendence is only imagination, let alone an illusion. It suggests, however, that whatever we discover as transcendence—however precarious and indescribable our approach may be—creates itself within this discovery, as it were. It appears as if Being and consciousness coincide on both sides of the final and ultimate reality; as if the question of the precedence of the Being or of being appropriated in mind were meaningless. Jaspers, however, does not state that; it

3. Ibid., 139.

is a mere suspicion, which is certainly difficult to avoid. Is God a God-for-us and, if yes, in what sense? Since existence is never complete, perhaps transcendence is never completed, either.

Certainly Jaspers left us his doctrine of ciphers. Ciphers indeed represent the language of transcendence. Yet this language is neither discursive nor aesthetic. Yes, the word is somewhat misleading, since we normally use it under the presupposition that deciphering is possible or that the deciphered meaning is known to somebody; at any rate, we suppose that something like a "genuine" text exists, even if it is hidden. But there is no genuine text behind Jaspers's ciphers. They are allusions to something that never reveals itself in a deciphered presence. Neither are they signs of God in a religious sense, which open a path from the sign to the source, however clouded it may be; though it is of course impossible that God reveals himself completely in his signs. The language of ciphers "replaces"[4] the revelation of transcendence, Jaspers says; and this language is audible only in the freedom of existence. The ciphers "are never the incarnation of Transcendence itself."[5] In other words, if we may speak of ciphers as symbols, then we can do it only in a sense singular to Jaspers. In ordinary linguistic usage, symbols are substitutes for texts—and as such they may be translated—or they are images through which the original can be recognized. In religious meaning, on the other hand, symbols are not images but real channels that provide a way to establish energetic contact with the divinity. Jaspers's ciphers are neither: they can neither be retranslated into the original, nor are they instruments to give us access to another reality. Rather, they are intimations of the hidden and desired as well as evidence of the invincibility of its being hidden. In the presence of ciphers we ascertain our irresistible striving for transcendence but also our fateful incapacity to satisfy this endeavor. In this sense, the ciphers reveal our fate as failure; they are signs of failure par excellence: we run our heads against the eternally closed door and, at the same time, we are aware that we can never resist the compulsion to repeat this futile attempt; for this attempt is part of being human, and in this sense, it is not futile. The unique in each one of us is confirmed by the effort. "The truth of the cipher elucidating, but not forcing, the decision of existence at an instance is measured by the circumstance of this instance, whether its decision will be forever recognized and adopted as one's own decision; whether I am identical with it and originally renew myself in repetition. . . . The truth of ciphers proves itself not by any cognition or dis-

4. Ibid., 156.
5. Ibid., 163.

cernment, but only through the elucidating force in the existential history of each individual."[6] It seems as if philosophical faith was nothing else but the will to face the presence of ciphers and never to let our situation in the presence of the indecipherable fall into oblivion.

Thereby it becomes apparent that philosophical faith is irreconcilable with the faith of revelation, and with positive theology as well. The faith of revelation is realized in obedience, which blocks our access to existence and thus to transcendence; and it freezes inevitably within the ecclesiastical institution. The faith of revelation cannot avoid the temptation of bringing about obedience by force and it cannot escape a notorious circle: I ought to believe because I possess revelation; and because of my faith, I know that the revelation is truly God's word. In the final analysis, positive theology is a crystallization of the deceptive certainty of the faith of revelation. The faith of revelation interferes with communication among human beings, and deceptive certainty kills the creative restlessness of existence.

Jaspers's critique of the faith of revelation and positive theology is basically that of the Enlightenment. Its inspiration should be sought in Kant's notion of human dignity as well as in the humanistic concept of the human beings as incomplete, open beings. Jaspers called himself a Christian, and by that he meant perhaps more than an accidental cultural affiliation determined by birth. He believed in the uniqueness of the Bible, yes, in its truth. But it is not truth in the ordinary sense. "Truth" in philosophy as well as in any thinking related to transcendence is defined by the source or by the original will to illuminate one's own existence, not by any *adaequatio*. In that sense, it seems as if all great philosophers and prophets were revealing a truth to us, even if their words are altogether incompatible when we confront them with each other as abstract ideas. In Jaspers we find analogues to many fundamental symbols of Christian belief; yet they are recast in such a manner that hardly any Christian may recognize himself in them. A list of such symbols can easily be assembled:

God—Transcendence
soul—Existence
revelation—ciphers
the satanic—passion for night
mystical experience—moments of eternity in time
Christian charity—existential communication
salvation—acceptance of one's own failure

6. Ibid., 173.

Missing from this list are symbols and terms without which it makes little sense to talk of Christianity in a historic sense or in conformity with its self-interpretation: there is no distinction between *sacrum* and *profanum*, no grace, no love of God for human beings, no mediator or savior, no final reconciliation. Certainly, all these symbols are important to Jaspers: they ought to be taken seriously as the attempts of human beings to express their relationship to transcendence. But their "truth" is not the one that people themselves have attributed to these symbols. They are ciphers, just as anything can be a cipher. For Jaspers, however, reading a cipher does not produce knowledge, whereas they are accepted as a universally obligatory truth within the mythical perception. Within the boundaries of our understanding, the interpretation of symbols given by believers, though explicable, is positively inadmissible and mythic, ecclesiastical, or theological in the pejorative sense. We may positively state that there is no revelation, no grace, no redemption, no incarnation of God, no savior—in the mode in which people ordinarily believe in these symbols. Philosophical faith excludes revelation. Jaspers is not a Christian. Some relationship may perhaps connect him with Catholic Modernists of the beginning of the century, but, to my knowledge, he makes no reference to them. It is a distant relationship, however. To the Modernists, who similarly separated knowledge from religious experience and intended to rescue Christianity from confinement in dogmatism and rigid institutional law, the encounter with God was real. But it is worthwhile to mention this kinship insofar as it may help us to locate Jaspers's thoughts within a broad stream as a cultural phenomenon.

Philosophical faith may be considered a draft for the religion of the enlightened. It is not only a philosophical faith but also a faith of philosophers claiming to be able to replace the religious. Often one has the impression that, for Jaspers, being human is defined by an accomplishment accessible only to a few, which gives rise to the suspicion that only a few philosophers reach the state of being human. It was one of the great accomplishments of Christianity to determine the meaning of its doctrine in such a way that no space remained for a distinction between the faith of the common man and that of the learned or enlightened. From this point of view, Jaspers's philosophical faith must be viewed as a proof of hubris or as unbelief.

Certainly, Jaspers considers the ability to comprehend oneself as "Existence" by reading ciphers to be universally human, and access to "Transcendence" is opened up by events which he calls *borderline situations* and which all of us experience—suffering, death, failure. Whether these situations necessarily show a way to transcendence is psychologically by no means certain, but if they do, the way rather leads to the personal god of the religion revealed—a way that Jaspers overall and in the spirit of the Enlightenment ought to denounce as a lapse into myth and a renunciation of existence. In this point, I believe, Karl Barth was right in attacking Jaspers's unspeakable and actually insubstantial "Transcendence" as being foreign to Christian tradition.[7]

Nevertheless, Jaspers's faith and the religion of revelation meet in a fundamentally human anxiety; namely, in the awareness of the self-insufficiency of the world and of the human existence within it. This is somewhat more than a simple negative self-demarcation from naturalism and scientism, since Jaspers believes that the insurmountable barriers of knowledge render those matters beyond by no means trivial or insignificant. Just the opposite: only by attempting to leap to "the other side" do we reach our existence, even though this attempt cannot be described in the language of universally valid categories. The meaning of ciphers, to be sure, is captured in the very uniqueness of existence: "The objective side of [a] cipher is only significant if it has existential import; as a mere state of affairs, it becomes a bare concept. The subjective side concerns the existential origin, which becomes transparent to itself in the objective side of [the] cipher; merely being subjective, it becomes the subject of a psychology."[8]

It is remarkable that Jaspers, who, in contrast to many other philosophers, did not think *against others,* but, like Hegel, intended to adopt in a positive way the entire Western philosophical heritage, himself intentionally obstructed the way of such assimilation of the faith of revelation and felt compelled simply to deny it. Nevertheless, he considered the vitality of the Biblical legacy as an indispensable requirement for the survival of Western culture. Did he really believe that the Bible—if its content was reduced to a collection of unspeakable ciphers so that it could no longer serve as the crystallization point of a religious community—could still maintain its spiritual force as the inspirational source of a culture? In his struggle against the faith of revelation and institutional religion, it appears on occasion as if the face of an obtuse school catechist, who stifled the mind of the talented boy, appeared continually before Jaspers.

But let us leave aside pedantic snappishness. The point is not to reproach

7. Ibid., 485, and Karl Barth, *Kirchliche Dogmatik,* vol. 3, 549ff.
8. Karl Jaspers, *Der philosophische Glaube angesichts der Offenbarung* (München: Piper Verlag, 1962), 309.

Jaspers for ambiguities, but to understand them within a larger cultural process. Obviously, Jaspers participated in the modernistic revolt against positivism and scientism. He directed his questions toward the whole and aspired to understand the whole. However, the whole is—as he knew—not an empirical or empirically constructable concept; it is not an object of reason. Still, without mastering the whole, the meaning of each detail remains doubtful. He rejected Kantian criticism in order to assume a truly Hegelian point of view, according to which reason, in order to comprehend the whole, must grasp the very process of understanding as a "moment" of the whole; otherwise, reason's position as an observer remains inexplicable. Positivism, however, is incapable of grasping the fact that reality, which it wants to grasp in cognitive acts, is precisely an object of cognitive acts, as Jaspers put it in his criticism. Consequently, the whole in positivism is not genuine.[9] But Jaspers was willing to accept some important results of the positivist approach as irrevocable: for instance, the impossibility of objectifying the ultimate reality. Indeed, we cannot talk about "Existence," since it remains conceptually inexpressible; on the other hand, we are forced to attempt discussing it because without such an attempt, genuine communication is unthinkable. By trying to comprehend the conditions of each objectification, we encounter freedom and thus leave the boundaries of knowledge. Knowledge cannot justify itself. Thus it sounds tautological to say that the substantiation of knowledge is no longer knowledge; but it is indispensable for a life of dignity to become clearly conscious of this tautology—Jaspers's message on this point perhaps may thus be paraphrased.

But we never leave the boundaries of knowledge, objectivity, and the world in the sense of finding ourselves in a new country, having forgotten the old. Incessantly we remain within empirical existence when we seek access to "Existence" and to the All-Encompassing. To freedom, the natural world is a place of resistance as well as a condition of its own existence, just as water is to the swimmer. I cannot comprehend myself directly, but only through the mediation of what I *am not*. That does not mean that my existence is sheer negativity—Sartre's void—but that it may never appear as substance. In addition—as we can read in a beautiful passage of *Vom Ursprung und Ziel der Geschichte*—all our attempts to leap out of the frame of historic reference and reach a base outside of history are not only indispensable but also unsuccessful, in the sense that they all must remain within

9. Ibid., 263f., 285f.

history.[10] We ought to remain faithful, however, to the Earth as well as to ourselves, and both obligations do not join on the same level of language.

Jaspers, if one may say so, brought to light the darkness of a cultural situation which had developed at the end of the nineteenth century and whose heirs we remain. It is defined by simultaneous awareness of the crisis between two enemies competing for domination of our spiritual and intellectual life: the Enlightenment and Christianity. On the one hand, Christianity felt increasingly insecure about its claims on scholastic rationality, and the criticism of the Enlightenment forced it more and more to seek other means of expression for its wisdom. On the other hand, the self-complacency of omniscient, optimistic rationalism collapsed, too. Christians were more and more prepared to accept, albeit reluctantly, that *Deus et anima* were absent from the world of knowledge. And rationalism increasingly proved its inability to find a foundation for itself and come to terms with questions which share in the determination of human existence and which cannot be banished through exorcisms and excommunications by the advocates of scientism. Jaspers excellently expressed both sides of this consciousness of crisis. He not only reacted to naturalistic anthropology, but he also noticed that human existence cannot be rationally understood beyond naturalism and psychologism. Furthermore, he aimed at describing this realization under the presupposition that the will to understand the unintelligible in myself is my human task par excellence. Hence, neither philosophical nor religious inquiry provides "truth" in the same sense as we speak of truth in the area of science. Since philosophical and religious truth are defined by their origin, their genesis, but not by their contents, there are no obstacles to simultaneously affirming ideas that collide with each other in content. The act of actual choice, and not the substance of choice, constitutes truth.

In other words, once we have crossed the borders of knowledge, truth is related to the uniqueness of existence and cannot be considered compelling to all human beings. Neither can the historically unique be generalized: revelation, a unique and unrepeatable fact, cannot bestow meaning on history. God's word is preached exclusively to me, and it appears that religious life as a common good is conceivable only *mala fide*. God realizes Himself only in my incurable desolation, and this is probably the reason why my encounter with Him inevitably culminates in failure: only in communication with others can I illuminate myself as "Existence"; but "Transcend-

10. Karl Jaspers, *Vom Ursprung und Ziel der Geschichte* (Zürich, 1949), 325ff., 331ff.

ence," which is the necessary pendant to "Existence," never becomes real as a field of communication. Ricoeur was right when he pointed out that for Jaspers guilt becomes the ontological state of human beings instead of a result of avoidable human offence. I shape my being human through free choice, and through free choice I become guilty. It even seems as if human misfortune and even human evil have their basis in the fact that we exist as separate persons; as if my limitation, my separate existence were a disease of being—as some trends of Buddhism and Schopenhauer affirm. Since there is no universally accessible God and consequently no salvation, I am faced with a dilemma: *Either* I slip into the ungenuine, by voluntarily submitting to authority, and thus lose my existence, *or* I accept my freedom and consequently accept failure as my ineluctable fate and affirm my dignity in the destruction of myself. In one particular sense, nobody is condemned, since the way suggested by Jaspers is always open to everybody; in another sense, everybody is condemned, since the best possible way ends in defeat.

In the final analysis it appears that the third way between rationalism and the faith of revelation may perhaps save us from self-delusion, but at the price of self-destruction in a state of reclaimed dignity. To repeat, Jaspers excellently expressed the simultaneous paralysis of the Enlightenment and Christianity. Against the Enlightenment he stressed the inexplicability and unintelligibility of the empirically accessible world from within itself. Against Christianity, he intended to show that this unintelligibility of the world can never be established as a common good of humanity, a universally valid achievement, or a field of communication. The result of his thinking had to remain ambiguous, and the ambiguity is not in the personality of our philosopher but of our civilization, whose double blockade was reflected in Jaspers's philosophy. While superbly expressing this ambiguity and paralysis, Jaspers offered no remedy for its elimination. But perhaps it is the call of philosophers to reveal crises instead of curing them.

Chapter Eleven

From Truth to Truth

Once I had a wonderful commercial idea: I would found an agency, a business nobody to my knowledge had ever thought of: a conversion agency. Its advertising slogan would be, We convert from anything to anything; whether you want to become a pious Jew, a Maoist, or Adventist—we arrange anything on demand, for a corresponding fee, of course.

The fees naturally would be determined according to the degree of difficulty for a given conversion. Following this plan, the most expensive conversions would be those to Albanian Communism and Khomeini's variety of Islam; the most inexpensive would be those to belief systems that are relatively comfortable and do not demand very much from their confessors, perhaps Anglicanism or liberal reform Judaism; Satanism would be located in the middle. Whether the schedule of fees should also account for the state of mind of the client, and whether the amount of payment should be adjusted for the degree of difficulty involved in freeing the person from the existing belief would remain an open question. Provided that people who called on my agency were mentally prepared to leave their belief or disbelief, such complications of the fee schedule could be dispensed with.

Psychologists and other experts of indoctrination shall then be entrusted with the actual work, which will in no way violate the freedom of the individual. The agency itself must remain strictly neutral religiously and ideologically; it could be named Veritas, "Truth," or Certitudo, "Certitude" (perhaps, "Happy Certitude").

It is difficult to estimate in advance how large the demand would be for this service. Since everywhere so many people are searching for intellectual and spiritual certitude, and since so many religious and ideological sects are being founded everywhere in the world—astonishingly absurd and grotesque ones among them—one could count on considerable success, I be-

Translated from the German by Wolfgang Freis from "Von Wahrheit zur Wahrheit," a lecture delivered over Bavarian radio, 1984. Revised by the author in English.

lieve. It is also likely that in democratic countries such an agency could operate on an entirely legal basis and would be able to pay its taxes legitimately; in ideological countries the business of the agency would probably be viewed as subversive and be punished with death, jail, or a concentration camp.

My laziness and lack of an enterprising spirit have prevented me from translating this inventive project into reality, but I am willing to license this idea for a small sum to more industrious people. So much for self-advertisement.

Is such an agency even imaginable? Yes, why not? In principle it is only a technique of indoctrination, which can be effective regardless of whether or not the technicians believe in the dogma to which they convert other people.

One could argue against it that it would not be true conversion, but only indoctrination. But what is "true" conversion? Certainly, in a Christian sense, true conversion is a gift of God, but even a priest who converts somebody to truth has no reliable signs of whether or not the conversion was genuine, that is, inspired by God's grace. For our purpose it suffices if the conversion is psychologically true, that is, if the converts believe in what they are made to believe. And that can be achieved by technical means. Otherwise my agency would not claim to be in God's hands.

No detailed technique has been drawn up for my agency so far. In this point, however, we are able to rely on century-old traditions. There are many possible procedures to make people follow a belief. At one end of the scale there is purely physical pressure: it is possible to make people sign or confess to a profession of faith. At the other end are the rational and irrefutable arguments with which one can convince people of truth. And there are many indirect and mixed techniques. Neither of the two techniques already mentioned would be used in our agency. Torture would be avoided, not necessarily because it would be unsuccessful, but because not enough volunteers would submit to the procedure. Rational persuasion would not be used because it is only applicable to a few truths, and it could not achieve total conversion—regardless of what was involved. Certainly, one does occasionally speak of conversions in very specific terms: It is possible to say that a scientist who resisted a certain theory for a long time finally came to acknowledge it or that somebody has turned to smoking a particular brand of cigarettes. But these are derivative and not quite correct uses of the word. The kind of conversion we are talking about, as it is usually understood, is something different. Above all it includes an imperturbable certitude, inured to all possible argumentation, which never can be obtained in a rational manner. But that is not enough, because imperturbable certitude also may be related to very specific convictions. Conversion in the proper sense leads to a belief operating as a universal ideology, which supplies conclusive answers not only to all important questions of human existence, society, and the universe, but it also gives practical direction for distinguishing right from wrong, and good from evil. In addition, belief provides more than abstract knowledge, namely, genuine energy and practical proficiency in translating all these truths and directions into the living reality. These three aspects of belief—knowledge, energy, and proficiency—can only be distinguished externally; theoretical truth, practical direction, and actual commitment in the mind of the believer are one and the same. Through conversion one gains not simply truth, but total truth—at least in respect to all questions that are important, interesting, and significant to life. One gains not only criteria to distinguish right and wrong, but criteria that are beyond any doubt, that are not afflicted by any argument, that grant moral certitude to the convert.

Thus, conversion is a radical intellectual or spiritual turning point leading to comprehensive understanding of the world, free of uncertainty, resolving all theoretical and practical questions, and eliminating all doubts. Considering conversion psychologically in this sense, it may apply, of course, to both religious faith and secular ideologies, as long as these ideologies claim to be all-inclusive and demand adherence to a certain life-style. Not to follow this life-style means not to have converted completely to the ideology: we do not call people true Christians who have adopted intellectually a Christian view of life but do not demonstrate that their belief influences their existence.

For that reason we also talk about conversion in the case of Christians who have never actually left the Church, but whose lukewarm loyalty suddenly changes to passionate faith permeating all of their lives. The biographies of many great figures in the history of Christianity testify to such conversions, including those of St. Katherine of Siena, St. Ignatius of Loyola, and Pascal. They did not turn from unbelief (or wrong beliefs) to belief as, for instance, did St. Augustine, St. Justin, or, to mention the most paradigmatic case, St. Paul; instead, they turned from an inherited affiliation, which they had never questioned, to an ardent and all-consuming act of self sacrifice, to an absorption in final certitude. A loss of faith, however, if it ends in indifference, ought not to be described as a conversion.

Sociology understands a conversion as an admission of an adult person into a religious congregation. As a psychological event, however, it must be related to its authenticity and effect, and it must not involve just any belief system, but only those that place absolute demands in intellectual as well as practical matters on the convert. Whether we can talk about conversion to a purely philosophical belief is uncertain. It is conceivable, though, that certain philosophical doctrines may qualify as requiring genuine conversion. In the fourth and fifth decades of the nineteenth century, it appears that various individuals converted to Hegelianism. If only temporarily, the young Russian intellectuals—Bielinski and M. Bakunin, for instance—found in the Hegelian philosophy of history, however correctly or incorrectly it was interpreted, an intellectual expression of their despair. This they had realized for themselves: If we can adopt the idea of historic inevitability, it is possible to accept what is necessary and discontinue the futile struggle against the fateful course of events. Thus, by living into destiny they could cloak their helplessness and despair in pathos and forge it into a quasi religion. To be sure, both of these thinkers soon reached a turning point and gave up their melancholic historic masochism to proceed to an ideology of radical revolt.

Whether or not their reading of Hegel was correct is irrelevant in the present context. Only the fact that an abstract philosophical construction may operate in special cases as a universal ideology and be the occasion of conversion is important here. I can also imagine that some people have converted, in the same sense, to Spinoza's philosophy, although I am not aware of any example that undoubtedly bears witness to that. Any philosophy promising both to solve metaphysical enigmas—or to eradicate them—as well as to answer the question, "How to live?" may assume such a function: for instance, stoicism, Nietzsche's doctrine, or perhaps even Heidegger's. Its attraction depends, of course, on the cultural circumstances at the time, the necessities of human beings, their willingness to be converted, and the authenticity of the philosophy. It is difficult to imagine, in contrast, a conversion to Cartesianism: the doctrine was intended to deal with metaphysical and cosmological questions, but it did not supply sufficient guidance to guarantee intellectual security, and did not bestow inspirational power to answer life's problems.

So far we have spoken only about conversions to beliefs that already exist. A conversion, however, may also consist of an illumination constituting an absolute beginning, a purely personal encounter with truth, a private revelation. An individual beholds the light, and nobody is able to convince him or her that it is an error or that he or she has been deceived. Mystical experiences in a strict sense of the word, as well as the revelations that some Buddhists experience at the end of their spiritual pursuits, belong to this category. Such cases do not involve an understanding and adoption of a certain wisdom, but rather an act of personal and not transferable spiritual initiation into a new world, where truth is not just known but lived in; or, better, where one becomes truth.

Something similar, though not identical, occurs perhaps in philosophical reflection as well, when a long struggle with metaphysical questions suddenly culminates in a single enlightenment, clearing away all doubts and leading the convert into a state of absolute certainty (or intellectual grace). Some great philosophers certainly have experienced such illuminations at some point, and there was no need to interpret them as a God-sent light. Reason, in such cases, could serve as a substitute for God; yet the feeling of possessing ultimate truth, one may suspect, was similar to a religious illumination.

In our times, a typical, yet not religious, conversion is of course related to secular universal political ideologies. They are often compared with religious movements or considered their surrogates in a largely secularized society. Such comparisons are partly, but not entirely, true. Political ideologies with global pretensions, such as Communism, operate—or rather, operated—psychologically in a manner analogous to religious belief in many respects; in this sense, conversion, too, is similar to religious conversion. The converts, first, gain complete certitude and, second, their belief is invulnerable against all argumentation and discussion. In religious belief, rational arguments are used essentially as weapons against followers of other religions, against heretics, and against skeptics. A rigorous belief remains invulnerable. Also, such political belief normally is constructed so vaguely that it is able to absorb all factual circumstances. As long as Communism and Marxism existed as living beliefs—which is hardly the case anymore in Europe, not to mention eastern Europe—one was converted to it, not convinced. A short credo was sufficient enough to become omniscient; to know human history perfectly, and to interpret it; to understand all circumstances of the present beyond doubt, and to predict the future infallibly. The difference between religious belief and political ideology, and thus between the two forms of conversion, is that the former presents itself as what it is: a belief consenting to a divine revelation. A universal political ideology, however, desires to be both; belief and rational knowledge. For that reason, it is always accompanied by a bad conscience. One ought to believe in it blindly, but at the same time one ought to be convinced of possessing a rational higher wisdom and call one's own blindness "science." In the event that an ideology includes elements that are formulated as empirical truths and may be critically examined, yet simply turn out to be false, one may say, as Lukacs and Bloch did (following the example of Fichte), "All the worse for the facts," and continue to adhere steadfastly to one's belief.

We are all striving for a comprehensive explanation of life, and we need certainty that we are living in reality. To live in never-ending insecurity, in fluctuation, and be unable to answer the basic questions with which the universe and the human world encircle us is hardly tolerable.

Psychologically conceived, conversion—leaving aside grace—originates in the desire for security, not in reason. This desire is human, all too human, and therefore any conversion, regardless of how it would be categorized theologically or socially, is an answer to a genuine, that is, anthropologically based, necessity. By giving us the ability to question, to be dissatisfied with the limited knowledge of direct experience, to be curious, and by inoculating us with the determination to understand the world, nature also gave us a desire for spiritual certitude; and only a belief that obtrudes upon the facts, instead of being derived from them, can satisfy this desire: knowledge alone, no matter how far it extends, does not fulfill it.

The desire for spiritual certitude, and thus for belief, is natural, and it is not to be expected that it will ever be eliminated. Consequently, the phenomenon of conversion is a constant part of human life as well. That individuals can live without satisfying this desire, that is, can live with frustration, does not speak against it. It is possible to live without satisfying sexual needs, which are also natural. If cultural or psychological factors prevent us from satisfying the desire for belief in religious form, a large number of nonreligious, and even antireligious, substitutes emerge to supply the same satisfaction. Actual intellectual domination of the world is not important to conversion; what matters is the certainty that, generally speaking, the world—in principle—already has been mastered intellectually. Thus, it is a question of "loyalty" to an existing view of the world; in order to be converted, it is necessary to know only a little, only the most fundamental aspects of this view. At any rate, this is what happens most of the time. Naturally, it is different in the case of prophets who *ex nihilo*—or apparently *ex nihilo*—discover a new, hitherto unknown truth.

Since conversion resembles *taking an oath of loyalty* to a truth that explains the world, and the conquest of a certitude, it is understandable that it is not easily realized in isolation. Normally—though not necessarily—taking such an oath requires a community in which the truth crystallizes, or which is

the proprietor or guardian of the truth. Thus, certitude usually also neces-
sitates association with those who serve or guard the truth, or with those
initiated into the truth: a sect, church, or ideological party. That is—I must
repeat—not completely indispensable, yet natural. Phenomena of mass conversion as they are known in history—when a sect or ideological movement
suddenly and for inexplicable reasons begins to spread like wildfire—are by
no means spurious. On the other hand, a collective conquest of absolute
certitude, psychologically seen, is quite comprehensible, and one often has
the impression that the desire for certitude is significantly more important
than the content of the belief. That becomes evident in cases of some sects
that are intellectually miserable and almost altogether without substance
and yet have significant successes in the marketplace of ideas. Gore Vidal's
novel *Messiah* presents a satirical example, in which a sect whose belief is
nearly bare of substance nevertheless conquers an unexpectedly large part
of humanity.

In today's world, where the desire for spiritual certitude is felt so painfully, and where the revival of the traditional churches and confessions—
especially among the young of various countries—may be observed despite
progressive "secularization," it cannot be ruled out that, for instance, a pres-
ently unknown sect, which today perhaps counts fifty members in Okla-
homa, will not one day abruptly and inexplicably expand and change the
situation of the world within a few years.

From this characterization it follows that a conversion achieved by force
is not inconceivable, and it is quite possible that the application of pressure
could produce a psychologically genuine conversion. The distinction between persuasion by pure force and indoctrination is one of degree, not of
substance. And indoctrination, for instance, in the case of children, hardly
differs from socialization. That does not necessarily concern religious education. In all matters of psychological development—moral as well as intellectual—the socialization of children, that is, their adjustment to a society,
consists of indoctrination: forcing something upon a defenseless person
(which we all were as children) that must be accepted as valid. The validity,
however, derives from the fact of the older generation's conviction. It cannot be any different: To give children complete freedom in their own development, that is, to leave them without any indoctrination, would mean
to raise them without any socialization; thus, they would remain on a bru-
tish level.

Indoctrination is not only present in religious education, and it does not
simply consist of children's instruction in distinguishing good from evil,

moral from immoral, and correct and incorrect thinking; it is included in the acquisition of *language* itself: Language offers a fundamental view of the world, a mode of dividing and classifying the world and that which is conceivable or unthinkable. Language already carries value-charged forms and distinctions. Hence, education without indoctrination is *non*education; it amounts to withholding humanity from young humans, and preventing their development as human. It does not follow, however, that every form of indoctrination is commendable and just as good as any other. The potential evil consists not in the act of indoctrination but in the fact that the indoctrinated person is deprived of the opportunity to compare various points of view, or is artificially isolated from a world that believes something different, or is not permitted to think critically. Indoctrination in this sense is characteristic of totalitarian education.

But even with adults, one can hardly maintain that a forced conversion was necessarily spurious. The border between an imposed way of acting and a true belief is not clearly defined, and behavior may lead to belief. The proof lies simply in the fact that forced conversions on a large scale were quite successful in the end: various parts of Europe were once converted to Christianity by force, and if it did not happen in the first generation, the second included mostly true believers. Even Pascal, wishing to help those people willing to convert, but not finding the spiritual power, gave simple advice: You should begin with "external" matters, and conduct yourself as if you were believing; do what believers do, yes, "stultify" yourself. And, not without reason, he hoped that true belief would grow out of purely external behavior.

So far I have talked about conversion on an entirely neutral level without expressing value judgments about the content of conversion. That is of course not my approach. It could not be farther from my mind to assume that every belief is equally valuable, or equally worthless. According to our historic experience it seems undeniable that there are misanthropic beliefs, and others that include a force with which the good rather than the evil in human nature may be encouraged and brought to light. On the other hand, I am not in a position to appear as priest or proselytizer of a specific confession. And to compare with each other all possible beliefs to which people may be converted is naturally an impossible task. I will make only a few remarks on possible methods of comparison.

There are forms of belief that reinforce hatred and others that strengthen love in humans. Naturally, we all carry the potential for hatred and love in us, and insofar as a belief is able to stimulate in us the energy of love and to weaken or destroy the store of hatred, to such an extent *a belief is good*. This is the most general and most essential criterion (though not the only one) with which we may compare and judge various forms of conversion.

According to this criterion, it will probably become apparent that universal political ideologies—those to which humans have to be converted in the true sense of the word—by their nature are more suited to release in us evil and not love: the diabolical and not the divine. Such ideologies subordinate the entire philosophy of life to political goals; thus good and evil are distinguished according to criteria of political usefulness, that is, the distinction is simply abolished. When a political goal—thus, domination—becomes the universal guideline, and when the focus of an ideology becomes the annihilation of an opponent, it appears obvious that the mobilization of hatred has become a natural means within such a philosophy. In a Christian sense, such ideologies must be labeled idolatry, or an absolutism and idolizing of relative goods which, through the fact of idolization itself, turn into tools of slavery.

Even if it is true that similar psychological mechanisms and certain social necessities may be observed in all conversions, and that the spiritual values gained by the convert also appear to be similar, such an analogy does not invalidate the distinction between a conversion to the diabolical and one to the divine. A conversion that furthers love in us and eradicates hatred *must* have part in truth, no matter what the content of the belief may be.

PART THREE

On Liberals, Revolutionaries, and Utopians

Chapter Twelve

The Death of Utopia Reconsidered

When I am asked where I would like to live, my standard answer is: deep in the virgin mountain forest on a lake shore at the corner of Madison Avenue in Manhattan and Champs Elysées, in a small tidy town. Thus I am a utopian, and not because the place of my dreams happens not to exist but because it is self-contradictory.

Are all utopias self-contradictory? This depends, of course, on the way we define the word, and there is no compelling reason why we should narrow its meaning down to those ideas of which either logical inconsistency or empirical impossibility are patent. In talking about utopia, we ought to stay reasonably close to the current usage of the word, even though we realize that this usage is to a certain extent shaky and imprecise. It is an interesting cultural process whereby a word of which the history is well known and which emerged as an artificially concocted proper name has acquired, in the last two centuries, a sense so extended that it refers not only to a literary genre but to a way of thinking, to a mentality, to a philosophical attitude, and is being employed in depicting cultural phenomena going back into antiquity, far beyond the historical moment of its invention. This fact suggested to some historians and philosophers that we had to do with an everlasting form of human sensitivity, with a permanent anthropological datum for which an English thinker in the sixteenth century simply invented an apt name. This may sound plausible on the assumption that we inflate the concept to such a size as to pack into it (as Ernst Bloch did) all human projections of something better than what is and, on the other hand, all the religious images of paradisical happiness. Thus enlarged, however, the notion is of little use, since everything people have ever done in improving their collective or even individual lives, as well as all their eschatological expectations, would have to be counted among "utopian" projections, whereby the concept would not be applicable any longer as a tool in any historical or philosophical inquiry. On the other hand, the adjective *utopian* has been given a pejorative sense in everyday speech and is applied to all projects, however trivial, which for any reason are impracticable ("it is utopian to expect that we shall be on time for dinner tonight"), and such a concept, again, is of no value in studying human culture.

Considering, therefore, that an amount of arbitrariness is unavoidable in trying to restrict the concept and that it is commendable to remain roughly within its current use rather than to employ an existing word for entirely foreign purposes, I suggest that we proceed with a double limitation. First, we shall talk about utopias having in mind not ideas of making any side of human life better but only beliefs that a definitive and unsurpassable condition is attainable, one where there is nothing to correct any more. Second, we shall apply the word to projections that are supposed to be implemented by human effort, thus excluding both images of an other-worldly paradise and apocalyptic hopes for an earthly paradise to be arranged by sheer divine decree. Consequently, conforming to the second criterion, the revolutionary anabaptism of the sixteenth century may be included in the history of utopias so conceived, but not various chiliastic or adventist movements, nor ideas that expect the Kingdom on Earth as a result of Parousia. On the other hand, according to the first criterion, I would not describe as utopian various futuristic technological fantasies if they do not suggest the idea of an ultimate solution of mankind's predicament, a perfect satisfaction of human needs, a final state.

Being thus restricted on two sides, the concept is widened insofar as it may be applied not only to global visions of a definitively saved society but to some specific areas of human creativity as well. We may speak, for example, of epistemological utopias, meaning the search for either a perfect certainty or an ultimate source of cognitive values; neither can anything prevent us from labeling as *scientific utopia* a hope for a definitive foundation of any science—in particular of physics or mathematics—or of all empirical sciences, a hope which, once fulfilled, would close the path to future progress except for applications of the ultimate equation in specific cases. It would be difficult instead to look for architectural or artistic utopias, as one may hardly find in the history of human thought—much as it teems with wild expectations of an Eschaton—the idea of an ultimate building or an ultimate poem.

Descartes may be called the founder of the modern epistemological utopia. He did believe—and perhaps rightly so—that if no source of an absolute, unshakable certitude can be found, no certitude at all is conceivable and therefore no truth, except in a pragmatic sense. And he believed that this ultimate cognitive assurance can indeed be discovered and that he had revealed it. He did not reveal it in the Cogito alone: had he been satisfied with the Cogito as the only truth resisting all possible doubts, he would not have been capable of going beyond this discovery, and the latter would have remained a self-contained, empty tautology leading nowhere. To proceed from this initial illumination to a trustworthy reconstruction of the universe, he had to be possessed of universally valid criteria of truth which he was unable to legitimize without the omniscient divine mind. A vicious circle which the first critics noticed in his reasoning (the criterion of the clarity and distinctness of ideas is employed in proving God's existence, whereupon God appears as guarantor of the reliability of clear and distinct ideas) and which would subsequently be discussed by philosophers to our day need not bother us now. Whether or not his proposal was logically sound, he asked (or revived) the formidable utopian question that has kept philosophy busy for centuries: is perfect certainty attainable at all; and if so, can it be reached without an appeal to absolute divine wisdom? If not—are we bound to give up, together with the ultimate foundation of knowledge, the very concept of truth in the usual, that is, transcendental, sense and to be satisfied with practical criteria of acceptability, renouncing forever the dream of episteme? Whatever the answer might be, the question was not trivial, and the crucial moments in the vicissitudes of modern philosophy are marked by clashes between empiricists and skeptics on the one side and the defenders of sundry forms of the transcendentalist approach on the other.

The epistemological utopia has never died away in our culture, and its most stubborn and bravest defender at the beginning of our century was no doubt Edmund Husserl. Untiringly and unceasingly he kept improving, correcting, and rebuilding the Cartesian project, drilling deeper and deeper into the layers of transcendental consciousness in the quest for the ultimate ground of all grounds, a ground we can reach without appealing to the divine veracity. He was driven not only by a philosophical gambler's curiosity but also by a conviction that the skeptical or empiricist renouncement of the idea of certainty, and thereby of truth, would spell the ruin of European culture.

The philosophical movement, however, did not go along the grooves he had started to furrow. Even among those who were ready to take up his ideas, the most important thinkers—Heidegger and Merleau-Ponty above all—abandoned the hope for a radical phenomenological reduction. They did not believe that we might ever set ourselves in the position of pure subjects of cognition who have gotten rid of all the historically relative, socially assimilated sedimentations of our consciousness, and start afresh, as it were, from a zero point. No matter at what moment we begin our reflection, we are already thrown into the world, we are molded by experience and compelled to express ourselves in a language we have not invented. However far we might go, or imagine we have gone, in hunting the perfectly unprejudiced, "presuppositionless" beginning of knowledge, we will always be in the middle of the road. There is no absolutely transparent distance (let alone abolition of distance) between us and the world, no cognitive void whereby the world, in its undistorted shape, could reach and enter our inner space. The division into the external and the inner world which the Cartesian tradition established and which was a condition of the quest for the ultimate epistemological foundation was, of course, repeatedly attacked in the nineteenth century, by Avenarius and Mach among others, and in fact by all post-Darwinian philosophers who believed that cognitive acts could be properly interpreted within a biological framework as defensive reactions and who thus dismissed the traditional search for truth as a result of metaphysical prejudices. It was against those anti-Cartesians that Husserl undertook his arduous journey into the unknown of transcendental consciousness and tried to reverse the trend of relativistic naturalism. He failed to discover or to rediscover the paradisical island of unshakable knowledge, yet he did open various new paths for thinking, and he left the entire philosophical landscape of Europe utterly transmuted; not unlike Descartes, Rousseau, or Kant before him, he compelled the next generations of philosophers, including those who refused to share his hopes, to define themselves in relation or in opposition to him.

A hidden nostalgia for an epistemological utopia was still active in some empiricist trends of the first decades of our century: not in the sense of transcendentalist expectations, to be sure, but in the form of the long-lasting quest for the ultimate data of knowledge or ultimately irreducible propositions. And this, too, has gone. Transcendental phenomenology has come to a dead stop in chasing the perfect transparency; logical positivism got stuck in its unsuccessful attempts to devise satisfactory definitions of verifiability and analyticity. A lot has survived from both, no doubt, but not the hope for an epistemological Ultimum. Transcendental research retreated in favor of existential ontology, which, in a variety of forms, expressed its refusal to believe that we might ever grasp either the subject or the object severally in their uncontaminated freshness, that either Being or human existence could be conceptually dominated. Logical empiricism has been replaced by the late Wittgenstein, by the ordinary language philosophy. Philosophical utopia seems to have died off. Whether it is truly and definitively dead or just temporarily asleep, we cannot say with any certainty; but even though we do not detect in this very moment any distinct signs of its resurrection, we may have reasons not to believe in its final extinction. I am strongly reluctant to admit that a philosophical life left entirely as prey to pragmatists and relativists is either likely or desirable. My reluctance is grounded on a certain understanding of what philosophy is as a cultural phenomenon, and this understanding in its turn is based, of course, on an interpretation of its historical vicissitudes.

My general attitude may be thus expressed: What philosophy is about is not Truth. Philosophy can never discover any universally admissible truths; and if a philosopher happened to have made a genuine contribution to science (one thinks, say, of the mathematical works of Descartes, Leibniz, or Pascal), his discovery, perhaps by the very fact of being admitted as an ingredient of established science, immediately ceased being a part of philosophy, no matter what kind of metaphysical or theological motivations might have been at work in producing it. The cultural role of philosophy is not to deliver truth but to build the *spirit of truth*, and this means never to let the inquisitive energy of mind go to sleep, never to stop questioning what appears to be obvious and definitive, always to defy the seemingly intact resources of common sense, always to suspect that there might be "another side" in what we take for granted, and never to allow us to forget that there are questions that lie beyond the legitimate horizon of science and are nonetheless crucially important to the survival of humanity as we know it. All the most traditional worries of philosophers—how to tell good from evil, true from false, real from unreal, being from nothingness, just from unjust, necessary from contingent, myself from others, man from animal, mind from body, or how to find order in chaos, providence in absurdity, timelessness in time, laws in facts, God in the world, world in language—all of them boil down to the quest for meaning; and they presuppose that in dissecting such questions we may employ the instruments of reason, even if the ultimate outcome is the dismissal of reason or its defeat. Philosophers neither sow nor harvest, they only move the soil. They do not discover truth; but they are needed to keep the energy of mind alive, to confront various possibilities for answering our questions. To do that they—or at least some of them—must trust that the answers are within our reach. Those who keep that trust are real diggers; and although I can not share their contention that by digging more and more deeply they will eventually reach the *Urgrund*, the foundation of all foundations, I do believe that their presence in the continuation of our culture is vital and indispensable. They are utopians and we need them. Next to diggers, however, we need healers who apply skeptical medicine in order to clean our minds from prejudices, to unmask the hidden premises of our beliefs, to keep us vigilant, to improve our logical skills, not to let us be carried away by wishful thinking. Philosophy, to survive, needs both diggers and healers, both reckless adventurers and cautious insurance brokers. They even seem to prop each other amidst their never-ending squabbles. The trouble is that whoever says so while being himself interested in philosophical riddles and thus involved in the conflict in one way or another cannot avoid the risk of antinomy or of contradiction: he is not capable of not taking sides in the conflict, and he asserts something that would ultimately compel him to be at both extremes simultaneously. We can escape the contradiction only by trying to place ourselves outside philosophy, to suspend our interest in the issues and to climb up to a vantage point from which philosophy itself appears as a part of the history of civilization. The trouble is, however, that to reach this point we almost certainly need some premises and some conceptual instruments that have been elaborated in the ambiguous realm of philosophy.

Still, it may be fairly said that today's life of the mind is antiutopian, that more often than not we are ready either to admit inescapable borders that limit the expansion of our cognitive passions or to argue, more consistently and more in keeping with the tradition of skepticism and empiricism, that the very notion of cognitive value or of "truth" metaphysically conceived is nothing but an aberration of mind which seeks to assert its illusory autonomy and self-reliance instead of seeing itself as what it is, namely, a useful defense device of our organism. It is possible that from a historical perspective some important achievements of twentieth-century science—Heisenberg's principle and Gödel's theorem—will be seen as contributions to the same antiutopian spirit of our age; they pointed out fundamental barriers that were imposed—by the nature of Mind, by great Nature, or by God—on our knowledge.

And when I say that the final extinction of the utopian drive in philosophy is neither likely nor desirable, I do not want to forget its intrinsic and apparently unremovable dangers. Whoever says that it is possible to discover a source of perfect certainty or an ultimate ground of knowledge says in effect not that it is possible but rather that he *has* found it. The expectations of an epistemological last judgment can certainly breed intolerance and self-righteous blindness. And they cannot escape the most traditional skeptical question about the infinite regression: *qui custodiet ipsos custodes?* Whatever criteria we establish, we may always ask what are the criteria of *their* validity.

The danger can be avoided, perhaps, if those ultimate criteria are considered—to use the Kantian idiom—as regulative, rather than constitutive, ideas; they serve us better if they are signposts which show the direction toward an unattainable goal instead of asserting that the goal has been, or is about to be, reached. In other words, the spirit of utopia has two versions: one of them corresponds to the Kantian maxim of pure reason and consists in actually building the ultimate ground, or at least in the belief that the premise of all premises is going to be discovered; the other is the search for a ground of any ground that we believe to have already unraveled, and it corresponds to what Hegel stigmatized as the "bad infinity." The former includes a hope of finding and intellectually grasping the Unconditioned in its very quality of Unconditionedness, and thereby a hope for a kind of philosophical theosis, for a finite mind which has acquired Godlike properties. The latter includes both the acceptance of the finitude of mind and the will to expand its potentialities without any definable limit being assigned to this expansion.

Analogous remarks may be made about social utopias. It might seem implausible to maintain that we witness the decline of utopian mentality when we observe so many movements promising us a secular or theocratic millennium around the corner and applying all kinds of instruments of oppression and violence to bring it about. I would argue, however, that the decline is going on, that the utopian dreams have virtually lost both intellectual support and their previous self-confidence and vigor. The great works of our century are antiutopias or *kakotopias,* visions of a world in which all the values the authors identified themselves with have been mercilessly crushed (Zamiatin, Huxley, Orwell). There are some works praising utopian thinking, to be sure, yet one can hardly quote an important utopia written in our epoch.

Apart from this matter-of-fact question, I would advocate an approach to the social utopias similar to the approach I tried to justify in discussing the philosophical ones. We know, of course, countless utopian fantasies, some revolutionary, some peaceful, some of socialist, others of anarchist character; and I am not going to make their inventory or to classify them.

I want to point out those general characteristics which are relevant to my subject.

First of all is the idea of the perfect and everlasting human fraternity. This is the common and permanent core of utopian thinking, and it has been criticized on various grounds. The strictures boil down to this: first, a universal fraternity is inconceivable; second, any attempt to implement it is bound to produce a highly despotic society which, to simulate the impossible perfection, will stifle the expression of conflict and thus destroy the life of culture by a totalitarian coercion.

This criticism is sound, but we should reflect upon the conclusions to which it leads. It is arguable indeed that, by the very fact of being creative and free, people are bound to strive after goals that collide with each other and to be driven by conflicting desires; by the very fact that they can never achieve perfect satisfaction, human needs can increase and expand indefinitely, and thereby the clashes between them are inevitable. This seems to be a constitutional framework of human existence; it was known to St. Augustine and, for that matter, to all the authors of Christian theodicies. We can imagine the universal brotherhood of wolves but not of humans, since the needs of wolves are limited and definable and therefore conceivably satisfied, whereas human needs have no boundaries we could delineate; consequently, total satisfaction is incompatible with the variety and indefiniteness of human needs.

This is what the utopian mentality refuses to admit and what makes the utopias fundamentally and incurably "utopian" (in the everyday sense). A feasible utopian world must presuppose that people have lost their creativity and freedom, that the variety of human life forms and thus personal life have been destroyed, and that all people have achieved perfect satisfaction of their needs and accepted a perpetual deadly stagnation as their normal condition. Such a world would mark the end of the human race as we know it and as we define it. Stagnation is an inescapable condition of the utopian happiness; those changes which we used to call progress or enrichment in whatever area of life—in technology, science, art, institutionalized forms of social communication—are all responses to dissatisfaction, to suffering, to a challenge.

Utopias which—like Campanella's or Marx's—promise us a world that combines satisfaction, happiness, and brotherhood with progress can survive only thanks to their inconsistency. Those which are consistent accept and praise a stagnant world in which all the variety has been done away with and human beings have been reduced to a universal, immobile mediocrity. The most consistent utopia was probably devised by Dôm Deschamps. This is a perfect society in which all people are completely exchangeable and entirely identical with each other; all the variety which might differentiate human beings has been eradicated, and people have become a collection of absolutely uniform specimens, not unlike coins forged in the same mint. Social perfection has irreversibly killed human personality. The denizens of this paradise could as well be stones and would be equally happy.

The ideal of equality—conceived of as identity, the absence of differences—is self-contradictory, to be sure, on the assumption that people are what they have been throughout the history known to us. The utopians, nevertheless, keep promising us that they are going to educate the human race to fraternity, whereupon the unfortunate passions that tear societies asunder—greed, aggressiveness, lust for power—will vanish. However, since Christianity has been trying to carry out this educational task for two millennia, and the results are not quite encouraging, the utopians, once they attempt to convert their visions into practical proposals, come up with the most malignant project ever devised: they want to institutionalize fraternity, which is the surest way to totalitarian despotism. They believe that evil has resulted from faulty social institutions which run counter to the genuine impulses of human nature, without asking themselves how these institutions were created and established. In the famous fragment on the origin of inequality, Rousseau seems to believe that private property was simply invented by a madman; yet we do not know how this diabolical contrivance, opposed as it was to innate human drives, was taken up by other people and spread through all human societies.

That—as a result of the institutional coercive abrogation of private property—human conflicts, the struggle for power and domination, greed, and aggressiveness will remain where they have been or perhaps increase was a prediction fairly frequently made long before the prescription for everlasting brotherhood—worked out on Marxist-utopian principles—was actually applied. This prediction was based on common experience, and it was to be infallibly borne out in the entire history of socialist societies.

An attempt to implement a conflictless order by institutional means can indeed be successful in the sense that it can, by applying totalitarian coercion, prevent conflicts from being expressed. Being incapable, however, of eradicating the sources of conflict, the utopian technology necessarily involves a huge machinery of lies to present its inevitable failure as a victory. A utopian vision, once it is translated into a political idiom, becomes mendacious or self-contradictory; it provides new names for old injustices or hides the contradictions under labels invented ad hoc. This is especially true of revolutionary utopias, whether elaborated in the actual revolutionary process or simply applied in its course. The Orwellian language had been known, though not codified, long before modern totalitarian despotism. Rousseau's famous slogan, "One has to compel people to freedom," is a good example. So is the announcement of the Paris Commune stating simultaneously that the compulsory military service has been abolished and that all citizens are members of the National Guard. So is the egalitarian-revolutionary utopia of Tkachev (an important source of the Leninist doctrine), which asserts that the main goal of the revolution is to abolish all the elites and that this task is to be carried out by a revolutionary elite.

In other words the two most common tenets of utopian projections— fraternity by coercion and equality imposed by an enlightened vanguard— are, each of them, self-contradictory. They are, however, compatible with each other, and more often than not they appear jointly in utopian dreams. One can notice nonetheless a difference in the distribution of emphasis in the utopian phraseology. To some utopians a conflictless community is the ultimate goal, whereas others depict equality as the highest value in itself. In the latter case the assumption is thus made that it is not human individuals, their suffering, or their welfare that matter, but only the fact that suffering and welfare are evenly distributed, so that we ought to aim at a perfect equality even if it is likely that all people, including the most underprivileged, will suffer more as a result of the egalitarian order being established. Apart from being obviously self-contradictory (perfect equality could conceivably be implemented only by a totalitarian despotism, and an order that is both despotic and egalitarian in a square circle), this ideal is a curious phenomenon in the history of civilization; the psychological forces that have sustained and stimulated it can be only a matter of speculation. The dream of a consistently egalitarian utopia is to abolish everything that could distinguish one person from another; a world in which people live in identical houses, identical towns, identical geographical conditions, wearing identical clothes and sharing, of course, identical ideas is a familiar utopian picture. To preach this ideal amounts to implying that there is an intrinsic evil in the very act of asserting one's own personality, even without harming other people—in other words, that there is something essentially wrong in being human.

Radical and consistent egalitarian utopias are thus antihuman. Based on the aesthetics of impeccable symmetry and ultimate identity, they desperately search for an order in which all variety, all distinction, all dissatisfaction, and therefore all development have been done away with forever; even the word *order* is perhaps inappropriate, as there is nothing to be ordered in a perfectly homogeneous mass. We recognize in the utopian temptation a vague echo of those oriental and Neoplatonic theologies to which our separation from the source of being, from the undifferentiated Whole—and this means individuality itself—was a sort of ontological curse that could be abrogated only when individuality had been destroyed. The perfect egalitarian utopia is thus a secular caricature of Buddhist metaphysics. It may be seen perhaps as a peculiar expression of the suicidal impulse of human society, a drive we detect in many historically relative versions all through the history of religious and philosophical ideas. Ultimately it amounts to this: life necessarily involves tension and suffering; consequently if we wish to abolish tension and suffering, life is to be extinguished. And there is nothing illogical in this last reasoning.

I am talking about perfectly consistent utopias, of which we have only a few examples. In the inconsistent ones we often discover the same temptation mixed up with ideas that are incompatible with utopian perfection: the praise of creativity, the glory of progress, and so forth. Few utopians (Fourier was no doubt the most notable example) were aware that the needs for variety and for personal self-assertion and distinctiveness were forces that it was impracticable to cancel or to suppress in specifically human life, and they tried to design their blueprints for universal happiness accordingly. They believed that those needs could be met without stirring up hostilities and struggles among people, that competitiveness might be preserved and aggressiveness channeled in harmless directions, thus producing a society which would happily combine satisfaction with creativity and the drive for distinction with universal friendship.

What made utopias look malignant in our century was clearly not the very dream of perfection; whether self-contradictory or not, descriptions of a celestial felicity on earth were in themselves no more than harmless literary exercises. They have become ideologically poisonous to the extent that their advocates managed to convince themselves that they had discovered a genuine technology of apocalypse, a technical device to force the door of paradise. This belief has been the distinctive characteristic of revolutionary utopias, and it was eminently embodied in various ramifications of Marxist doctrine. Having become, as a result of many historical accidents, the main ideological self-justifying and self-glorifying support of the totalitarian cancer devouring the social fabric of our world, the Marxist or quasi-Marxist utopia naturally called our attention to the apocalyptic-revolutionary literature of old, which had displayed similar features.

The second important characteristic of this utopia was the belief that the glorious future is not simply predetermined by the course of history hitherto, but that the future was already there, not empirically noticeable and yet more real than the empirical present about to crumble. This belief in a "higher" reality which, albeit invisible, was already embedded in the actual world could be traced back, to be sure, to its Hegelian sources; more exactly, it was an extension into the future—illegitimate in strictly Hegelian terms—of the Hegelian way of investigating the past. This enviable ability to detect in what appears to be something that appears not to be but that in fact *is* in a more eminent sense than what is "merely" empirical was itself, in Hegel, a secularized version of the Christian concept of salvation which, though not perceptible directly, is not just inscribed in God's plan but has already occurred, since in the divine timelessness whatever is going to happen has happened. It justifies the unlimited self-righteousness of those who not only are capable of predicting the future but in fact are already its blessed owners, and it gives them the right to treat the actual world as essentially nonexistent. The imminent, ultimate revolution being not simply a fortunate step in the succession of historical events but a rupture in continuity, a total beginning, a new time, the past—including everything that might yet happen before the great breakthrough—is not, properly speaking, a progress. The latter means cumulation, gradual improvement, growth; whereas the Ultimate Event, ushering in the new time, does not add more wealth to the existing stock we have already capitalized but marks a leap from the infernal abyss to the kingdom of supreme excellence.

These three characteristics of revolutionary-utopian mentality supply justification for three less innocent political attitudes. A hope for the brotherhood into which an illuminated elite can coerce people by decree provides a natural basis for totalitarian tyranny. Believing in a higher-order reality that is set into the present and, though undiscernible to the naked eye, is the genuine reality, justifies utter contempt for actually existing people, who scarcely deserve attention when contrasted with the seemingly nonexistent but much more important generations of the future. The idea of a new time gives legitimacy to all kinds of cultural vandalism.

In this sense the strictures of utopia are well substantiated. We may even say more: considering that the most perfect specimen of the genre was written in the eighteenth century by the just-mentioned Dôm Deschamps, it is arguable that the socialist utopia had killed itself by its own consistency before it was born.

The same, for that matter, may be said of the individualist quasi utopia. Probably the most consistent individualist-anarchist utopia was devised by Max Stirner in 1844. Starting with a fairly reasonable premise that social life as such—not any particular form of social order—necessarily imposes limits on our aspirations and our exclusive concern with ourselves, it suggested a "liberation" which everyone could separately achieve by abandoning all the norms, restrictions, and requirements that the "society" dictates, including logical and moral rules and presumably the language as well. I am talking about "quasi utopia" because the point is less to invent a perfect society and more to abolish the society for the sake of the highest value, which each human person is to himself.

And yet there is another side to the story, which we may not lightly dismiss. The utopian mentality, I should repeat, is withering away. Its intellectual status has sunk to the level of a pathetic adolescent gibberish surviving in leftist sects; in the established communist ideologies the utopian language and utopian imagery have been less and less noticeable throughout the last decades.

It is legitimate to ask whether this demise of utopia, however justifiable in terms of the gruesome history of utopian politics, may be seen as a net gain. My argument on this point is analogous to what I have just said about the epistemological utopias. I do believe, indeed, that the dream of an everlasting universal brotherhood of humankind is not only unfeasible but would cause the collapse of our civilization if we took it seriously as a plan to be materialized by technical means. On the other hand, it is too easy to use all the well-founded antiutopian arguments as a device whereby we may accept or even sanctify any kind of oppression and blatant injustice if only they are not supported by utopian phraseology. This, again, is not a matter of an abstract possibility but of a well-recorded historical experience. For centuries the intrinsic evil of human nature has not only been invoked as an argument against the attempts to restore paradisical conditions on earth but has justified resistance to all social reforms and democratic institutions as well. Therefore, the antiutopian critique requires important differentiations. The utopian dogma stating that the evil in us has resulted from defective social institutions and will vanish with them is indeed not only puerile but dangerous; it amounts to the hope, just mentioned, for an institutionally guaranteed friendship, a hope on which totalitarian ideologies were founded. Yet it might be no less pernicious to replace this optimistic fantasy with the opposite one, implying that in all human relationships there is nothing but hostility, greed, and the lust for domination, and that all expressions of love, friendship, fraternity, and sacrifice are no more than deceptive appearances concealing the "real," invariably selfish, motivations. Whether based on the anthropology of Hobbes, Freud, or the early Sartre, this creed makes us naturally prone to accept all man-made monstrosities of social life as inevitable forever. It may be reasonably argued that the fallacy of those who view human nature as hopelessly and utterly corrupted is safer and less sinister than the self-defeating confidence of the utopians: a society in which greed is the dominant motivation is much preferable, after all, to a society based on compulsory solidarity. The total corruption theory may be nevertheless employed as well to support a totalitarian or a highly oppressive order: examples abound, starting with the theocratic doctrines and practices of early Calvinism. And the grounds for this theory are speculative, not empirical; there is no evidence to refute the commonsense platitude that the potential for disinterested friendship and solidarity is in us as well as the seeds of hatred, envy, and greed. To state that whatever is good in us is but a mask of evil, far from being a report of experience, is a metaphysical axiom; it even makes social life unintelligible: if there is nothing in us but evil, what might the mask be for?

It might be true that the most notable examples of fraternity known to us have often had a negative background and could be found most easily when they were forced on people by a common danger, wars, or disasters. It is true that the experience of all voluntary communist associations—not to speak of compulsory ones—is not very encouraging; nothing of value has survived from the communities established in America by early socialists—Cabet, Weitling, Considérant—or by the hippies. The most lasting and most successful communes are perhaps the Jewish kibbutzim, brought to life by joint socialist and Zionist ideals. Some monastic or quasi-monastic communities as well as many informal groups may serve as positive examples. Undeniably, however, people are able to create conditions in which aggressiveness, hostility, and selfishness, if not eradicated, are really minimized.

The general conclusion of these remarks might sound somewhat banal but, not unlike many banalities, worth pondering. It says that the idea of human fraternity is disastrous as a political program but is indispensable as a guiding sign. We need it, to use the same Kantian idiom again, as a regulative, rather than a constitutive, idea.

In other words, both Kant's theory of radical evil and his belief in the indefinite progression of rationality—a progression which can go on amid the unremitting tension between our love of freedom and our sociability, between individual aspirations and societal order, between passions and reason—are useful to us. In the standard sense of the word *utopia,* Kant was clearly an antiutopian, as he had never expected an ingenious technical contrivance that would bring about the actual state of perfection and bliss. He did believe, though, in the calling of the human race, in a teleologically propelled movement, the end of which we can never achieve or locate in time—an asymptotic growth, as it were—and which we nonetheless always have to keep in mind if we want to remain human. These two complementary sides of his "as-if" philosophy—a belief in a perpetual motion, loaded with struggles and contradictions, toward a goal, and a disbelief that the goal might ever be effectively reached—are certainly reconcilable in philosophical terms. It is unlikely, however, that humankind as a whole could ever be converted to Kantian philosophy. Therefore it is likely that two kinds of mentality—the skeptical and the utopian—will survive separately, in unavoidable conflict. And we need their shaky coexistence; both of them are important to our cultural survival. The victory of utopian dreams would lead us to a totalitarian nightmare and the utter downfall of civilization, whereas the unchallenged domination of the skeptical spirit would condemn us to a hopeless stagnation, to an immobility that a slight accident could easily convert into catastrophic chaos. Ultimately we have to live between two irreconcilable claims, each of them having its cultural justification.

Chapter Thirteen

The Idolatry of Politics

It is proper on this occasion to look for a moment at what is probably the most famous single sentence ever written in the Western hemisphere, that is, the sentence, "We hold these truths to be self-evident: that all men are created equal, that they are endowed by their Creator with certain inalienable Rights, that among these are Life, Liberty, and the Pursuit of Happiness." (If not the most famous, it is the second most famous sentence after the saying, "Coke is it!"). Once we glance at it, we immediately notice that what seemed self-evident to the patron saint of our meeting tonight would appear either patently false or meaningless and superstitious to most of the great men who keep shaping our political imagination: to Aristotle, to Machiavelli, to Hobbes, to Marx and all his followers, to Nietzsche, to Weber, and, for that matter, to most of our contemporary political theorists. If "self-evident" means "obvious," or deriving its truth from the very meaning of the concepts involved, the truths just quoted are not self-evident at all. They are now reserved for pontifical messages or Sunday sermons, yet they are banned beyond recall from the permissible philosophical or theoretical idiom; there are few thinkers who still stick by the belief that the criteria of good and evil, instead of being freely invented and freely canceled, if needed, by the human race, or of expressing, at the best, its biological invariants, are somehow embedded in the order of things. Those adventurers are well aware of treading on a perilous and slippery soil.

That this change of perception does matter there is no need to prove. The rationalist refusal to take for granted any inherited order of political or moral rules was, as we know, a side of the same centuries-long process whereby the modern idea of negative freedom and the principles of freedom of economic activity and of legal equality were established. Market economy, rationalist philosophy, liberal political doctrines and institutions, and

Jefferson Lecture in the Humanities, 1986. Reprinted by permission from *The New Republic*, 16 July 1986. Copyright © 1986 by The New Republic, Inc.

modern science emerged as interconnected aspects of the same evolution, and none of them could have asserted itself separately. The reasons for this interdependence are reasonably clear and well investigated by many historians.

Even though the prime target of attack of this entire ideological and political development was once the Church with its claims to spiritual and political supremacy, an important part of the Enlightenment was ideologically inconsistent in its attitude to the Christian legacy and in the scope of the effective debt it owed to this legacy. It often affirmed the rights of autonomous reason, the principles of personal rights and of tolerance, against ecclesiastical institutions, yet not against Christian tradition, in a way similar to the way the Reformation and medieval heresies, earlier on, appealed to the Gospels in order to destroy the institutional and dogmatic framework of the Roman Church. And it was more than a matter of ideological self-blindness or political expediency. One may reasonably argue that modern liberal doctrines were historically rooted in the biblical belief that in a basic sense all human beings are equal and equally precious. However tortuous and self-contradictory was the path from the religious to the political meaning of this insight, however often it was strewn with conflicts and struggles, it was historically real.

It has been largely forgotten by now. The ideas of religious tolerance and of the separation of the Church from the State—and by extension, of ideology from the State—belong to the natural equipment of the republican tradition. They were established against clericalist, if not, strictly speaking, theocratic, forces in Christianity, and they won in Western civilization. They imply that no religious body is either privileged or discriminated against by law, that there is no compulsory religious teaching in public schools, that religious loyalties are irrelevant to the rights and duties of citizens, and so forth. The few possible or real deviations from the principle of strict neutrality of the State are either largely ceremonial, like the status of the Anglican church, or of little importance, like the special positions of churches in taxation and charity law in various countries.

Yet we may ask, To what extent can this religious and ideological neutrality of the State be consistently upheld? In democratic countries, ideas as well as religions are governed by the rules of the market: a consumer has countless options and countless possibilities of choice. However, this freedom of producing, advertising, and distributing religious and ideological goods is itself a result of an ideological—and indirectly religious—option. If we believe that freedom is better than despotism; that slavery, that is, the ownership of a person by another person or by the State, is contrary to the very notion of being human; that equality is right, and legally established privileges are unjust; that the spirit of religious tolerance ought to be supported, and oppressive fanaticism opposed, and so on, we are not "neutral" in matters concerning basic values. Neither is a State which, in one form or another, has inscribed those values into its constitutional framework; otherwise it would be neutral toward its own neutrality, whereby the neutrality would defeat itself. If such values are directly or indirectly of biblical origin, there is no reason why stating this would undermine the principle of separation. In terms of both its historical origin and its prevailing norms, it would be silly to say that any State within the realm of Western civilization, by being neutral, is non-Christian in the same sense as it is non-Muslim or non-Hindu.

During the recent discussion in the United States about voluntary prayer in schools, one could not help being struck by the almost hysterical tenor in those who attacked permission for such prayers, as if not to forbid a few pupils to say the Lord's Prayer during a break in the school day amounted to throwing the country into the abyss of a sinister theocracy.

To be sure, this particular issue is a fragment of a larger conflict that includes more serious questions like abortion and capital punishment as well as pressures from various intolerant or even fanatical religious groups. I believe, however, that it would be advisable to impose certain moderating restrictions on the general framework of the debate about relationships between politics and religious tradition.

It is undoubtedly true that over the last years we have been witnessing, in various regions of our planet, the growing role of religious bodies and ideas in political conflicts. This might be an effect of the increasing disappointment of many people with the dominant political ideologies we inherited from before the First World War, when the political landscape seemed—rightly or wrongly—mild and promising by comparison with ours. It might have resulted from the natural need for rules of conduct that are both simple and absolutely valid. It might be due in part to the simple fact that in many countries of the Third World the available political ideologies seem to be of little operational use, whereas the need for an ideologically grounded legitimacy of the existing power system is more pressing. While we may observe this process with alarm, it is fair to say that it has not produced any significant growth of theocratic tendencies in Christianity—in contrast to Islam, where this tendency, however explainable by the historical vicissitudes of Islamic faith and its content, is quite vigorous. To fear that the Western world is likely to fall prey to a totalitarian theocracy seems groundless; the opposite tendency, which reduces Christianity to a political ideology, thus cutting off its roots, appears instead fairly resilient.

The other part of the same political framework is this: we try to survive in a world torn asunder by a conflict which cannot be simply seen as the competition of big powers vying for enlargement of their respective areas of influence; it is a clash of civilizations, a clash which for the first time in history has assumed a worldwide dimension. However distasteful our civilization might be in some of its vulgar aspects, however enfeebled by its hedonistic indifference, greed, and the decline of civic virtues, however torn by struggles and teeming with social ills, the most powerful reason for its unconditional defense (and I am ready to emphasize this adjective) is provided by its alternative. It faces a new totalitarian civilization of Sovietism, and what is at stake is not only the destiny of one particular cultural form but of humanity as we have known it: not because this new civilization is militaristic, imperialistic, and aggressive, but because of its educational goals, because it promises us to convert human persons into perfectly replaceable parts of the impersonal state machine, each of them having no more reality than this machine is ready to confer on it, and each having a mind that would be, ideally, a passive replica of a lifeless robot, with no will, no ability to revolt, no critical thought of its own. While we have arguments to assert that this ideal is unattainable for reasons that are inherent in human nature (the abysmal economic ineptitude of this civilization, its retreats and reluctant concessions reveal them), a strong movement toward it has already brought about unspeakable cultural disasters and is likely to cause more.

I would go further and repeat what Karl Jaspers once wrote. Jaspers, who was extremely sensitive to religious intolerance and fanaticism in Christian tradition, said that if he had the distressing choice between Christian (he meant Catholic) and Communist totalitarianism, he would opt for the former, after all, because the spiritual source of Christianity, the Bible, is the source of European culture, and therefore our civilization, even in such an oppressive form, would not lose its continuity or be severed from its origin.

Needless to say, those of us whose minds have been shaped to a large extent by the Enlightenment and who are not prepared to dismiss its legacy altogether, no matter how self-defeating its upshot might appear, abhor the prospect of such a choice. And we might be wrong in thinking that it is no more than an abstractly concocted possibility; it is not imminent, to be sure, but it is not a fanciful or surrealistic vision either, considering the energy of the movements that make it conceivable.

It has been the contention of many people that if we want to confront the danger of our civilization collapsing into a nihilistic sluggishness and becoming an easy prey for tyranny, and to confront it in a broader historical perspective rather than in terms of direct political or military technique, the spiritual legacy of the Enlightenment calls for revision; there are indeed at least three crucial points in which humanist beliefs seem to have reached a suicidal stage.

The first point is the belief in so-called absolute values. To sneer at "absolute values" has been extremely easy, of course, since the movement of the Enlightenment managed to convince us that all human beliefs about good and evil are culture-bound, historically relative, and that we had already suffered enough because of struggles between various religions and doctrines whose adherents, on all sides, were deeply convinced of being the only privileged carriers of the absolute truth. Humanist skepticism, including its dismissal of "absolute values," forged a powerful weapon against the fanaticism of sectarian strife and laid a foundation for the institutional framework of a pluralist and tolerant society.

It revealed its danger, though. It made those very ideas of pluralism and tolerance as relative as their opposites. We got used to shrugging off many horrors of our world by talking about cultural difference. "We have our values, they have theirs," is a saying that we frequently hear when dealing with the atrocities of totalitarianism or of other forms of despotism. Do those who say so seek really to state that it is pointless and arrogant to make value judgments about the difference between pluralistic forms of political life and those societies in which the only known method of political competition is to slaughter the rivals? When we extend our generous acceptance of cultural diversity to all the rules of good and evil and aver, for example, that the human rights idea is a European concept, unfit for, and unintelligible in, societies that share other traditions, do we mean that Americans rather dislike being tortured and packed into concentration camps, but Vietnamese, Iranians, and Albanians do not mind or enjoy it? And if so, what is wrong with the racial laws of South Africa, and why should we not be satisfied with saying that the Afrikaners simply "have some values of their own" and that we have no way to prove that ours are any better? Or, to put it crudely, shall we say that the difference between a vegatarian and a cannibal is just a matter of taste (even if taste is admittedly involved)?

To be sure, we usually do not express our enlightened tolerance in such a daring manner, but this might result from our reluctance to make explicit the consequence of our faith. It is easier to say, vaguely, "Societies have various values," or "The belief in absolute values is obsolete and naive," than clearly to admit that slavery is as good as freedom, granted that nothing is intrinsically good or evil. More often than not we are simply inconsistent, less for cognitive, and more for political reasons: we like to profess our relativistic complacency in cases that we prefer, on political grounds or because of cowardice, to treat with civility and to reserve our moral intransigence and "absolute values" for other cases; for example, we like to be moralists in problems concerning South Africa but Realpolitiker and courteous relativists when dealing with Communist systems ("They have their values . . .") or vice versa; this means we convert our political commitments into moral principles, and this is precisely what the idolatry of politics means: to fabricate gods for an ad hoc use in a political power game.

To say this does not solve any particular political issue and by no means implies that moralistic inflexibility provides a good basis for all political decisions or that one could infer the entire policy of a country, say, from the concept of human rights. This is clearly impracticable. In many decisions moral cost is inevitably involved, alas. Bloodshed is always evil, but we have to admit that it is not the ultimate evil. All through history, people have accepted bloodshed for good cause and it would be silly to decide that we ought to avoid bloodshed in all circumstances and at any price, since in some cases not to avoid it is the only way to avoid worse calamities and greater bloodshed. This might be unpleasant to say in a world living in the shadow of a possible war and facing the daily horrors of terrorism, but this is trivially true all the same. The point is rather to be aware of our choices and call things by their names, which is infrequent in political conflicts.

But, let us repeat, to believe in intrinsically valid rules of good and evil *and* to admit that it is not feasible to base political decisions exclusively on them does not settle any specific political issue. However, there is nothing extravagant in a reflection which, without being directly useful in political affairs, aims at examining the nonpolitical source of diseases that affect political life: not our technical inability to cope with problems but rather our inability to handle problems which are not technical and not soluble by technical devices. And it is arguable that this inability of ours is a part of the mentality we inherited from the Enlightenment and even, one may say, from the *best* aspects of the Enlightenment: from its struggle against intolerance, self-complacency, superstitions, and uncritical worship of tradition.

Even if the great masters of the Enlightenment did not necessarily unfold their relativistic ideas in a form which, as I am arguing, exerts a paralyzing influence on our current ability to oppose evil and intolerance, they planted a good seed which turned out to produce dangerous fruit. The denial of "absolute values" for the sake of both rationalist principles and the general spirit of openness threatens our ability to make the distinction between good and evil altogether; to extend tolerance to fanaticism amounts to favoring the victory of intolerance; to abstain from fighting evil on the pretext that "we are imperfect" might convert our imperfection into barbarity.

The second point in which we notice the self-degrading movement of the Enlightenment is the uncertain and conceptually fragile status of human personality. The saying about the social nature of human creatures has been repeated for twenty-three centuries. Its meaning, however, is at least two-fold: it might mean something trivially true or something that is not only highly controversial in philosophical terms but, if generally accepted, very damaging, perhaps disastrous to our civilization. It is, of course, trivially true that the language, knowledge, ways of thinking, emotions, and aspirations of each of us have been shaped by what we have experienced in our human environment, that we could not survive either physically or mentally without sharing our experience with others and communicating with them. Still, this platitude does not entail that the reality of each of us is entirely reducible to what others have given us, that apart from participation in communal life, a human creature is literally nothing, as if each of us were only a collection of masks that are put on an empty space, as if there were no other humanity but collective, no self save Rousseau's *moi commun*. The belief in an irreducible and unique core of personality is not a scientifically provable truth, certainly (apart from its description in genetic terms, which is not what is meant), but without this belief, the notion of personal dignity and of human rights is an arbitrary concoction, suspended in the void, indefensible, easy to be dismissed.

The belief that the human person is entirely society-made, even if molded from a raw material (which is physical, and not human) has a number of alarming consequences. Many people have noticed and investigated the erosion of both the very concept and the feeling of personal responsibility in contemporary civilization, and it is difficult not to perceive how this process is linked to the belief I am talking about. If "I" am not "I," if the word *I* is a pronoun to which no reality corresponds, at least no morally constituted reality, if I am totally definable in "objective" terms of social relationships, then indeed there is no reason why I, rather than the abstract "society," should be responsible for anything. I remember seeing on American television a young man who was convicted of brutally raping a child, a little girl; his comment was, "Everybody makes mistakes." And so, we now know who raped the child: 'everybody,' that is, nobody. Let us think of the famous recent trial when a tobacco company was brought to court by a family which charged it with being guilty of the cigarette addiction of their deceased member. Shall we see a rapist suing the "society," that is a school or the government, for being a rapist? Or a wife demanding that the government order her husband, who eloped with another woman, to love her again? There is no point in dwelling on this subject or multiplying the examples; the general tendency to devolve the responsibility for the individual's acts (in particular their wrongdoings and shortcomings) on anonymous collective entities is well known and can be documented only too easily.

The more sinister side of the same loss of our ability to assert the separate, irreducible, ontological status of personality is that it makes us conceptually defenseless in the face of totalitarian doctrines, ideologies, and institutions. There are obviously no grounds for attributing to the human person an absolute and irreplaceable value on the assumption that a person is no more than an expression of an impersonal aggregate; and therefore there are no grounds to oppose the idea that individuals are organs of the State and that all aspects of their lives, and life itself, are to be treated accordingly, that their worth is entirely to be measured by their usefulness—or otherwise— in the service of the State. On the same assumption, we are helpless to resist those aspects of democracy which in some conditions—empirically observable—are compatible with totalitarianism; the principle of the majority conceived of as an absolute rule is an example.

The distinction between the personal and collective sides of life, though banal and investigated for centuries by philosophers and social thinkers, does not cease to be worth inspecting. It takes on special significance in modernity, when it is politically expressed in two requirements, always distinct and sometimes limiting each other: participation in power on the one hand and personal rights on the other. The right to participate in power, expressed in democratic institutions, does not by itself assure the protection of personal rights. The latter, far from being an extension of the principle of the majority, puts limits on it, considering that personal rights can be suppressed with the approval of the majority, and a despotic or even totalitarian order which enjoys the majority's support is not only conceivable but can actually be shown by examples. A society shattered by despair and dread, thrown into panic, can look for a solution in a tyranny that robs individuals, including those who support it, of personal rights. The majority gave power to Hitler, to Khomeini, perhaps to Mao, if not always by active assistance, then by inert submission to the rape. In the normal course of things all the revolutions that establish a tyranny end in a bitter hangover very soon, but usually too late for people to shake off the self-imposed yoke.

It is possible to argue that to guard personal rights is more important in our world than to defend the system of participation in power. If personal rights can be brought to ruin with the active or acquiescent support of the majority, the reverse is true, too: they can be protected in a condition where there is very little participation in power. We can show in various historical periods and in various countries examples of a mild autocracy or oligarchy where participation in power was restricted to a tiny privileged section of the population, where no universal suffrage existed, and where personal rights were nonetheless protected—if not perfectly, then reasonably well—where people normally did not fall prey to lawless brutality, and where the law was enforced, and cultural life suffered no severe restrictions. The most superficial glance at European history can convince us that life in a nondemocratic order does not need to be an unceasing horror, that individuals—rich as well as poor—can survive reasonably well and arts can flourish, that an autocracy can be, if not quite generous, at least not cruel. And to support this line of argument, some people argue that participation in the democratic process is largely illusory or is reduced—as the much underrated French thinker Jacques Ellul says—to the so-called political commitment, which means nothing but the surrender of one's own will to professional politicians. We may add that in democratic countries, according to many signs, the degree to which people identify with the government they brought to power in free elections is not impressively high. It is enough to ask a childish question: if people have the government they elected, that is, a government they wish, and consequently have the law they wish, including the taxation law, why do millions cheat on their taxes? One should suppose that in a good democracy people are required to pay in taxes as much as they wish to pay, but to draw this conclusion, in full naïveté, from constitutional principles, can only reveal the grotesque hiatus between principles and psychological reality.

Those arguments are probably reasonable, but they are only half of the truth. The other half is that, while we can find examples of a benign autocratic or aristocratic order, they come from the past and not from the present. Benevolent tyrannies, enlightened and tender-hearted autocracies, are not in existence any longer; perhaps they have become culturally impossible. We can only speculate about why it is so. Power has always been desired and sought after as a good in itself, not only as a tool to gain other benefits. But the idea that everyone has a right to participate in power is of relatively recent origin, and it so much belongs to the ideological armory of modernity that it is verbally admitted in the most hideously despotic regimes. Once it has been established, it cannot be canceled, and participation in power in a democratic process, however dubious it might appear to individuals (who often perceive in it a proof of their own helplessness, rather than a device whereby they can influence events) is the only reliable defense against despotism; therefore, in our world, it is a necessary condition for the protection of personal rights as well as cultural pluralism.

It is not a sufficient condition, though, and therefore I believe it important to keep in mind that personal rights set limits on democratic principles rather than being their natural consequence. And personal rights are defensible only on the assumption that there is a realm of personal reality that is definable in moral, not biological, terms; they have to be vindicated on moral grounds, much as their implementation depends on political conditions. In a world where everything has become politicized, it does matter to repeat the time-honored truism that political goals have to be assessed in terms that are not political. This truism carries perhaps more weight today, as there is no agreement on even the most general framework of political ends, and no one can define in a noncontroversial manner what the Aristotelian "good life" as a political objective means. We have been taught by long experience that basic goods which we might be ready to approve are in conflict with each other: security and freedom, freedom and equality, equality and personal rights, personal rights and the rule of the majority.

Personal rights, moreover, insofar as they include the right of property, inevitably conflict with the idea of distributive justice. It would be futile to assert both without qualification. The normative notion implying that all people are entitled to have a share in the wealth of nature and in the fruits of civilization, that they may make claims to a minimally decent life, that the institutions of the welfare state are to be upheld as a matter of justice, not only of political necessity, is incompatible with everyone's right to enjoy legally acquired property.

In vain do we repeat slogans that mix up all our "values," as if we knew how to implement them jointly. When we say "peace and justice," we have always to bear in mind that forty years of peace in Europe have been based on glaring injustice, on the enslavement of Central and Eastern parts of the continent. However precarious and unstable this peace—in the sense of the sheer absence of war—might be, it has been preserved for four decades. And so, when we use generalities like "peace and justice" as expressions of our good wishes, more often than not we simply avoid real issues and real choices.

We thus go back to Max Weber's classic distinction between the ethics of intention and the ethics of responsibility. A politician's good intentions clearly do not count in his performance; he is assessed according to his skills in foreseeing the foreseeable consequences of his acts—in fact he is usually called to account for the unforeseeable effects as well. We cannot avoid the notorious fact that acts which we are ready to deem noble when performed by an individual for moral reasons might be not only inexcusable but disastrous when they are converted into political acts, let alone into rules of politics. These pacifists of old who, on religious or moral grounds, refused to carry a sword but were ready to serve on a battlefield as stretcher-bearers or nurses and to share the dangers of soldiers, deserved full respect, since they proved that their refusal was morally motivated rather than being just a search for safety. Those pacifists who today act as political bodies have to be assessed by political criteria, that is, by their ability to calculate the consequences of their actions and not by their intention to secure peace—as though anybody might now wish to provoke global war. If one may reasonably argue that their actions make war more rather than less likely (as I believe is the case with the advocates of unilateral disarmament in Europe), they have to be judged accordingly. Still, the intended consequences, whether actually materialized or not, obviously have to be judged as well by nonpolitical criteria; otherwise, the efficiency in pursuing any goal, however hideous, would remain as the sole measure.

Owing to the tradition of the Enlightenment, we once got used to the belief that all the pillars on which human hope for a good world rested— freedom, justice, equality, peace, brotherhood, prosperity, abundance—can be built jointly in a harmonious progression. Very few of us can now preserve this belief and take it seriously. European liberals and socialists who spread this faith were time and again accused by conservatives of their failure to perceive the inherent evil in human affairs or to explain it. They saw evil, according to this criticism, as a technical blunder, something contingent that could be eradicated by an adequate social technology. Liberals and socialists, in their turn, accused conservatives of using the doctrine of ineradicable evil as a pretext to oppose all reforms that could make our lot more tolerable and reduce human suffering. There is some justice in both charges, and therefore it is probably safer for us that progressives and conservatives coexist in unremitting conflict rather than that one of those irreconcilable mentalities should gain the definitive victory.

The third point at which the legacy of the Enlightenment has become destructive in our civilization is the erosion of historical consciousness. I do not mean, of course, historical research, which is flourishing and apparently in robust health; nor do I mean historicism as a philosophical doctrine, which has continued to grow as an ideological device since the end of the eighteenth century. I do not even mean the amount of historical knowledge people get in schools or from books and television. I have in mind the progressive decline of the awareness that our spiritual life includes the sedimentation of the historical past as its real and active component and that the past is to be perceived as a never-fading frame of reference in our acts and thinking. That human life actually does include this component and hinges on this frame of reference might be true without our being aware of it. It is the withering away of this awareness that I am getting at.

This is, of course, hardly a new tenet: it has been worrying many people for several decades, and by broaching it I do not pretend to discover new continents. But it is worth discussing as we usher in an epoch when children, from the earliest age, are going to sit at their computers and, as a result, their minds will be entirely shaped by the acts of calculation, with historical self-understanding sinking into irrelevance or oblivion.

The Muse of history is gentle, learned, and unassuming, but when neglected and deserted, she takes her revenge: she blinds those who scorn her.

An important trend within the Enlightenment, since Descartes, used to shrug off the historically defined notion of human existence for obvious reasons: first, because it appeared irrelevant to the progress of science, technology, and the future happiness of mankind (and is not the past, after all, a huge mass of irrational passions, ignorance, and foolish mistakes?); second, because the respect for history included worship of tradition as such, the veneration of what is old and established for no better reason than that it is old and established. In conformance with this mentality, it is we, the moderns, who are old, whereas the ancients were children—as many thinkers, since Francis Bacon, have claimed—and there is no reason for the elderly to look for wisdom in the minds of infants. And what profit, apart from a possible entertainment, can we get from being informed that Zorobabel begat Abiud and Claudius was done in by Aggripina? To be sure, hardly anyone today expresses the rationalist contempt for history in such a simplistic fashion, but the natural disposition of the rationalist mind seems to have gained the upper hand over historical curiosity in general education and in the mental habits of modernity. We have been told time and again that we do not learn from history. This saying, too, is trivially true in a sense and perniciously wrong in another. It is trivially true in the sense that historical events and situations are by definition unique, and the stuff historical processes are made of is countless accidents, unrepeatable coincidences, disparate forces unpredictably interfering with each other. Apart from commonsense platitudes, we cannot acquire from historical studies any useful rules of conduct that would be applicable in new situations. A politician—to take a Machiavellian example—does not need to study the vicissitudes of Roman emperors in order to discover that he cannot rely on the unconditional loyalty of people he has promoted; to be aware that lost wars are likely to provoke domestic upheavals, we can do without immersing ourselves in the chronicles of modern Russia.

To derive from such observations a general principle to the effect that "we do not learn from history" implies, however, that historical knowledge would be useful only if it provided us with a technical guidance we could subsequently apply in governing, in vying for power, or in warfare, as if we were consulting a manual to repair a broken vacuum cleaner. Since historical studies are demonstrably futile in this sense, they are worthless *tout court*. This manipulative, technical approach to the past is a natural consequence of the general rationalist view of life, and it may prove ruinous to our civilization.

We learn history not in order to know how to behave or how to succeed, but to know who we are. And what matters is not the scope of our learning. From a good historical film about, say, Richard III, I can learn more than I have ever known on the subject and even with reasonable accuracy. But I know this as a matter of amusement, and my newly acquired knowledge in terms of my mental life does not differ from the "knowledge" I gain from a purely fictitious thriller. Educated and even uneducated people in preindustrial societies, whose historical learning was very meager, were perhaps more historical—in the sense I mean here—than we are. The historical tradition in which they lived was woven of myths, legends, and orally transmitted stories of which the material accuracy, more often than not, was dubious. Still, it was good enough to give them the feeling of life within a continuous religious, national, or tribal community, to provide them the kind of identity that made life ordered (or "meaningful"). In this sense it was a living tradition, and it taught people why and for what they were responsible and why, as well as how this responsibility was to be practically taken up.

It would be difficult, on the other hand, to refute the objection that history which is conceived not as an object of scientific inquiry, a mundane knowledge, but as an imperative force tying people together by the awareness of common destiny and common responsibilities, is bound to be a mythological history—unquestionable and immune to rational scrutiny. Moreover, historical myths have usually confined their power to tribal or national entities, and the universal history—either as a framework of our mental life or even as reality—has only begun to emerge. The myths of universal religions have come the closest to all-encompassing, meaning-generating social memory, but none of them has proved so far to be capable of becoming truly universal. Buddha and Jesus have certainly provided us with the memory of events of universal significance, not restricted to any tribal perception, but even the powerful radiation of those events has broken the resistance of tribal self-containment only to a small extent. And while historical self-understanding has the virtue of giving sense to a particular community, it has the vice of dividing the human race as a whole.

I do realize that this might sound like old reactionary prattle. It is old. It was not new when Sorel taunted the utopian dreamers who, ignorant of historical realities, were building in imagination their world of perfection. It was not new when Dostoyevski scoffed at the apostles of progress who hated history because they hated life itself. It was not even new when Burke argued (in part against Thomas Paine) that all legitimate social contracts involve past generations. But I do not believe that whoever is interested in, and worrying about, the spiritual fragility of young people can deny that the erosion of a historically defined sense of "belonging" plays havoc in their lives and threatens their ability to withstand possible trials of the future.

And we have reasons to worry about the decline of historical awareness in a more specific and politically more pertinent sense. A manipulative and rationalist (as distinct from "rational") approach to historical knowledge is an organic part of the general belief that the potential of social technology is unlimited; in other words, that the society is "in principle" as malleable as any material; that we can, step by step, eliminate chance from historical processes as efficiently as we eliminate it from our machines; and that, if we are clever enough and benevolent enough, we can, by employing those technological skills, produce a society without evil and hostilities, without scarcity and suffering, without frustration and failures. Once we let ourselves be convinced of the idea that the past is pointless because it fails to provide us with reliable prescriptions for solving any specific current problems, we fall into a paradoxical trap. On the one hand, by losing the clear awareness of the continuity of culture and thus losing the historical frame of reference for our issues, we lose the ground on which those issues can be properly stated at all; on the other hand, we easily imagine that the past—ignored or reduced to nothingness—is not a real obstacle to our dreams of perfection, that political technique, properly improved, can reach the point of near-omnipotence, and that all human worries are soluble by political means. To expect that chance can be removed from social processes, that history can be simply canceled, is a deadly illusion. To believe that human brotherhood is a political "problem" amounts to imitating the Saint-Simonists of old, who designed special jackets that were buttoned from the back, so that people could not dress or undress themselves without the help of others; this was supposed to promote universal fraternity. It is reasonable to hope that various forms of human suffering can be successfully fought against—that hunger can be overcome and some diseases rendered curable—but to imagine that scarcity as such, scarcity *tout court,* shall be eradicated is to defy all historical experience, because scarcity is defined by wants, and human wants can grow indefinitely. In all those hopes we perceive the same spirit of idolatry.

There are no "laws of history," but there are layers of reality—climatic, demographic, technical, economic, psychological, and intellectual—which change and move at different rates, combining their energies in irregular ways and surprising us time and again with unexpected extravagances and caprices. Historical knowledge cannot prevent those surprises from occurring; it gives no clues for predicting the unpredictable, but it can at least protect us against foolish hopes and reveal the limits of our efforts, limits defined by physical and cultural invariants, by permanent aspects of human nature and of Great Nature, and by the burden of tradition. The conditions of political competition are so tough that professional politicians and statesmen have no time or energy to spare for disinterested study; to succeed, they usually have to start their careers early in life. They must restrict their knowledge to what might be useful and relevant to their day-to-day preoccupations and cannot afford to keep that distance from current events which a larger historical perspective might help them to acquire. Those few politicians of the last decades who were on more intimate terms with the historical past—like de Gaulle and Churchill—were not protected against making blunders; but if their influence was more profound and longer-lasting, this was perhaps due to their sturdy awareness of living within, and being limited by, a continous historical stream.

In all three areas in which, as I have tried to point out, the ambiguities of our cultural heritage matured into immobilizing self-contradictions, we cannot be comforted, alas, by a hope of discovering a well-balanced *juste milieu*. The belief or disbelief in "absolute values" is often offered to us as a choice between fanatical intransigence and nihilistic indifference. To assert or to dismiss the intrinsic and irreducible value of personal life might easily mean either simply to reject the idea of distributive justice or to yield to the totalitarian temptation, that is to say, to accept either the unacceptable sides of liberalism or the unacceptable sides of collectivism. To experience the historical dimension of our life as a source of meaning, or to deny the validity of this experience often amounts either to going back to the inert romantic worship of a mythological past or to decreeing that history as such is irrelevant and thus demolishing all nonutilitarian grounds of communal life. To state that one is "in between" those options or that one has reconciled them in a synthetic view is most easy in general terms and most difficult when the detailed choices are to be made. One is rather tempted to locate oneself on two irreconcilable extremes simultaneously.

In political decisions and attitudes, people can appeal to divine law, to natural law and the theory of the social contract, or to the feeling of historical continuity, of which they are agents even if they revolt against it. It appears that we are about to lose all three of those reference points; thus we either reduce politics to the technical rules of success or try to dissolve our existence in a mindless and fanatical devotion of one kind or another, or else we are escaping from life into drugs and other self-stunning devices. Perhaps we can be cured, but not painlessly.

An objection might be raised that what I have said could well borrow its title from the famous treatise of Abelard: *Sic et non*. I would be in trouble in trying to rebut this charge, except by saying that *Sic et non* is a suitable title for most of the stuff our minds are made of.

Chapter Fourteen

The Self-Poisoning of the Open Society

As I was browsing through *The Open Society and Its Enemies* again after many years, it struck me that when Popper attacks totalitarian ideologies and movements, he neglects the reverse side of the threat.[1] By this I mean what could be called the self-enmity of the open society—not merely the inherent inability of democracy to defend itself effectively against internal enemies by democratic means alone but, more importantly, the process by which the extension and consistent application of liberal principles transforms them into their antithesis. Adherents of totalitarian doctrines are external enemies, even inside an open society; but if "openness" itself can result in the paralysis of openness, then we are dealing with self-destruction. It would even seem that the Hegelian philosophy of development by self-negation, attacked by Popper, is to a certain extent vindicated (I myself have no desire to support such a view, however; quite the contrary). Debatable as it may be, I shall not consider the question of how far Plato, Aristotle, Hegel, or Marx have contributed to the dissemination of the totalitarian world view. Whether and in what sense the open society becomes its own enemy, whether this self-destructive mechanism is driven by some necessity of fate—which I do not believe at all—is the disturbing enigma of present-day political confusion, one which is perhaps more than any other worthy of discussion.

At first, it might appear that the reason Popper did not touch upon it is that the various intellectual and social phenomena observable today in advanced stages of development were embryonic and hardly perceptible

Translated from the German "Selbstgefährdung der offenen Gesellschaft," in *Liberalismus—nach wie vor* (Buchverlag der Neuen Zürcher Zeitung, 1979), by Susan MacRae. Reprinted with revisions by the author by permission of the publisher from *Survey* 25, no. 4 (Autumn 1980):113. Copyright © 1980 by the Eastern Press, Ltd.

1. K. R. Popper, *The Open Society and Its Enemies*, 5th ed. (London: Routledge, 1966).

thirty-five years ago. However, that is not quite true in this case. The self-destructive potential of liberalism was noted by great conservative thinkers in the nineteenth century, Dostoyevski among them; the classic liberal writer John Stuart Mill referred to it several times. But the question why it is so difficult for the champions of liberalism to recognize this potential has to be asked. Perhaps it is that liberal philosophy has a certain innate optimism, which does not of course consist in a historical theodicy, but rather in the attitude of tending to believe that there is a good solution for every social situation and not that circumstances will arise in which the available solutions are not only bad, but very bad.

But enough of generalities. My purpose is to examine some qualities of the open society and in doing so to evaluate the concept once again.

□

Briefly mentioning Bergson's theory of the "open society,"[2] Popper distinguishes it from his own as follows: for Bergson the distinction between the closed society and the open society is to be understood in religious terms, the open society being seen as the product of mystical intuition; but as mysticism is an expression of the yearning for the closed society and a reaction against rationalism, his theory, including the "hysterical" acceptance of change, must be looked upon as contrary to Popper's theory.[3] According to Popper, "closedness" is, above all, characteristic of a tribal community, where rigid magical taboos operate, where any change is regarded with fear and suspicion, where critical debate and the use of reason are stifled, where democratic, individualistic, and egalitarian ideologies are forbidden, and where a tendency to economic autarky prevails. The open society, on the other hand, is characterized by a general spirit of criticism and antidogmatism, by a readiness for public debate and the subordination of authority to reason, by the abandonment of irrational taboos, by faith in scientific methods, by a belief in the universal brotherhood of people (in contrast to the exclusiveness and self-sufficiency of a tribe). This contrast, exemplified by that between Sparta and Athens in the time of Pericles, is today manifest in essence in the clash between totalitarian and pluralistic ideas and systems. The open society, Popper notes, needs a system of ethics which encompasses the early Christian virtues, which in effect challenges

2. Expounded in Henri Bergson, *Deux sources de la morale et de la religion.*
3. K. R. Popper, *The Open Society and Its Enemies*, 5th ed., vol. 1 (London: Routledge, 1966), 202, 314.

the values of success and reward, and which encourages the capacity for self-sacrifice and selflessness.[4]

Quite apart from the judgment, which I find derogatory, on Bergson's social theory and on mysticism, the sharp contrasting of a closed and an open society seems to me highly questionable for the reasons which follow.

The open society is described less as a state constitution and more as a collection of values, among which tolerance, rationality, and a lack of commitment to tradition appear at the top of the list. It is assumed, naively so I think, that this set is wholly free of contradictions, meaning that the values it comprises support each other in all circumstances or at least do not limit each other.

I would raise the following reservations about this optimistic interpretation of social life: (1) among the essential values of the open society are those which for empirical, not necessarily logical, reasons clash with each other and are to be implemented only through mutual limitation; (2) therefore, any attempts made to introduce some of these values in a completely consistent way inevitably threaten the continuation of the open society; (3) no society, not even the open society, can do without trust of tradition in some degree, or—to put it another way—some "irrational" values that are characteristic of the closed society are indispensable to the open society. In short, not only is a clear-cut contrast between the two forms of society empirically unfeasible (the same might be said of virtually all empirical distinctions), but a completely open society does not allow itself to be depicted as ideal, in either a normative or a methodological sense. That this is so is probably more obvious today than ever before, especially since the self-defeating power of liberal principles has become sharply evident in various ways.

□

It would hardly be disputed that the idea of personal freedom as well as the political institutions which guarantee it have developed historically in connection with the development of trade and the power of the market. This connection has been well researched and described in historical studies. That does not mean that the idea of freedom was produced causally by the market economy, or that it did not exist in any form previously. It seems beyond doubt, however, that in recent history political and economic liberalism nourished and supported each other. In this sense it is true—as the conservative critics of revolution, the Romantics and the early socialists

4. Ibid., vol. 2, 277ff.

in the first half of the nineteenth century repeatedly stressed—that "negative" freedom is a bourgeois idea. This origin or connection has, of course, just as little to do with our evaluation of the idea as information about the genesis of a phenomenon has to do with value judgments on it; the fact that the art of El Greco might have had something to do with his defective sight does not influence the aesthetic evaluation of his paintings. When the Romantics contrasted the society that was based on the negative bonds of egoistic private interests with their longing for the "organic" solidarity of a tribe, village, or nation, they were justified in the sense that what they branded as the misery of the new social order was obviously firmly bound up with economic freedom. To put it briefly, the market meant political freedom, the growth of rationality, technical progress, scorn for tradition, and it also meant the merciless struggle of private interests, egoism, obsession with money, indifference to one's neighbors, the decline of religious value, the poverty and exploitation of workers, and the victory of reason over history, authority, and sentimentality.

It should soon have become evident that it was no inescapable "either-or," no unambiguous "package deal," either a society as described by Balzac or one as dreamt up by the Romantics. The choice is not necessarily between an absolute liberal marketplace and a medieval village; but in each instance we observe the same conflict between mutually limiting needs. Universal suffrage, political freedoms, freedom of the press, pollution, pornography, freedom from hunger, social insurance, criminality, open frontiers, insoluble problems of giant cities, cultural diversity, decline of the school system, the rule of law—we enjoy all this in advanced Western societies, everything at once and interdependent. Certainly, on several negative points and on all positive points of this list, including pollution (and excluding pornography, thanks to censorship), the record of the totalitarian countries looks worse. Why then is there anxiety in western Europe about "the totalitarian temptation"? Why are there widespread doubts about the ability of the pluralistic society to withstand successfully totalitarian despotism (in the political, not the military sense)? From where inside the democratic order do the totalitarian ideologies derive their strength?

□

I wish to touch upon only a few of the countless aspects of this question, those which seem to me to be related to the tradition of liberal ideas.

It was pointed out long ago that the growing economic role of the State in democratic countries bears an enormous potential for totalitarian development. Although it is also true that in the Western welfare states citizens have been deprived of no essential freedoms as a result of this expansion of state interventionism, the feeling is very widespread that the legislature seeks to control more and more areas of individuals' lives (expressed the world over in complaints about "big government"). There is no need to emphasize the fact that the welfare state does nothing to distribute economic power fairly or to "democratize" it; rather the contrary is true.

The traditional liberal world view presupposes that freedom of economic activity is a necessary, though certainly insufficient, condition of political freedom; this was revealed as much by the demonstrable interdependence of social life as by direct experience; as for the second part of the argument, the history of the Communist countries is deemed an *instantia crucis:* despotic forms of government, the total destruction of citizens' freedoms and human rights are obviously closely linked with the state monopoly of production and trade. To this, adherents of democratic socialism reply that, historically, Communist despotism came about not by state acquisition of the means of production, but without exception by the prior use of political violence: political expropriation preceded economic expropriation. This weakens the liberals' argument. Moreover, say the democratic socialists, the partial nationalization undertaken in the Western countries, and the considerable use of state power to regulate prices, income, foreign trade, and investment have certainly not brought with them a totalitarian society; this proves that the connection pointed out by the liberals has no basis in reality.

This is, of course, a healthy rejoinder, but the extent of its validity depends on how we define freedom in economic affairs. In unlimited form this freedom brings with it the equally unlimited action of the laws of accumulation through competition, thereby creating monopolies, so that the original principle of freedom in competition destroys itself if consistently applied. This is a fact which has long been stressed by the socialists and which has given grounds for various attempts at antimonopolistic legislation. But all present-day examples of pluralist societies have mixed economies, and not one demonstrates the possibility of an order that combines total nationalization and political freedom, for common sense and all the available evidence clearly contradict this.

□

It would seem that what is essential for the survival of political freedom is not any one particular method of distributing property, but just the existence of the market itself. As long as the market operates, it is not economically important whether the ownership of the means of production is private, individual, corporate, or cooperative, however important this may be for the distribution of noninvested profit or for efficiency. "Not economically important" means here "not directly relevant to exchange." One can well imagine an order in which ownership is predominantly cooperative, in which there is hardly any private ownership by individuals of the means of production, and which is built entirely on the principles of unlimited competition and free trade, with all the economic consequences of a pure liberal economy. In effect, the anarchist ideal of total autonomy of productive units and total self-government by workers represents a model of nineteenth-century liberal economics; this ideal, if it could be implemented, would inevitably produce all those social consequences which the socialists denounce in the capitalist economy: extreme inequality, unemployment on a huge scale, crises, bankruptcies, and misery.

The abolition of the market, on the other hand, is conceivable only if the State monopolizes the means of production and trade, which would imply a totalitarian political order. The abolition of the market means not only that the consumers—that is all members of society—are robbed of virtually all choice of consumption and all influence over production; it also means that the instruments of information and communication are monopolized by the State, as they too need a vast material base in order to operate. The abolition of the market means, then, that both material and intellectual assets would be totally rationed. To say nothing of the inefficiency of production convincingly demonstrated in the history of Communism, this economy requires an omnipotent police state.

Briefly, the abolition of the market means a *gulag* society.

□

One might perhaps ask, Given that this is the case, why should it be impossible to combine state ownership of all means of production with the operation of the market? Surely there is no physical, let alone logical, incompatibility here?

I would answer by making a further distinction: ownership rights are, in effect, disposal rights. All laws which limit the freedom of disposal also limit the right of ownership; in many cases such laws are well justified on social grounds, but one may not say that they do not affect ownership rights. Let us then imagine that the State does indeed own the means of production, but that the right to use these means freely remains in the hands of private persons, cooperatives, corporations, workers' councils, and so on. Here the State is owner no longer, and the fewer tools of intervention and control it has, the less of an owner it is. And all the limitations which the State today imposes upon private owners' disposal rights are so many limitations on ownership rights. In other words, state ownership of the means of production is compatible with the operation of the market only insofar as this ownership is fictitious. Real ownership, which means unlimited power of disposal, excludes the market but includes total planning (whether it be real or apparent), which means the political as well as the economic expropriation of the whole of society.

If we imagine, on the other hand, that the State is not the nominal owner of the means of production, but that it has an unlimited right to control the use of these means and of the products themselves, it can carry out total expropriation, in all but name, and do away with the market; in this case the political consequences already mentioned would soon follow.

□

What does this have to do with the application of liberal principles? It appears that the inclination to abolish the operation of the market directly contradicts those principles. But that is not the case. Already by the end of the nineteenth century, the liberal tenet that the State had virtually no right at all to intervene in economic life had only a few supporters left. If we read L. T. Hobhouse's classic work, *Liberalism* (1911), we see liberal philosophy setting out on the path of inordinate consistency leading to its own death. Hobhouse convincingly derives what was later called the *welfare state* from liberal premises: freedom for all can be secured only if the State protects the weak from the strong and suppresses private or corporate power by legislative coercion. But in economic life, too, these circumstances arise: the workers are weak in relation to their employers, and where the market situation allows the former no real freedom of choice, he is forced to accept the terms of the latter, with no mention of a "free contract." Therefore, the principle of liberalism demands that in this case too, the State should take the weaker side into its care, which is actually what industrial law does by restricting exploitation and controlling working hours, child labor, remuneration, and so forth.

So far so good. The welfare State will hardly be attacked by anyone on principle. But if we justify the institution of social security on the principle that it is the State's role to protect the weak from the strong, then it is not difficult to appreciate that, applied in full force, this principle would lead to the total abolition of the market and to a totalitarian State. The market necessarily involves competition, a form of struggle, and by definition, the stronger wins the struggle (no matter if the "strength" in any particular venture comes from industriousness, from sheer luck, or from previously won advantages). The socially undesirable, indeed catastrophic, results of unbridled competition can be mitigated through a system of safeguards and state control, but competition itself can be removed only with the complete elimination of the market.

But if we accept what has been said above, that there is a fatal and recip-rocal connection between totalitarianism and the abolition of the market, then it becomes apparent that the liberal precept that the State should look after security and protect the weak from the strong ultimately demands the totalitarian order. Needless to say, however, the totalitarian state in no way ensures the protection of the weak, but establishes the omnipotence of the state machine over the individual. One can say, therefore, that the liberal principle by its own consistency transforms itself into its opposite, or that its completely consistent application is simply impossible.

This is no abstract juggling with ideas: all totalitarian ideologies do, in fact, rely on the same liberal idea of the security and defence of the weak by state law, and they fight competition, which means the market, in the name of this idea.

□

An analogous line of reasoning can be conducted in the case of another recognized value in the legacy of liberalism: equality of opportu-nity. Liberal philosophy has, of course, never prized equality as an ideal; neither has it ever demanded of political institutions measures intended to promote it; on the contrary, it accepted the need for distinction as an ines-capable fact of social life and emphasized that the conditions for general progress are most likely to be fulfilled where this need and the inventiveness and creative energy that it generates are given the widest possible space in which to develop. Whereas in the utopian-totalitarian brands of socialism, equality was seen not only as a value in its own right, but also as the highest value, liberal philosophy stressed that it was madness to put equality above the welfare of all. Utopian egalitarianism forces us to believe that we must accept equality as an ideal, even if it lowers the living standard of all, in-cluding the disadvantaged, and forces us to condemn every form of inequal-ity, even if it eventually furthers the prosperity of all. But ever since the theory of the survival of the fittest was discarded as the philosophical basis of liberalism, and the normative concept of justice introduced, there has no longer been any reason not to adopt the idea of equality; not, of course, equality in the sense of the desired final result, but in the sense of equal opportunity for all.

It was not difficult to observe, however, that when interpreted unconditionally and thought through logically, this concept created just as powerful a legitimation for totalitarian ideology as equality *tout court*. Obviously, universal education does not equalize opportunities, it does not abolish the variety of familial milieu; meanwhile, any inequality today is a source of inequality in the next generation. Complete equality for individuals in the social conditions in which they develop (leaving aside the inequalities people are born with) requires the complete equalization of all living conditions; furthermore, if it is to be consistent, such a plan would not only have to take into account full equality in material conditions but also in intellectual conditions, or the identity of educational milieu; but this means the abolition of the family and the collective compulsory education of all children in state institutions, realizable only through extreme forms of totalitarian power. It is clear indeed that in the continuity of the family environment various advantages and inequalities persist and that thereby the "privileged start in life" is to some extent perpetuated. In pluralist societies, where the correlation between personal achievement and social position is fairly high, such "privileges" may, in effect, be limited in favor of genetically inherited differences, but not completely abrogated. If we take the principle of an equal start in life seriously and wish to remain faithful to it to the end, we have one foot on the road to totalitarian slavery.

Direct experience, however, together with an understanding of human passions, teaches us that, once introduced, the totalitarian order does not bring with it equality of opportunity in life, let alone equality in material things. The opposite is the case. Two things are especially highly valued and important in modern society: free access to sources of information and participation in power. Under totalitarian systems, both are denied to the overwhelming majority of the population and are strictly rationed out to small privileged minorities. Inequality in the distribution of material goods is, then, associated with enormously increased inequality in access to knowledge and power. And, the social inheritance of these privileges has an even greater effect than in societies where inequality remains purely quantitative, where it can be calculated in terms of money.

Thus we find that in this case too, if followed consistently, liberalism leads us eventually to the opposite of what is sought.

□

The essential characteristic of the open society is said to be spiritual freedom. It is not so much the institutions guaranteeing freedom of political activity, of speech, and of the press within the law that count, but rather the social conditions in which a general spirit of reasonableness and tolerance prevails, where all irrational taboos are abolished, where nothing is seen as sacred simply for reasons of tradition, where the people are capable of taking socially important decisions through rational discussion, and where no authority may operate against the verdict of reason.

Put like this, the rules of "openness" seem quite unobjectionable, at least for those educated in the tradition of the Enlightenment. On closer inspection, however, doubts arise. A society with no tradition or taboo, with no historically sanctified moral principles, would have to be a society mature in age and spirit. However, as that is impossible, there are at least two institutions which are constructed on the principle of authority and are inconceivable otherwise: family and school. One may say that the effect of authority can and should gradually decrease as children grow older; but this does not alter the situation. In each case both moral and intellectual education must start from authority and depend on it for a long time.

However, this is not the only reason why total freedom from authority and unconditional antidogmatism are empty catchphrases. In moral affairs there is a more fundamental impracticability. There are no rational criteria of good and evil in the moral sense, that is, no criteria sufficiently grounded in experience and logic. To the rationalists—who otherwise admit for the most part that moral judgments cannot be inferred from empirical judgments—this normally seems to cause no great social inconvenience, as all people are prepared to agree with many fundamental values, so that to all practical purposes it is important to discuss the means and not the value-goals, and such discussion can and should take place within the bounds of empirical criteria. This is, unfortunately, an intellectualist self-delusion, a half-conscious inclination by Western academics to treat the values they acquired from their liberal education as something natural, innate, corresponding to the normal disposition of human nature. Nothing is further from the truth than this supposition. That we should be kind, unselfish, and helpful to all our fellow humans is not at all obvious or natural. Since the empirical criteria that divide the normal from the pathological must be constructed on the basis of frequency and not on moral norms, it appears, unhappily, that hatred, envy, tribal exclusivity, racism and aggression are normal.

It does not follow from this that they are hopelessly ineradicable; nor does it mean that there is no potential in people for the development of countervirtues. It does, however, follow that moral education may not rely on instincts, that it is, to a certain extent, contrary to nature, otherwise it would hardly be necessary; nor can empirical knowledge create a foundation for it. To educate people to be tolerant and unselfish, to overcome tribal customs in favor of universal moral standards, cannot be done without the strong base of a traditional authority, which up till now has derived from the great universal religions. Very often, though not always, the net result of education freed of authority, tradition, and dogma is moral nihilism. The Hobbesian contract of mutual security can, of course, be founded on "rational egoism"; but there is no such thing as a rationally based brotherhood. The liberal slogan that exhorts us to strive for complete liberation from tradition and the authority of history is counterproductive: it leads not to the open society, but at best to one in which conformity enforced by fear keeps strict control over the struggle of private interests: precisely the Hobbesian model. There is, however, no mechanism whereby the dissemination of rationalist attitudes would produce universal friendship and love.

Here too, as in the cases already mentioned, we are not merely playing around with ideas. The attacks on the school and family upbringing have normally been conducted under the banner of liberal slogans (freedom from authority); often supported by totalitarian enemies of democratic values, they are often presented as a continuation of the old liberal struggle against the stupefying rigidity and cold formality of the nineteenth-century school system. By now this struggle has become irrelevant in virtually all advanced countries (perhaps not everywhere to the same degree); what are actually attacked in similar words are not Prussian or tsarist *gymnasia,* but the liberal schools themselves, schools with fairly flexible regimes, but still based on the principle that their main duty is to impart to the pupils knowledge, intellectual skills, logical standards, and mental discipline.

□

A similar pattern is to be observed everywhere: the institutions which make the survival of the pluralist society possible—the legal system, the school, the family, the university, the market—are attacked by totalitarian forces using liberal slogans, in the name of freedom in other words. Freedom appears as the absence of law and responsibility, in the anarchistic sense, and thus promises all the consequences which European social philosophy has pointed to for several hundred years: unlimited freedom for everyone means unlimited rights for the strong or, according to Dostoyevsky, in the end, absolute freedom equals absolute slavery. Wherever freedom finds itself in opposition to the law, to intellectual standards or to tradition, it turns against itself and becomes the weapon of its enemies. The ideology of anarchism derived—not with compelling logic, but not quite groundlessly either—from liberal principles works in the service of totalitarianism, not necessarily because it suits the intentions of its adherents, but because the totalitarian order is the only possible outcome of the pure negativity of anarchism.

What is at stake is the pluralist society, whose chances of survival depend, for sure, not only on the continued existence of its institutions, but also on a belief in their value and a widespread will to defend them. However, the reverse side of the welfare State is psychological changes that contribute to the weakening of this belief and this will. These changes may be roughly described as society's *retreat into infantilism*. Many technical, demographic, and social circumstances conspire to devolve the responsibility for more and more areas of life onto the State. We are accustomed to expect from the State ever more solutions not only to social questions but also to private problems and difficulties; it increasingly appears to us that if we are not perfectly happy, it is the State's fault, as though it were the duty of the all-powerful State to make us happy. This tendency to bear less and less responsibility for our own lives furthers the danger of totalitarian development and fosters our willingness to accept this development without protest.

□

It is well known that inherent in the pluralist order is a perpetual antinomy: how can pluralism defend itself against its enemies without using means that contradict its own essence? The dilemma is a pressing one and not intended for theoretical purposes. A constitution, which guarantees citizens' rights as well as political freedoms, works against itself if it outlaws totalitarian movements and ideas, and it works against itself if it ensures their legal protection; both tolerance and intolerance of the enemies of tolerance contradict the basic principle of pluralism, and no one can tell how far this tolerance can extend without causing democracy to collapse.

The totalitarian movements struggling for power, however, are finding more and more scope for their destabilizing activities, as the increasing interdependence for purely technological reasons of all spheres of social life makes it ever easier for relatively small groups to paralyze the whole economic mechanism of society; in every technically advanced country there is a vast network of links, each one of which, once immobilized, can bring the whole economic machinery to a halt; experience has given us many examples of this. And so, in the moment of danger every democratic order can be caught on the horns of a fatal dilemma: either allow itself to go under, or take refuge in unconstitutional coercive measures. In "favorable" circumstances this may mean the appalling choice between a totalitarian and an authoritarian-military order, a choice which can put it in an admittedly extraordinary but quite conceivable situation.

In other words, it is difficult to protect democracy by democratic means; difficult, but feasible on condition that democracy has the resolute will to defend itself. Tolerance is not necessarily indifference; the pluralist order is obviously founded on the recognition of particular values, and is not "value free" or neutral; also, the indifference of the law presupposes no neutrality of values; it is anchored in a social philosophy. In order to defend itself, the pluralist order should voice these values ceaselessly and loudly. There is nothing astonishing or outrageous about the fact that within the pluralist society, the defenders and enemies of its basic principles are not treated with exactly the same indifference; it is quite possible to treat them differently without harming citizens' rights or the principle of tolerance. A pluralism that acquired from its own norms carelessness about its existence and made it a virtue would condemn itself to death.

And among the dangers threatening the pluralist society from within—they include racism, nationalism, communist and para-communist movements, and the growing role of the State—what seems to bode most ill is the weakening of the psychological preparedness to defend it.

All this does not mean that the pluralist society is heading inevitably for destruction. Not only does it have powerful inner reserves for self-defense; its strength also lies in the abominable features and irremediable economic inefficiency of totalitarianism. The end result of the collision between the opposing forces that are tearing our world apart—one furthering the retention and dissemination of pluralism and the other promising totalitarian reorganization—can be known by nobody and is by no means decided; too many unaccountable circumstances play a part. The very fact that the totalitarian side feels forced to appropriate the language of liberal social philosophy and to make deceitful use of liberal phraseology may be taken as proof of the vitality of democratic values. The cause of the "open society" is not lost as long as it does not transform its openness into its own sickness and weakness.

Chapter Fifteen

Politics and the Devil

1

According to the traditional Christian teaching, the devil is incapable of creating; whatever is created, having been created by God, is unqualifiedly, unrestrictedly good; the whole of nature, God's diffusion, is good by definition, whereas the ill will, diabolic or human, is a pure negativity. Consequently the devil, in order to carry out his work of destruction, is bound to exploit the divinely supplied material and to foil its proper use; his evil activity is entirely parasitic upon the excellence of the creation. In human affairs this perversion consists mainly in that the devil—catching hold, of course, of the wickedness we all share as a result of the original sin—tempts us to see relative goods as goods in themselves, to worship some secondary goods as though they deserved divine reverence, thus substituting creatures for the Creator. This is in fact of what most of our sins consist. Our natural drives, instincts, and desires are good as such; their use is legitimate to the extent that they ultimately direct themselves to God as the highest good instead of being used for their own sake. Our physical and mental needs and wants are worth being satisfied if only we keep in mind that God is their ultimate goal. Knowledge is laudable and desirable if we employ our reason to fathom the mysteries of nature with the purpose of knowing better the divine order and thereby the author of this order. The pleasures of life are worthy insofar as they serve life and as we realize that the purpose of life is to sing the glory of the Lord. We love other people properly when we love God through them.

This applies to political affairs no less than to all others. To the extent that politics is the sheer struggle for power, it is bound, in Christian terms, to be the realm of the devil by definition; it then simply releases our *libido dominandi* as a drive that expands, as it were, for the sake of its own expansion and has no objectives beyond itself. As in all other areas of human life,

Previously published in *Encounter,* No. 400, December 1987.

however, the devil distorts and poisons the good natural order. The domination of nature is a biblical privilege of man; so is the necessity of political
order, which is to assure peace and justice on earth as a way of serving God
and fulfilling His designs. Once political goods acquire autonomy and become ends in themselves, they are at the service of the devil. Thomas Aquinas built the most admirable, all-embracing conceptual order, which—
without dismissing or despising instrumental goods, relative values, and
secondary causes and thus without encouraging a theocratic temptation—
found a proper and legitimate place for all kinds of human activity: cognitive, political, artistic, and technical. This order was vaulted by the divine
wisdom and goodness toward which everything naturally tends as the final
goal. There was no place in this order for any sharp distinction between law
in purely normative sense and law as a natural regularity, between the rules
concerning good and evil and the rules that govern the natural succession
of events, both kinds of rules deriving their validity from the infallible verdicts of a Being in Whom wisdom and goodness coincide. Even though we
can, to be sure, violate by our acts the rules of good and evil, which we
cannot do in case of natural regularities, in neither case is the validity of the
law broken. We are punished by natural order if we try to forget its laws,
and we are punished by God if we breach the commandments. Natural law
has no validity in itself; it derives from the eternal law: it is the way in which
eternal law operates in rational creatures; *lex est aliquid rationis,* as Thomas
Aquinas says, anticipating Kant;[1] it cannot be abrogated by the "human
heart."[2]

This elegant order, in which all areas of human life, including politics,
had their proper place in the universal hierarchy, has crumbled irreversibly
(or so it seems), and we may reflect for a while on the metaphysical meaning
of this collapse. The entire development of modernity, starting with its late
medieval roots, may be seen as a gradual movement whereby politics, arts,
science, and philosophy had asserted, step by step, their autonomous status
and independence from divine and ecclesiastical supervision. Each of them
had to look for its own criteria of validity instead of inferring them from
the biblical tradition and from the teaching of the Church, and it could
never be obvious any longer where this normative foundation was to be
discovered and how an area of thinking and acting could produce *ex nihilo*
its own principles without making them simply a matter of arbitrary choice
or caprice and without ending up with the idea that no such principles were

1. Aquinas, *Suma Theol.* la 2ae.Qu. 91. art. 2.
2. Ibid., Qu. 94.

available at all. This last stage of nihilistic liberation was eventually to be achieved in art, less so in philosophy, and not at all in the sciences, whereas in political doctrines it has never been accepted unambiguously and universally, even if the Machiavellian and Hobbesian analyses came close to this result.

One should expect, in conformance to Christian and, in particular, Augustinian teaching, that any area of life, if it achieves independence and issues for itself all verdicts about what is good, valid, excellent, or proper in it, falls under the sway of the devil. Those verdicts, one could argue, then become a matter of free human choice, and human choice, not informed by grace, naturally opts for evil; whether in making those choices we surrender to an actual diabolic temptation or to our own rotten nature, the result will inevitably invigorate the infernal forces.

If art, instead of being edifying and initiating people into Christian truth, becomes a matter of sheer amusement, of formal experiments, of unrestricted personal expression, or of flattering the impure tastes of the public, it becomes not just morally indifferent; it is bound to promote sin. If secular knowledge, instead of trying to disclose in the world the wisdom of the Creator, disregards revealed truth and works for the satisfaction of human curiosity, it becomes, fatefully, an instrument of godlessness. Indeed, St. Bernard in his treatise on the degrees of hubris lists curiosity among the manifestations of this horrible sin, and the same tenet has been repeated time and again in devotional literature.[3] As to the evil of secular politics, it is so obvious and so glaring in terms of traditional Christian wisdom that there is no need to dwell on the subject. If political affairs have no foundation in natural law, which in turn derives from the divine legislation, it seems self-evident that there is no reason at all why justice (whatever this means) rather than injustice should be praised, and the human city is left with no ground except for the unbridled movement of blind passions fighting against each other. Peace could then be no more than a temporary equilibrium of mechanical forces, and justice would be reduced to never-ending attempts by each of the struggling sides to extort concessions from the other. Political thinkers, after having discarded the gospels, might still, no doubt, have recourse to their Aristotle—as in fact they did—but Aristotle, much as he was venerated by many Christian and non-Christian philosophers alike, had no divine authority, was by no means infallible, and his advice could be shrugged off by anybody with impunity.

3. St. Bernard, *De gradibus humilitatis et superbiae,* Migne, Patr. Lat., vol. 182, 941–977.

That this was in fact the standard way of thinking in the Church's teaching we can easily see from innumerable official and semiofficial documents and from the large body of Christian literature devoted to the subject. It might be argued that Hobbes's philosophy was a kind of triumph of Christianity: it vindicated the idea that all normative principles of politics, once they have been cut off from their religious foundation, are bound to disappear, and the entire fabric of society will be based on the sheer distribution of forces, ruled by fear, greed, and thirst for power, simply because this is how the world is arranged.

If indeed the supremacy of the divine law in all realms of human life, including politics, is an essential part of Christian teaching, if no political order can enjoy legitimacy unless it is explicitly a fragment of the all-encompassing divine order, if social life, deprived of this legitimacy, unavoidably slides down into the clutches of Satan, should we not suppose that the Church may not, without inconsistency, renounce its claims to supremacy over civil authorities, indeed that according to its own doctrine, it ought to strive after theocracy, lest it surrender to the prince of this world?

And if so, how are we to view all the recent pronouncements of the Church and the popes, especially since the Second Vatican Council, that clearly renounce theocratic pretensions, accept the autonomy of science, and so on? Are they not just concessions, made under duress, to the spirit of the age, to modernity, and are they not at odds with the entire tradition of Christianity?

To be sure, some theorists of natural law among the deists and atheists in the seventeenth and eighteenth centuries argued that we can get to know natural law directly, without the support of the revelation, because it is a matter of innate insight; we simply know instinctively what is wrong or right, just or unjust, since nature has inscribed such intuitions in the mind. This amounted to saying that the presence of God and his legislation is irrelevant to the principles of justice; those principles stand on their own feet, whether or not a supreme legislator exists.

This belief, however, was naturally eroded both by the simplest skeptical arguments and by the fact—which became more patent as people learned more about other civilizations—that the notions of natural justice and natural law are by no means historically or geographically universal, and therefore we cannot rely on their being immutably engraved in the human heart.

And indeed, since the struggle of kings and princes against papal authority was not only expressed in practical political measures but found a theoretical foundation as well, one could see, among the defenders of secular politics and of the autonomy of civil authorities, a certain uneasiness in the face of the political order that had been robbed of its celestial legitimacy. This is expressed in the view that it is proper and useful for political rulers who do not believe in God and an afterlife to employ religious imagery, rites, clergy, and divine sanctions in promoting their interests and assuring social order. Marsilius of Padua made this point quite clearly,[4] and Machiavelli, of course, more emphatically;[5] so did Hobbes and—less explicitly but unmistakably—Spinoza, who also averred that one should govern people in such a way that it *seemed* to them that they governed themselves. Even Montesquieu says, through the mouth of his Usbek, that if justice depended on human conventions one should conceal this horrible truth even before oneself.[6] The reason for this fraudulent use of religion for political purposes was simply that most people are either stupid or wicked or both, and without the horror of hell their blind passions, constantly threatening the social order, cannot be tamed. While God was supposed to be the supreme judge, the devil as the executor of His verdicts seemed to be more powerful in affecting human imagination. Political theorists who preached this approach worked therefore on this assumption: if there is no devil, one should invent him.

And although those completely "secularized" teachers unwillingly confirmed the traditional Christian tenet—politics cannot dispense with religious justification—this did not mean that the priest or the pope should control the emperor or the prince; on the contrary, the prince should hire a priest to serve him. It was thus admitted that a sound political order needs a divine protection—if not real, then imaginary—and a kind of perverse theocracy (though not a clerocracy) seemed to be encouraged even by the implacable Church-haters.

2

There is, however, another side to the story. The devil tries, often successfully, to convert good into evil, but God is not idle; He knows how to outwit His foe and to reforge evil, havoc, and destruction into instruments of His own designs. The devil might have managed to tear asunder the healthy arrangement that had kept politics in its proper subordinate

---

4. Marsilius, *Defensor of Peace* 1.5.11.
5. Machiavelli, *Discourses* 1.11–15.
6. Montesquieu, *Lettres Persanes* 83.

place and had made the power of the emperor void unless sanctified by the pope; he might have offered independence and the right of self-determination to the realm of politics as well as to art, science, and philosophy (or at least taken the profit of their independence). But this fragmented world has never slipped out of the divine control, and from the disorder a new order emerged which was to defeat the satanic plot and start a new round of wrestling.

To understand God's way of proceeding we have to keep in mind the reasons why He cannot simply command the devil to evaporate or shackle him and make harmless. The answer that Christian theodicy has been repeating for centuries was that reason and the ability to do evil (i.e., freedom) are inseparable; consequently God, by producing rational creatures— human and angelic—had to suffer the inevitable evil results.

This kernel of theodicy was well shaped in early Christian thinking. The whole of it is virtually included in St. Basil the Great's remark in a homily that to blame the Creator for not having made us incapable of sinning amounts to preferring the irrational and passive nature to the rational, active, and free one.[7] Origen, who made a similar point earlier, avers that if human beings are weak, if they have to suffer and to toil in order to survive, this is because God wanted them to exercise their ingenuity, skills, and intelligence, and this would not have been possible if they could have enjoyed an idle life amid abundance.[8] Briefly, if the suffering that nature inflicts on the human race is a condition of progress, the suffering that people inflict on each other results from their ability to do evil, and this ability is an unavoidable part of their being free and thus capable of doing good as well.

The main point of Christian theodicy boils down to this: God's creation is an act of love, and the mutual love between the Maker and His creatures is conceivable only if the latter are reason-endowed beings who can do good of their own will; compulsory good acts are not good at all in a moral sense, and the ability willingly to do good implies the ability to do evil. Evil is therefore a necessary condition if a loving creator is to be conceivable at all; without it the creation would be pointless. It is implicitly admitted even in the earliest theodicies that God is bound by the standards of logical consistency and incapable of creating self-contradictory worlds.

It is therefore as a result of logical necessity that the course of world affairs is a continuous game in which good and evil attempt to outsmart

7. St. Basil, Migne, Patr. gr., vol. 31, 346.
8. Origen, *Contra Celsum* 4.76.

each other; that the game is going to end with the ultimate victory of the good is, of course, a matter for the revelation to promise.

3

Even if we assume that it was the devil who, through his patient and painful work, robbed the Church of its worldly power and eventually made politics—both as a practical activity and as a theoretical effort—independent of religious bodies and doctrines (at least in Western civilization), it is natural to reflect on God's countermoves. But it is far from obvious that this process of "autonomization" was initiated by the devil alone. Certainly the development whereby politics, science, art, philosophy, and technology gained their independence and had to build their own foundations, rather than taking them ready-made from the religious legacy, was the absolute condition of all the successes and failures of modernity. To break out of the tutelage of religion was indispensable for the further expansion of human potential. This story may therefore be seen, in Christian terms, as a new *felix culpa*, a simulation of the original sin; had it not occurred, the first couple would have been stuck in a hopeless stagnation, producing a race without history and without creativity.

While the Enlightenment granted autonomy to all the fields of human activity, it could not have prevented evil from sneaking into all of them. Being independent, however, they inevitably conflict with each other, producing a kind of metaphysical check and balance system. Religion is not trying any longer (again, in Western civilization) to impose its rule on science, art, and politics; as a result, the devils who were dispatched to those particular areas of life cannot cooperate smoothly and have to weaken one another's work.

At first glance politics seems obviously to be the favorite hunting ground of the devil (next to sex), as it is directly responsible for wars, persecutions, and all imaginable and unimaginable atrocities which the struggle for power brings about. But in historical processes we are never sure about where the ultimate responsibility lies. Art, science, and philosophy look innocuous by comparison, but their innocence might be deceptive because they operate on a much larger time-scale, and their evil results are for this reason usually diluted, difficult to trace, uncertain, and elusive. The demons from the department of politics can be simpletons or debutants, whereas those who operate in art, philosophy, and science must be much wiser, subtler, and more farsighted. The evil produced by tyrants and conquerors is intentional, easily identifiable, and in part even calculable; but who can identify and calculate the evil that resulted (unintentionally) over centuries from the minds of great philosophers and artists, from the creative toil of Plato, Copernicus, Descartes, Rousseau, or Wagner? What a craftsman does it take subtly to poison the fruits of all noble and clever benefactors of mankind, to foresee and control the changes in human mentality that their work would effect, and to exploit those changes for the profit of hell!

4

The above description might suggest that a drive toward theocracy is somehow naturally built into the spiritual framework of Christianity, and that diabolic forces were eventually to foil it. This is by no means certain or even likely.

Despite everything we know about the Church's claims to temporal power, Christianity has never been theocratic in the strong sense. The Church of the martyrs was certainly not; Christians naturally tended to see themselves as an alien enclave in the pagan world, and they viewed secular authorities as their natural enemies. But even the triumphant Church at the peak of its temporal might cannot properly be called theocratic. To be sure, the famous official document which comes the closest to theocratic pretensions and is routinely quoted in this sense, the bull *Unam Sanctam* by Bonifatius VIII (1302), states clearly that the physical sword is to be subordinated to the spiritual one, that earthly powers, if they deviate from the good, should be judged by the Church, and the churchmen by their own superiors, that all human creatures are subject to the pope as a matter of salvation. The doctrinal basis of those claims is the unrestricted capacity of the Church to define what is sin or virtue; in all matters involving sin and requiring its suppression—by sword if necessary—civil authorities are in duty bound to be at the service of the Church.

Practically, the extent of real papal claims depended on contingent historical circumstances, and what was actually meant to fall under the heading of "spiritual matters" could never be unambiguous, since most human activities, potentially at least, have a moral aspect. Two sayings, "The Church has no power in secular matters," and "The Church has power in spiritual matters," seem to be logically compatible or complementary, but because there are various ways in which to separate those two areas, we know that in practice they clash with one another; those who use the former phrase want to restrict or even abolish ecclesiastical power, whereas adherents of the latter want to enlarge it. In theoretical terms everything depends on the criterion whereby the temporal is distinguished from the spiritual. On the assumption that our conduct in temporal affairs is always relevant, in one way or another, to our salvation, theocratic claims seem to be vindicated.

In fact it is plausible to argue that not only are they not, but that semi-theocratic aspirations were brought into Christianity as a result of diabolic sophistry.

Even the most extensive claims to secular power—whether in theoretical statements like the previously mentioned bull and the writings of Aegidius Romanus, or in the practical policy of papacy, say, in the times of Innocent III—were not, strictly speaking, theocratic; they never aimed at the replacement of royal, princely, or judicial authorities by the direct rule of the clergy, or tried to abolish the distinction between two kinds of power.

The most frequently quoted scriptural basis for the division of power was, of course, Jesus' saying, "Render unto Caesar . . ." (Matt. 22:15–22; Mark 12:13–17). We learn from the gospel that this was how Jesus evaded the trap laid by the pharisees. What trap it was is easy to see: had He said, "No, you must not pay taxes," He would have denounced Himself openly as a political rebel; had He said instead, "yes, do pay taxes," He would have become a loyalist or a collaborator. The answer therefore was bound to be ambiguous. To read into it a general theory of two independent, or partially independent, legitimate sources of power was an extremely inflated and distorting exegesis. Still, Jesus' saying is quite in keeping with his teaching if it means, "Give to Caesar the earthly goods he desires, his power is short-lived anyway in the face of the imminent descent of God's kingdom. Caesar is not important; all his glory will soon evaporate without a trace." The oncoming Apocalypse is the never-fading framework of Jesus' preaching.

Thus Jesus provided his disciples with neither theocratic aspirations nor a clear theory of the double source of authority, however defined. He preached moral rules that were universally valid. It was therefore natural that His successors were supposed to pronounce moral judgments in all matters and all areas of life, including politics, wars, sex, trade, and labor. Their task was to say what is good or evil. There is no basis in Jesus' teaching on which they should demand any instruments of coercion or violence in order to implement—directly or indirectly—their teacher's rules. Indeed, a morally good act performed under physical coercion is an obvious contradiction in terms.

5

The devil is never asleep, but neither is God. The general history of their struggle in the area under scrutiny may be depicted as follows.

The devil instigated the persecution of Christianity, but this direct assault proved to be counterproductive; the blood of martyrs, as they predicted, fertilized the soil on which the Church was to flourish. Once Christianity emerged as the victor, the devil decided to spoil it with the glory of secular power and with the temptation of evangelizing the world by the sword. He convinced the Church that it ought to dominate political institutions: since God alone is to be worshipped, and the sin of worshipping anything else has to be extirpated, he argued, political activity cannot have its own goals but must take them up from the Church and bow before its verdicts. This was a misleading non sequitur which the devil, we should admit, instilled into Christianity with tremendous efficiency. The success was not perfect, however. Christianity had some built-in barriers that prevented it from demanding a full-fledged theocracy. One of those barriers was the previously mentioned wrong interpretation of Jesus' reflection on a Roman coin; it suggested that secular politics has legitimate rights in its own domain and thus a certain autonomy; the interpretation which, I believe, was more plausible would have been a stronger barrier, but the prevailing one was working, too. The other barrier against the devilish fraud was Christianity's strong belief in the devil, evil, and original sin. Theocracy is a Christian, or rather pseudo-Christian utopia, a dream about the perfect world, built on earth under the Church's control and designed to destroy sin, or at least "external" sinfulness. The legacy of both the gospels and the Church of martyrs was there to resist the utopian delusion: it suggested that the blood of martyrs would be shed, here or there, until the end of time and that evil, no matter how opposed, cannot be abrogated; an earthly paradise—moral or material—before the second coming is a superstitious product of human self-conceit.

Moreover, the theocratic dream includes, implicitly or explicitly, a vision of humankind that has done away with contingency, hazard, and freedom as well, a stagnating perfection in which people would be robbed of the opportunity to sin and thus of liberty: both are inseparable in Christian teaching. The relative autonomy of politics has to be accepted as a part of the unavoidable human imperfection, whereas a forcible attempt to abolish it would produce incomparably more evil; the Church as *corpus mysticum* might be infallible, but every individual churchman is fallible and sinful, and so is the Church as a sublunar organism. The concentration of all power in its hands would spell disaster both to human advancement and to Christianity itself. The devil knew that, of course; after all, his first venture in the Christian era, about A.D. 30, was to tempt Jesus with the prospect of earthly splendor and kinghood; Jesus did not surrender, but most people no doubt would.

The drive toward theocracy was nevertheless strong, if never completed. It was rooted not in the doctrine or in a wrong reading of the gospel but in the very fact of the secular power in the hands of the church—the result of a number of historical accidents.

6

And so the third phase of the battle, which was to unseal new avenues for further human development, had to consist in the progressive dispersion of power and in giving more and more independence to politics and to other fields in which human energy could expand. This was to be a dangerous game. God employed the tactics which, as we know from the Old Testament, had been tested many times when He scourged His people with disasters and wars brought on by its—and His—enemies. In the course of our modernity He apparently had no other choice either, granted that He refused, as He consistently had done, to correct the human race by taking away its freedom. Once more, He had to visit our iniquities upon us by employing for the job His own foes, that is to say, the Enlightenment.

One major task of the Enlightenment, among others, was to free politics from the fetters of religion. Since religion itself, by assuming so many political responsibilities and so much power, had become more and more contaminated with secular interests, more and more involved in military adventures, in diplomatic intrigues, and in amassing wealth for wealth's sake, the other part of the same assignment was to purify Christianity itself and to reduce it to what was its proper business. This part was to be given to the Reform movement within the Church. Again, two sides of the same Roman coin.

The devil, as one should have expected, was operating relentlessly on both sides of the process, and quite successfully. Within the Enlightenment proper, his idea was to convince people that it was not enough to liberate politics from religious control and to sever the State from the Church but that the progress of humanity consisted in forgetting its religious tradition altogether and, if necessary, doing it by violence. He gave the Enlightenment its anti-Christian shape and worked out, with the help of many fine and virtuous minds, the idea of humanism, which defined itself primarily by godlessness. Thereby it opened the door to the concept of politics as a sheer vying for power, power being a supreme good in itself; this went far beyond the Aristotelian tradition.

This was the easier and not very complicated half of the devil's job. Properly to wreck and to exploit the ideal of Christianity, which would have gotten rid of the secular pollution and returned it to its original purity, was a much harder task, but the devil proved to be up to the challenge.

The yearning after the innocence of the apostolic faith, after the unspoiled beginning of the New Time, was the most powerful ideological message of medieval popular heresies up to and including the great Reformation. And the destiny of the Reformation was to reveal how the devil took up the seemingly unassailable slogans of the poor Church, of the Church that makes no claims to worldly power and glory.

This happened within a few years after Luther's glamorous entrée into European history.

Since what Christianity is about is the salvation of the individual soul; and since, according to Luther, salvation is a matter of faith, which is God's gift; and since, further, neither a priest nor the Pope nor the Church as a whole has the power of forgiving our sins—and whatever is done by us without faith is a sin—the conclusion seems natural that the visible Church has nothing to do and should be abrogated. Various radicals of the Reformation drew this very conclusion and blamed Luther, who failed to do so, for his inconsistency. At the beginning, Luther thought only about mending the conscience of Christian people and seemed to assume that the world, hopelessly corrupted and ruled by Satan, does not lend itself to reform. Once he decided to reform it nonetheless, he was compelled to make compromises, as no material is perfectly malleable, and if we want to mold it to our vision, we have to take into account its immutable qualities; that is, to renounce the ideal shape and think of a possible one, looking for a compromise between the dreamed-of product and the actual stuff we work on. We have to give up the radical dichotomy of "all or nothing" and try to improve the world, thus implicitly admitting that it can be improved and is not incurably rotten, after all. Still, while the Lutheran reform accepted the necessity of the visible Church, it broke with its divinely protected continuity by doing away with the sacrament of priesthood and with the apostolic succession; it made the Church a branch of secular life. The conclusion was that the Church had to be subordinated to secular authorities, and this is what was eventually to happen.

This was an impressive triumph of the devil. Starting with the attacks on the adulteration of Christianity with earthly passions and interests and on secular power of the Church, the Reformation ended up with the idea that perversely turned theocracy upside down: it made the Church a maidservant of secular authorities!

That was not all. The Church was supposed to be nationalized, and, as the reverse side of the same coin, secular authorities were sanctified and bestowed with a divine dignity. This hallowing of secular power encompassed all its facets, as we can see from Luther's famous tract on civil authorities from 1523. The state obviously needs not only artisans and peasants but hangmen, judges, and soldiers as well, and therefore there is as little wrong with being a hangman as with being a cobbler. With impeccable consistency, Luther argues that if Jesus Christ was not a cobbler or a hangman, this was only because He was busy with other things. In other words, one may well imagine Jesus Christ as a hangman! (His earthly father was a carpenter, and it is quite plausible to think that Jesus, before He embarked on His mission in Galilee, had been a carpenter as well, and this is a perfectly respectable job, so why not a hangman?)

That was not all. The Reformation not only secularized Christianity as an institution, it secularized it as a doctrine as well, which amounted to stabbing itself in its own heart, as no greater abomination could ever have been imagined by its founders. Here, the devil's performance was indeed spectacular. This is how he proceeded.

In order to restore the pristine purity of Christian life, the Reformation rejected outright the tradition preserved in the dogmatic pronouncements of the popes and Councils as a separate source of authority, next to the Bible; the Scriptures were supposed to be the only norm of faith. But then there was the question of who is authorized to interpret it? In principle anyone who listens to the voice of the Holy Ghost is capable of doing that. But then the Church, as an organized community, simply could not exist, because everyone, including heretics or the devil-possessed, would make claims to a special revelation or inspiration, and no binding canon could be enacted. Therefore the exegetes, having no support in the historically formed, continuous ecclesiastical authority, had no other instruments for interpreting the Holy Writ but their own reason, which was otherwise condemned, declared corrupt, and dominated by the devil. As a result, in glaring opposition to its original intention, the Reformation produced the horrifying idea of rational religion; it was to become a hotbed of deism and rationalism. Bossuet in his *Histoire des Variations des Eglises Protestantes,* the masterpiece of counter-reformation literature, grasped the issue with a laudable clarity: "The true tribunal, one says, is the conscience wherein everybody ought to judge . . . matters and listen to the truth; this is easy to say. Melanchthon said this, as others did; but he felt in his conscience that another principle was needed to build the Church. . . . Should one leave the door open to anybody who would pretend to be a messenger of God? . . . Whatever one does, one has to go back to the authority, which is never assured or legitimate unless it comes from above and is not self-established;[9] . . . If he [Melanchthon] had properly understood this, he would never have imagined that truth could be separated from the body in which the succession and rightful authority were laid."[10] He goes on to say, "The cause of [the] changes we saw in separated bodies consists in that they did not know the Church's authority, the promises it got from above; briefly they did not know what the Church is"; the heretics therefore "were thrown upon human reasoning, upon their particular passions."[11]

In other words the devil transubstantiated the Reformation into the Enlightenment: not a mean achievement. God, in order to counteract the dangers of theocracy—that is, of the corruption of Christianity with secular power on the one hand and the stifling of human creative potential on the other—had to loosen the relationship between religion and politics and grant the latter a certain (institutional, we may guess, not moral) autonomy. The devil caught hold of this process and deflected it in two directions, which were eventually to converge: he favored nationalization (and this means secularization or devastation) of religion, and he gave the Enlightenment a strongly antireligious shape, thereby compelling politics to create its own rules *ex nihilo* and reducing it to the sheer thirst for power.

7

The effects were not quite satisfactory in the devil's eyes, though. In order to accomplish his purpose, he had to promote freedom, and freedom is divine, however it might be exploited by the devil and whatever Luther might have believed. Politics, once it had to rely on itself, was to abandon *truth* in favor of *consensus* as its foundation. It is indeed one of the cornerstones of democracy: consensus by no means implies that its participants are blessed owners of truth. The majority is to rule not because the majority is right but only because it is the majority; nothing more is needed.

This was not what the devil intended. Despite what he presumably (and rationally) expected, politics, which had to build its own foundation instead

9. Jacques-Bénigne Bossuet, *Oeuvres*, vol. 19, 1816, 296–97.
10. Ibid., 311–12.
11. Ibid., vol. 20, 449.

of finding it in divine commandments, became not more but less cruel (to be sure, he may comfort himself with the idea that this unpleasant outcome resulted from the lingering energy of the religious legacy; I leave aside the question whether or not this explanation holds good). And the divine gift of freedom had more and not less opportunity to expand and to assert itself.

The devil had to design a new counterforce, and he came up with the cleverest idea ever devised. This is the fourth phase of the contest, and it is being played out in our century for all of us to see.

The devil decided to go back to the old notion of politics based on *truth*—as opposed to contract or consensus. He invented ideological states, that is to say, states whose legitimacy is grounded in the fact that their owners are owners of truth. If you oppose such a state or its system, you are an enemy of truth. The father of the lie employed the idea of truth as his powerful weapon. Truth by definition is universal, not tied to any particular nation or state. A nation or a state is not just a nation or a state, trying to assert its particular interest, to defend itself, to expand, to conquer new territories, to build an empire and so on. It is a carrier of universal truth, as in the old days of the crusades.

The devil, as the medieval theologians used to say, is *simia dei,* an ape of God. By inventing the ideological states he produced a caricatural imitation of theocracy. In fact the new order was to be much more thorough and complete than any Christian state of old, as it dispensed with any distinction between secular and religious authorities, concentrating instead both spiritual and physical power in one place; and the devil gave it not only all the instruments of coercion and education but the entire wealth of the nation as well, including the nation itself. Theocracy, or rather aleteiocracy, the rule of truth, had, at a certain moment, achieved an almost perfect form.

It changed, naturally, the character of war. Since the Second World War, most wars are about universal truth, that is to say, they become civil wars. As in a civil war, no rules of warfare are operating; prisoners are often slaughtered or compelled, under the threat of death, to take the side of the former enemy—which is not a betrayal, as they simply abandon falsehood for truth, and to embrace truth is a conversion or enlightenment. The concept of betrayal has changed; it can be applied only to those who renounce the side that is the vehicle of truth.

The devil seems to have succeeded admirably with his new invention, but there are signs that his triumph will be short-lived, for all the horror his new historical toy has caused. Ideological states did emerge, and many proved to be impressively resilient. But they clearly have reached the phase of decline. Ostensibly, they are still embodiments of truth, which gives them the principle of legitimacy. But whenever they want their people to be motivated to do something, they do not appeal to the universal truth but to national sentiments, imperial glory, *raison d'état*, racial hatred; this is particularly glaring in communist ideocratic states. They do succeed to some extent, but their very successes reveal the grotesque gap between the reality and its verbal disguise. That their truth is fake has become irreversibly patent. Openly to admit their reality as it is would be, however, disastrous. They try awkward and intermediary solutions, thus patching up the crisis.

The devil has other resources, no doubt. Apart from constructing the towers of truth, he tries surreptitiously to reintroduce truth into democratic institutions as an alternative to contract and consensus. He takes up the principle of majority rule and distorts it by suggesting the attractive idea that the majority as such is right and is therefore entitled to do anything, including abolish the very principle of the majority. This is, as we know, a real problem. Can a democratic constitution, by the consent of the majority, vote itself out of existence? Can it be abrogated, that is to say, commit suicide, in accordance with its own principles? (There is an analogous question: Can a pope infallibly declare that he is not infallible?) A number of people reflected upon this question, from Carl Schmitt (before he became a Nazi, that is) to James Buchanan. If the majority is right as such, this can easily happen, because the minority, being by definition a vessel of falsehood, deserves to be destroyed.

I do not expect that the devil will succeed in either of the two ways he has embarked upon in order to do away with freedom, that is, to abolish human existence. People need mental security, no doubt, and this makes them susceptible to the devilish temptation of an ideocratic order. But they need to be human as well, and thus to use their freedom to question the existing order, to suspect every truth, to venture into uncharted realms of the spirit. The need for security is not specifically human; the need to take risks in exploring the unknown is. Clausewitz in his classic work makes this remark:

> Although our intellect always feels itself urged toward clarity and certainty, still our mind often feels itself attracted by uncertainty . . . it prefers to remain in imagination in the realm of chance and luck. Instead of living yonder in poor necessity, it revels here in the wealth of possibilities; animated thereby, courage then takes wings to itself, and daring and danger make the element into which it launches itself as a fearless swimmer

plunges into the stream. . . . There is therefore everywhere a margin for the accidental, and just as much in the greatest things as in the smallest. As there is room for this accidental on the one hand, so on the other there must be courage and self-reliance in proportion to the room available.[12]

Clausewitz knew well what he was talking about. What applies to wars between states applies as well to the war between good and evil in history. This war may never end, as the stuff we are made of feeds both sides. If the present phase, just described, is going to close with the devil's designs being frustrated, he will certainly be clever enough to open new avenues for his energy. But to speculate upon his future inventions would be futile.

This endless game is not a matter of intellectual delight. St. Augustine wrote indeed in *The City of God* that God "enriches the course of the world history by the kind of antithesis which gives the beauty to a poem . . . there is beauty in the composition of the world's history arising from the antitheses of contraries—a kind of eloquence in events, instead of words."[13] Hegel made a similar symphony of historical dialectics. After what we have been witnesses to in our century, we rather tend to think, with Kierkegaard, that to find this sort of aesthetic and intellectual delectation in the grandiose historical panorama is like enjoying the charm of the music emitted by the bull of Phalaris (according to the legend, the Sicilian tyrant Phalaris had a brazen bull, empty inside, in which his enemies were slowly roasted alive and the bull was so ingeniously constructed that the horrible howling of the victims came out, through an acoustic device, as a pleasant melody). No, the struggle between the devil and God in history is not a merry spectacle. The only comfort we have comes from the simple fact that we are not passive observers or victims of this contest but participants as well, and therefore our destiny is decided on the field on which we run. To say this is trivial, and, as many trivial truths, worth repeating.

12. Carl von Clausewitz, *On War,* chap. 1.22, ed. by A. Rapoport (Penguin Books, 1983).
13. St. Augustine, *The City of God* 11.18.

Chapter Sixteen

Irrationality in Politics

That *rationality* has little to do with *rationalism* is not, I assume, a matter of controversy. The latter, defined in opposition to either *irrationalism* or *empiricism,* is an epistemological doctrine, a normative definition stating what has or does not have cognitive value, whereas *rationality* and *irrationality* are characteristics of human behavior. We might measure the rationality of behavior by standards of *rational human nature;* for the time being I leave aside this question and concentrate instead upon the current sense. In this sense rationality is related to, without being identical to, efficiency. What we usually seek to say when describing an act as irrational is that the act is predictably counterproductive; what matters is the relationship between goals and means within the limits of available knowledge. This last restriction is obviously necessary, as inefficient or counterproductive actions are not irrational if the outcome depended on circumstances that the agent was unable to know; the pharaoh who destroyed his army by pursuing the fleeing Jews could not have predicted the miracle on the Red Sea, and thus he did not behave irrationally.

The goals or the hierarchy of values which guide our actions cannot be qualified according to the criteria of rationality; consequently our opinions on the rationality of human behavior involve no moral judgments. For the same reason we cannot describe irrationality in terms of the self-destructive or the self-damaging effects of our actions, considering that self-destruction can be intended; it would be silly to state, for instance, that suicide is irrational by definition. Therefore it is fair to say that even though the same root, *ratio,* is involved in both pairs of words, the *ratio* we have in mind when talking about rationality or irrationality is close to its original sense of "calculation," unlike the *ratio* which various doctrines of rationalism imply. An action is irrational whose outcome the agent can calculate but fails

Reprinted by permission of the publisher from *Dialectica* 39, no. 4 (1985), with revisions by the author.

to (and not of which the outcome is, as a matter of fact, disastrous, self-destructive, morally inadmissible, and so on).

Thus far this description seems reasonably clear and unlikely to generate much controversy. At second glance it becomes more dubious, at least as to the extent of its usefulness and applicability, both in real life (as opposed to situations artificially concocted in seminars on ethics and action theory) and in political issues.

There are a number of reasons why assessment of human actions in terms of rationality, thus defined, is often doubtful, useless, or impossible. The most obvious reason amounts to the simple fact that all of us, both in politics and in private life, pursue various independent objectives, irreducible to each other, inexpressible in homogeneous units, and unattainable jointly; the means we employ to achieve one objective usually limit, sometimes even destroy, the hopes of achieving another. Since we may not evaluate the objectives or the hierarchy of preferences in terms of rationality, we are often helpless in assessing the rationality of actions if they imply a choice between incompatible or mutually limiting aims.

Do I behave irrationally if I continue smoking despite a probability of 0.3 that I will die of lung cancer? I do behave irrationally if I first decide that to extend my life-span is the supreme value to which everything else is to be unconditionally subordinated and that I would take no action that might decrease, with some probability, my longevity; these actions would include, for instance, flying airplanes, driving cars, climbing mountains, walking on the street, exposing myself to stress, being engaged in conflicts, having or not having a family (both are dangerous), visiting New York, and taking part in politics, wars, or business. The life strategy based on such an assumption is probably not rationally constructible: I should follow, for instance, all the dietary rules, which change from one year to another; not a week elapses without my reading new warnings about one food or another—sugar, butter, eggs, meat, coffee or whatever (actually, the only food about which I read something positive in recent years is alcohol), and if I tried to be consistent in my behavior, I would most likely die rationally of worry or of hunger. And, after all, the knowledge that as a smoker, I have a 0.3 chance of dying of lung cancer repeats only, without the slightest addition, the fact that 30% of smokers die of lung cancer. I do not carry any probability in my body; if I die of cancer, I do not die with a 0.3 probability, I just die. However, even if a perfect strategy based on the integration of all known probabilities were constructible, it would be "rational" only in the light of my previous decision about the monistic hierarchy of values, and there is nothing rational or irrational in this decision. The same can be said about political choices. For instance, it has been repeatedly pointed out that the extermination of the Jews by the Nazis in the last phase of the war was harmful to the Third Reich in "technical" terms, that is, in terms of warfare, and was thus "irrational." This assumption would be true only if genocide was to the Nazis a means to win the war. Yet it was clearly not so; the extermination of the Jews was a goal in itself, which might have collided with other goals, as is usually the case. Or, to take an example from the other side, the massive extermination of the military cadres by Stalin, in the face of an imminent war, appeared to many as an act of madness which nearly brought the Soviet state to ruin. It is by no means obvious that this was so. Stalin could rationally expect that during a war, when the role and the independence of the military is bound to increase enormously, a military coup might easily have led to his assassination, if the army had not previously been brought to obedience by massacres and intimidation, including the extermination of the best cadres. Stalin wanted to win the war, of course, but he also wanted to survive as an undisputed despot. And he succeeded, thus disproving the charge of irrationality. That uncountable human lives were sacrificed in the process as a result of military incompetence is a fact which might be of relevance to the question of rationality only on the premise that saving the lives of his subjects was one of Stalin's objectives; and there is little evidence to support this premise.

The same kind of unanswerable questions may be asked about all major political decisions. Was the revocation of the Edict of Nantes, with its nefarious effects on the French economy, an irrational act? Or the Byzantine foreign policy in the first half of the fifth century? The answers depend on the objectives which Louis XIV and Justinian respectively aimed at.

There is another reason why it is often a hopeless task to evaluate the rationality of our actions, political or otherwise: the options we face are frequently offered as package deals. Many voters in democratic countries would like to vote for only half of a given candidate's objectives or a given party program, and rarely have such an opportunity. They inevitably find themselves in the company of people they dislike, sometimes intensely. Many liberal (in the European sense) and enlightened American intellectuals who voted for Reagan in 1980 hold little in common with the ideology of the "moral majority" or the Southern rednecks who also voted for Reagan. Many liberals (in the American sense) who voted for Carter were in compulsory but unwanted alliance with the leftist extremists who voted for Carter in the absence of better options. Everybody, save the utopian daydreamers, knows that more often than not we have to expect and to suffer the unpleasant consequences of our best choices: we cannot eliminate pornography without preventive censorship and state control of printing, we cannot have a welfare state without a huge and cumbersome bureaucracy; we cannot achieve full employment without compulsory labor in a police regime, and so on. This is a commonsense banality, to be sure; it was, in general form, well known to the authors of Koheleth and of the Talmud, and it is worth mentioning to the extent that it might be useful in explaining the feeling of helplessness we often experience when trying to assess the rationality of political decisions.

A particular case of this conflict is the inescapable tension between short-term and long-term goals. This seems to be an ineradicable aspect of human affairs, whether political, economic, or private, and quite often, given the infinite complexity of causes and effects, the rationality of the decision made can never be unequivocally established. Politicians elected for a limited term tend naturally to support decisions that will pay off in the short term, but are often harmful in the longer perspective: is this necessary and always irrational? Since knowledgeable people very frequently disagree about the overall effects of certain decisions, there is never a shortage of plausible but opposed arguments. And a lapse of time often changes our views on the "ultimate" outcome of some previous actions. Poles today still passionately argue about the wisdom or folly of the uprisings against the Russian oppressors during the partition period. The uprisings failed, to be sure, but— so one of the arguments goes—if the Poles had not repeatedly asserted their will to independence in unfavorable conditions, they would have been unable to assert it successfully when the proper moment arrived. This was not, of course, the intention of the unsuccessful fighters, who fought to win, not to become just fertilizer for future generations. Yet the arguments that point out unintended or "historical" rationality sometimes cannot be lightly dismissed when we deal with long-term processes. To take a quite recent example, the question is still unclear about the wisdom of signing the Helsinki Agreement, which obviously brought some profits and some disadvantages both to the democratic countries and to the Soviet bloc. Most likely no conclusive proofs about the final balance will ever be provided to general satisfaction.

Conflicts of desires or goals can work without their victims being clearly aware of them. Many people who have always voted for one particular party keep voting for it after either they themselves, the party, or both, have changed to such an extent that their continuing allegiance seems absurd in terms of their professed values. There is, however, another side to their irrational conduct: consistency in political loyalty comprises part of the feeling of self-continuing identity, whereas violent breaks in long-lasting loyalties are highly damaging in this respect. In terms of moral self-preservation, this kind of behavior is therefore less irrational than it appears. Usually such people try, more or less awkwardly, to explain away or to rationalize their inconsistency. Many cases of cognitive dissonance, analyzed by Leon Festinger, are of a similar character. People who continue to live with these kinds of contradictions, which they try to conceal from themselves or of which they are only half aware, may perhaps be blamed for moral reasons (bad faith), but not necessarily for irrational conduct. The commandment, "Thou shalt be consistent" might be justifiable within a rationalist philosophical creed, but it is not—at least not as a universal rule—an aspect of rationality in the sense under scrutiny. Neither is the Lockean supreme principle, which requires that we conform the degree of our convictions to the degree of justifications of a given belief. On the contrary, if we made every effort to abide strictly by these two rules, we would probably become paralyzed and unable to act, politically or otherwise.

It does not follow that irrationality in this Machiavellian or Hobbesian sense is a non-issue or that it is pointless to make a distinction between its various degrees. However, the relativity of our judgments in such matters does not result merely from uncertainty in assessing the global effects of some important decisions and from the variety of interdependent forces which are at work in all human affairs. In saying that people behave irrationally when they can, but fail to, calculate the results of their acts, we should ask about what this *can* means. We have seen many cases of predictably disastrous decisions taken by despots who perhaps "could" foresee, but were mentally unprepared to foresee, the results because of their primitivism: Mao's "great leap" or the absurd "reforms" initiated by the dictators, say, of Uganda and Zaire may serve as examples. It took only rudimentary knowledge to predict that the tyrants would bring ruin and havoc to their countries, yet they lacked this rudimentary knowledge. In what sense could they have been better educated? In other cases disastrous results, though predictable, are accepted because other considerations outweigh them. There is no doubt, for instance, that socialized or collectivized agriculture is bound to be very inefficient in terms of productivity. It is easy to see why, and the examples abound to bear out the prediction. If, however, the point of collectivization is to assert totalitarian power and to leave no segment of the population independent of the omnipotent state, productive inefficiency and the consequent misery of the population are the price to be paid.

The charge of irrationality appears more plausible when we are talking of people who certainly are mentally prepared to perceive obvious fallacies in confronting goals and means. Intellectuals who identified themselves with monstrous tyrannies—National Socialism, Stalinism or Maoism—for the sake of freedom and justice have provided us with countless examples of astonishingly poor judgment and self-inflicted blindness; they can be blamed not only for moral but for intellectual failures. The two kinds of blame cannot easily be separated; blunders in judgment are very often caused by moral irresponsibility, by the inability to see facts through the veil of passions. Ultimately, when irrationality is spoken of as a failure for which a person is rightly blamed, it is a moral rather than an intellectual failure.

Since conflicting objectives are usually irreducible to comparable units, and since the global results of important decisions are rarely predictable (and even if some predictions are in fact borne out, their soundness can easily be dismissed and the results attributed to other causes, as happens every day in political quarrels), we have little reason to expect that the art of politics might actually be rationalized in the sense here discussed. It does not seem likely that if active politicians were acquainted with game theory, they would perform more efficiently in terms of their goals. Whether or not such progress is desirable depends, of course, on our attitude towards those very goals. There is no reason to be happy about the rationalization, that is, growth in efficiency, of torture and genocide, and most of us would not like the regimes that practice those measures to become more efficient.

The passions that drive human actions (I take the word in the Cartesian or Spinozist sense, which implies no special intensity) are neither rational nor irrational. To be sure, the struggle between passion and reason has been for centuries a persistent and favorite topic of philosophers and moralists, starting at least with Seneca and Cicero. Yet this conflict has usually been discussed in terms of "rational human nature," of a reason which was capable not only of applying adequate means to achieve the desirable effects, but of establishing the goals as well. Once reason, as I assume here, is reduced to the power of calculation, human acts do not become irrational when motivated by passions. We may still talk about this conflict, having in mind cases in which the distance is drastically reduced or abolished between the power of passions or emotions and the acts themselves, so that we become unable to think of the other effects of our conduct—for instance, when we act in panic or are blinded by hatred, love, rage, and so on. To ask whether or not in such cases we "can" be more rational amounts to asking about the validity of psychological determinism, and I am not going to venture into this area. It appears, however, that in individual political actions and decisions made by men in power, this kind of blindness is not very frequent, most probably because people who are altogether unable to calculate the effects of their actions are not likely to reach important political positions. We remember many stereotypical images of rulers who acted out of pathological hatred, envy, vindictiveness, and lust for power—from Tiberius and Empress Theodora to Stalin and Hitler—and it is by no means obvious that such psychopaths were as a rule unable to calculate their actions rationally.

The same does not apply to spontaneous mass movements and revolutions in which the power of calculative reason is usually abrogated. We are acquainted, of course, with the persistent psychological patterns of revolutions and civil wars, starting with Thucydides' famous description of the civil war in Corfu. In such conditions appeals to reason are impotent and turn naturally against their authors. If a revolution succeeds, it is not in spite of, but on account of, the irrationality of the actors' conduct; the energy that is needed, if a revolutionary movement is to prevail, cannot be mobilized without the power of illusions, deceptive hopes, and impracticable claims. Therefore the success of a revolution is bound to be spurious and ambiguous; a revolutionary movement can succeed in the sense of imposing its will on the society, but it always fails in the sense of being incapable of keeping its promises and fulfilling the expectations that are a necessary component of its energy. No revolution has ever succeeded without bringing bitter disappointment almost in the very moment of victory.

Passions that work in political processes—tribal or national sentiments, envy or lust for power, desire for justice, freedom and peace, identification with the oppressed, or the hope of being the oppressors—can in some conditions produce an incurable individual or collective blindness and thus an inability to act rationally. When a major crisis affects a society, causing widespread panic, fear, and desperation, and leaving no time for calculation and reflection (it is after all an important aspect of this discussion that rational conduct often requires more time than we feel we have before an irreversible disaster), rationality becomes, as a matter of fact, a non-issue. If, in such conditions, a providential figure, a "charismatic" leader (I dislike this much abused adjective, but I find no substitute) can instill the feelings of safety and hope, the problem of calculation becomes pointless. Such charismatic figures often lead a society into an abyss, but they are sometimes helpful in mobilizing social forces that are able to find a noncalamitous solution to the crisis. Among such leaders in our century we can count Gandhi, Lenin, Hitler, Mussolini, De Gaulle, Peron, Castro, and Mao. In facing such situations our reactions are safer if guided by purely moral considerations, rather than by the uncertain use of calculating "ratio."

It thus appears that even the most modest and apparently most trivial advice—"we act more rationally, that is, more efficiently, if we know more, rather than less, of the conditions that are relevant to our actions"—may by no means be accepted without qualifications. Considering that in so many human affairs, political and personal, the strong expectation of success is an important condition for success, strong self-delusions might often be rational, even though they cannot be, of course, consciously programmed or decided. In other words, in all human efforts the seemingly most rational strategy can be counterproductive. This most rational strategy can be summed in the simple rule: In order to succeed we should assume that the uncertain or unknown aspects of the situation relevant to our action are the worst possible for our success. This rule seems sound insofar as it is obviously rational to build all the safeguards against possible adversities, but it runs counter to the principle of rationality insofar as it produces discouragement and enfeebles the will. Granted that—to speak in the somewhat pretentious Lukácsian idiom—the object and the subject of cognition partially coincide in our knowledge of social affairs, ignorance might be an asset and be in this sense rational, although its rationality is not ours; it is rather the cunning device of human nature. Self-fulfilling prophecies—both positive and negative—are a well-known phenomenon; this is why defeatists have so often been shot during wars, and not without reason. It is true that self-defeating prophecies occur as well when excessive self-confidence breeds carelessness: if the victory of a party in an election is so certain that many voters do not bother to go to the polls, their absence might assure the success of the adversary. It is unlikely that we could produce a theory to define in general terms the conditions in which more ignorance and optimism, or rather more knowledge and more room for defeatist expectations, would be strategically "rational." If we could elaborate such a theory, it would probably be of no great practical use anyway, as it is rather difficult consciously to produce self-delusions on rational grounds.

Neither do we have any certainty whether or not and in what circumstances self-delusions about one's own motivations and goals are "better" in strategic terms. By broaching this question we enter the shaky ground on which the combat between psychoanalysis and existential philosophy was waged. To the advocate of the former, human consciousness is inherently self-opaque; more often than not we are necessarily unaware of our "real" motivations. To an adherent of existentialist phenomenology, especially in the Sartrean version, the "unconscious psyche" is a square circle; our consciousness is self-transparent, and unconscious motivations are those we deliberately conceal from ourselves in bad faith—we are always able, though often unwilling, to be aware of what we are "really" after. Whichever approach is closer to the truth, it appears at first glance that it is more rational to have a clear idea about one's own objectives and not to lie to oneself. Yet this is not necessarily so. It might be strategically helpful to substitute loftier ideas for the less noble ones, not only for the use of other people, but for one's own use as well. A good self-image is an element of strength; complete cynicism and self-awareness of one's own objectives are, therefore, not frequent among politicians.

Can we evaluate political "systems" in terms of rationality? It might appear that the notion is not applicable as long as it implies the relationships between means and purposes, and only people, not systems, can have purposes. Yet there is nothing wrong or logically suspect in slightly extending its meaning; people who identify themselves with the values that a given system is supposed to embody consider themselves agents or carriers of those values. Thus we may reasonably ask which systems are "more rational" in the sense of being more efficient in supporting and reinforcing the values which, in the people's opinion, they stand for. Needless to say, systems can only be assessed on their own presuppositions, not in terms of good and evil.

We might be tempted to believe, on this assumption, that systems which embody liberal values are more rational than despotic ones, since they provide a much greater chance for decisions to be made on rational grounds. They give room for open conflicts and discussions, thus compelling decision-makers to be responsive to various arguments, and they let the large mass of information be freely divulged, which is an obvious condition of rational planning. Meanwhile, totalitarian regimes, with so many built-in barriers to information and with an inherent inability to discuss political issues publicly (or any other issues, for that matter), are bound to limit severely their chances of acting rationally.

On closer inspection this argument is not very convincing. Both kinds of systems have, no doubt, some weaknesses and some advantages in terms of their self-perpetuating efficiency. The rulers of totalitarian states sometimes fall prey to their own lies: since the flow of information is normally provided by the same people who are responsible for the management of a corresponding area of activity, the carriers of bad news often denounce themselves to higher authorities and risk punishment. On the other hand, freedom of information and public debate have disadvantages of their own in terms of efficiency; by making decisions depend on various conflicting views and calculations, the system easily produces uncertainty, hesitation, and lack of determination. Besides, the processing of the immense amount of information that is the basis of decisions in both political regimes is so difficult that the risk of blunders is perhaps not significantly greater in either. And so, judging by the global results, there is no strong evidence for granting one of those systems a clear advantage in rationality of conduct. The great totalitarian Soviet empire, despite numerous and sometimes almost disastrous blunders resulting from its despotic character, has survived for more than two generations and has vastly expanded its area of domination.

Besides, freedom is seen in democratic countries as a value in itself, as is the unlimited extension of the State's power in totalitarian regimes; they are not only instruments for acquiring other goods. It would be unreasonable, therefore, to think that a highly despotic totalitarian regime might improve its efficiency—in terms of its values—by becoming less oppressive. This would undermine the scope of state power, whose increase is the main and autotelic good. To be sure, on various occasions compromises with reality are made under duress in both kinds of regimes, when, for instance, democratic countries introduce various forms of censorship during a war, or when totalitarian regimes allow some limited economic freedom to cure in part the devastating effects of centralization. In both cases the concessions run counter to the basic values on which the systems are respectively founded, yet in both cases the point is to sacrifice a part in order to save the whole. In neither case are the fundamental values abandoned.

The results of the foregoing remarks are not encouraging. It appears that irrationality in politics—if we stick to the sense of the word as defined—is not a very promising topic. It is unlikely that general criteria of rationality that are applicable—apart from extreme cases—to political life could be reliably worked out. Even if they could, it is unlikely that their existence might have any real impact on political life. And if such an impact were possible, it is by no means certain that it would be desirable.

I do not see how we can escape these three meager and philosophically less than stimulating conclusions if rationality and irrationality are defined in "technical" terms, and this is probably the only framework that empiricist philosophy is ready to legitimize.

The terms of the discussion are radically changed, of course, when the "ratio" we refer to is defined as a transcendental category in the Platonic, Kantian, Hegelian, or Husserlian manner. As with most philosophical issues, we ultimately go back to the conflict between empiricist and transcendentalist approaches, each of them self-supporting and incapable of justifying its own validity without a vicious circle. I am not trying to discuss this issue, which naturally involves the very foundations of modern philosophy, except for a brief remark. On empiricist assumptions, human nature or human "normality" has to be described by reference to frequency: rationality is to be measured by efficiency, and consequently the worst man-made monstrosities might in certain conditions turn out to be rational; there is no natural law, no valid distinction between good and evil, and no goals which are in themselves more or less rational. Transcendentalists believe in rational nature, which provides us with standards whereby our acts and goals, as well as political institutions, can be assessed. What we do or fail to do can be judged as "human" or "inhuman," that is, conforming to or contrary to a model of nature which is there, no matter to what extent, or even whether or not we can show empirical examples of its being fully materialized in actual human conduct or institutions. In empiricists' eyes this rational nature, capable of issuing normative verdicts on our conduct and values, has, at the worst, the same status as fairies and is, at the best, a matter of arbitrary faith or of sheer, rationally unjustifiable commitment. As the question cannot be now investigated any further, I will end with a very brief *confessio fidei*.

The rules of empiricism, as has been repeatedly pointed out, cannot be empirically grounded and are no less arbitrary than the transcendentalists' "ratio." Assuming—which seems to be a plausible hypothesis—that the rules of bivalent logic belong to the cultural invariants, that is, that they have governed human thinking in all civilizations, they do not become valid in a transcendental sense and may still be seen as contingent characteristics of the behavior of a species. If so, the very concept of truth in the current sense seems to be not only redundant, but inconstructible. And I tend to believe that consistent empiricism is bound to dismiss the concept of truth in any but the pragmatic or utilitarian senses. Transcendentalists, while admitting that we can become aware of cultural invariants only in communication with other people and by using the language that is necessarily contingent, believe that those invariants result from our participation in the realm of "ratio," which precedes any actual civilization. And often, though not invariably, they are ready to include in those invariants the distinction between good and evil, that is, to accept a doctrine of natural law. They would argue that the experience of good and evil is as universal as logical rules, even though, of course, the distinction does not run along the same lines in all civilizations.

I do not see how this fundamental opposition of two mentalities could be resolved by appeal to ground common to both. Apparently there is no such ground, and therefore two mutually irreducible notions of rationality will probably continue to coexist in unremitting hostility.

Practical considerations often invoked in this discussion are not likely to be conclusive. Empiricism has been constantly accused of paving the way to moral nihilism, or at least of breeding helplessness in moral and political issues (Bertrand Russell remarked—I am regrettably unable to quote the source—that after Nazi atrocities it is difficult to be satisfied with saying, "De gustibus . . ."). We are aware, on the other hand, of the dangerous totalitarian potential hidden in Hegelian transcendentalism, and I am very suspicious of the Frankfurt School's *Vernunft,* which in some interpretations, such as Marcuse's, can easily be reforged into a justification of tyranny. I am much more sympathetic to the Kantian approach, which includes the belief that by being free and taking part in the transcendental realm of rationality, all people, each of them separately, are given the same rights and are bound by the same duties. This leads directly to the Kantian idea of the human person which is an unexchangeable, self-grounded, and supreme value. This assumption might not suffice to solve any particular political issue, but it is good enough to make the distinction between political freedom and slavery a matter of rationality, rather than of taste or of whim.

Chapter Seventeen

Marxism and Human Rights

In the German version of the "International," the refrain ends with the words *Internationale erkämpft das Menschenrecht* (the "International" wins human rights). The song, while written without Marxist inspiration, was adopted as the official hymn of the Third International, which was supposed to be the only political embodiment of Marxist doctrine. From this it might seem that the idea of human rights was part of the ideology of the Communist movement. Alas, on closer view, we find that this was not so. The expression, which appears neither in the French original nor in other translations of the song, seems to have been inserted into the German text principally to rhyme with the preceding line (*auf das Letzte Gefecht*). This is an oddity not only in the history of the hymn, but in the history of Marxism as well. *Nous ne sommes rien, soyons tout!* is certainly a more accurate rendering of Marxist ideology.

In inquiring into the relationships between Marxism and the theory of human rights, it may be useful to define both terms, a difficult task, given the enormous variety of definitions that exist and the controversies they generate. While no set of definitions will satisfy everyone, if we reduce the problem to its theoretical core—dismissing the many peripheral variants of Marxism and setting aside the intricate questions that relate to what may be included as human rights and the extent to which their implementation depends on contingent historical conditions—we may be able to make some progress.

□

When we say that we accept human rights, we are saying in effect that we accept human rights as *valid*. But what does that mean? It does *not* mean that those rights make up, or have always and everywhere made up, a part of all legal systems. Such a statement would be false and in any case irrelevant to what most people believe to be true about human rights—that these rights would be valid even if no positive law included them, explicitly

Reprinted by permission of the publisher from *Daedalus* (Fall 1983). Copyright © 1983 by the American Academy of Arts and Sciences.

or implicitly. Conversely, if all legal systems in the world guaranteed them, this by itself would not be sufficient grounds for accepting them. Their validity, then, does not depend positively or negatively on actual legislation, past or present.

Nor do those who accept the concept of human rights claim that it is an arbitrary norm which they accept simply because they like it, and that it achieves validity by the force of their decree. To assert the validity of human rights is not a sheer act of commitment of which the justification lies in its very performance. It amounts to more than simply saying that "we (I) decide that everybody *ought* to be given these rights," but rather to declaring that "it is the case that everybody has these rights." The idea of human rights, in other words, has no firm basis except in terms of natural law theory, which may, in turn, have a theological or transcendentalist (say, Kantian or Husserlian) justification.

Natural law theory does indeed imply that stealing, for example, is wrong; rightness or wrongness are inherent properties of certain human acts, according to whether they conform to or conflict with the rational nature of man. Those immanent moral qualities may or may not depend on divine decrees. In the tradition of late medieval nominalism (and in Cartesian metaphysics as well), they resulted from God's free verdict, which might have been different from—indeed, opposite to—what it actually was. God decided that it was wrong to kill one's father; given the irreversibility of God's law, patricide has since been inherently and immutably sinful. Seventeenth-century natural law doctrines rejected the "decretalist" theology and instead made a distinction between natural law and divine positive law, arguing that while the latter resulted from God's decree alone, natural law was inherent in the nature of things and could not be changed, even by the Creator himself. Grotius, for one, took this position.[1] Leibniz argued that God orders what is immanently good and forbids what is immanently evil, instead of making acts and things good or evil by the force of His own free decision.[2] The very idea of *homo*, Puffendorf argued, included his inherent dignity.[3] While making the moral order of things independent of our knowledge of God, natural law theory was based on a metaphysical principle which stated that the order of nature displayed immutable moral characteristics, and that it was not only an order of causes and effects but of values as well.

To the extent that the idea of human rights was logically dependent on

1. Grotius, *De iure belli ac pacis* 1.1.10–15.
2. Gottfried Wilhelm Leibniz, *Discours de metaphysique*, 2.
3. Puffendorf, *De Officio* 1.7.1.

the belief in natural law, it was clearly unacceptable to the adherents of empiricism and of all varieties of historicism, including Marxism. A distinction on this point is necessary, however. The human rights concept includes three characteristics, among others, that are important for this discussion: first, these rights are valid because of the inherent dignity of being human, and they make up part of the natural order, rather than being established by decree or by positive law; second, this order is immutably valid wherever human beings live together and interact with one another; third, these rights, however specified, are rights vested in all individuals and *only* in individuals, not in social groups, races, classes, professions, nations, or other entities.

On these assumptions, it appears that a Marxist's case against human rights would be much stronger than the one made by an empiricist. The latter, while not accepting the first of the three premises, dismissing the notion of an "objective" order of values and rights, and the idea of their permanent validity—insofar as it is not a validity established by specific legislation—might still, without fear of contradiction, commit himself to the idea of human rights. He might not believe that God or nature made certain human actions wrong or right, but he could admit that there is nothing improper, illicit, logically unsound, or empirically forbidden in our reacting to human actions by saying, "this is wrong," "this is noble," "this is good." An empiricist qua empiricist is not bound to preach moral nihilism. He may believe, for example, that torture is wrong and that we ought to support and fight for a society in which all people enjoy guarantees against being tortured.

In a limited sense, an empiricist may even accept the second premise; he may, without being inconsistent, state that though no universal validity may be spoken of in a particular case, he himself is ready to stand up for human rights in all imaginable conditions. To be sure, since his position cannot be defended in terms of "validity," he is helpless before the challenge of an adversary, and must concede that, in cognitive terms, those who deny the idea of human rights are in a no worse position than he. Barred from committing himself intellectually or theoretically to the doctrine of human rights, he is nevertheless free to abide by his practical commitment to it.

A historicist may find himself in a somewhat analogous position. While believing that all values and standards, both cognitive and moral, "express" specific needs, aspirations, and conflicts of the particular civilization in which they happen to arise, he knows that it is pointless to dwell on their ahistorical, let alone eternal, validity. This, however, does not prevent him from admitting that as a participant in a particular culture, he shares its norms, and that he is not being inconsistent if he "believes" in those norms, aware though he may also be of their historical relativity.

A Marxist's position is far more radical. Within his conceptual framework, he is not only bound to take the historicist's standpoint, dismissing all the claims of natural law theory, all beliefs in everlasting moral order or in immutable rights, but, to be consistent, he must positively oppose the concept of human rights even in its historically relative form; he is ideologically committed to reject the very idea.

The conflict between Marxist doctrine and human rights theory consists in something more than the idea that all values and rights, in Marxist terms, are nothing but the temporary products of particular relationships of production, nothing but the opinions that particular classes use to express their vested interests, to give them an illusory ideological shape. For to the Marxist, both the concept of liberty and the idea of human rights, as defined by Enlightenment thinkers and ideologists of the French Revolution, are the specific expressions of a bourgeois society that is on the verge of collapse. Marx's writings, from the "Jewish question" onward, wholly dismiss all claims made to the lasting validity of "bourgeois freedom" and unremovable human rights. The idea of the individual's rights, Marx explains, implies a society in which the interests of each person are naturally and inevitably opposed to the interests of others, a society incurably torn asunder by the clash of private aspirations. The dominant motivations in this society are bound to be egoistic—not as a result of the corruption of human nature, but because of the character of the economic system, which is inevitably conflict-laden. All rights and liberties in bourgeois society simply assert and codify the fact that each individual's aspirations and interests inevitably conflict with, and are limited by, the interests and aspirations of others. Since the civil society is a place of incessant and all-pervasive war, where no real community is possible, the State steps in to provide an illusory unity, to set limits to the conflicts by imposing restrictions on hostilities. These restrictions appear in the form of civil liberties, which necessarily take on a purely negative character. Ideological legitimacy is given to the system by various social contract theories. Communism, in its promise of abolishing classes and class struggle, thereby cutting out the roots of social conflict, makes the bourgeois "negative freedom" and human rights—rights of individuals isolated from, and hostile to, one another—useless. The division between civil society and the State, indeed the very distinction between the two, is done away with; "real life" and spontaneous community, having absorbed the

State, law, and other instruments of the government that kept bourgeois society, with its privileges, exploitations, and oppressiveness intact and served to perpetuate it, has no need of such supports. Communism ends the clash between the individual and society; each person naturally and spontaneously identifies himself with the values and aspirations of the "whole," and the perfect unity of the social body is recreated, not by a return to the primitive community of the savages, as the Romantics would have it, but by a movement upward on an "ascending spiral" that restores human meaning to technological progress. Human rights, in other words, are simply the facade of the capitalist system; in the new, unified society they have become utterly irrelevant.

Although Marx despised "bourgeois" rights, he never argued, as the anarchists did, that it did not matter whether those rights were valid in bourgeois society. The difference between a despotic and a liberal order within the "capitalist mode of production" was an important one to Marx. During the 1848–49 revolution and thereafter, he urged workers' parties to ally themselves with the democratic bourgeoisie to fight against tyrants; republicans were to be supported against royalists. This, however, was not a matter of principle but of tactics. While it was true, according to Marx, that no imaginable political changes in a capitalist society could have a socialist meaning, and that the iron laws of the market economy could be obliterated only by a revolutionary upheaval, resulting in the expropriation of the bourgeoisie and the centralization of all economic levers in the hands of the State, the workers needed to participate in the fight for democracy; it would improve the political condition of their struggle, preparing them for the final battle against capitalism.

Marxists, therefore, behave consistently when they fight for civil liberties and human rights in despotic nonsocialist regimes, and then destroy those liberties and rights immediately upon seizing power. Such rights, according to Marxist socialism, are clearly irrelevant to the new conflictless, unified society. Trotsky stated clearly that democratic regimes and the dictatorship of the proletariat should be assessed according to their own respective principles; since the latter simply rejected the "formal" rules of democracy, it could not be accused of violating them; if the bourgeois order, on the other hand, did not abide by its rules, it could be rightly blamed.[4] This standpoint cannot even be viewed as cynical, so long as Marxists who fight for guarantees of human rights in nonsocialist despotic regimes do not pretend that

4. Leon Trotsky, *Writings 1932*, 336.

it is a matter of principle nor that their moral indignation has been aroused, and furthermore make no promise to guarantee these rights once they are themselves in power. (As it turns out, they usually do all three.)

Marx himself did not pretend that capitalist society deserved to be condemned because it was unjust, or that the revolutionary struggle was about *justice*. He abandoned the moralistic approach to social problems early on, and from the moment he defined himself in opposition to the so-called German true socialism, he tried consistently to convince his readers and followers (and himself) that the proper attitude to social changes consisted not in denouncing the moral failures of capitalism, but in analyzing the "natural" tendencies that would inevitably cause it to collapse and bring about the new society. In this society, all would have an opportunity to develop their potential to the fullest, asserting their individuality not against the society but in contributing to its general progress. There was, he believed, no reason to condemn capitalist exploitation in terms of social justice or injustice; the labor force itself was a commodity; the worker, in selling himself to an employer, usually does it according to the principle of equivalent exchange. The conflict between capitalists and workers, according to Marx, was one of right against right; force alone would decide between them.[5]

Marx's dismissal of the moralistic approach, to a large extent, was of course a self-deception. Normative premises are hidden in all his basic concepts, particularly in his idea of alienation and in his theory of value, as well as in his belief that Communism would restore the truly human character of human life. He knew how to achieve the conformity of the empirical man with the idea of *humanitas*, and this was no less value-laden knowledge than Plato's acquaintance with the world of *ideas*. He failed to explain what motivations people might have for taking part in the struggle for Communism; he would have resisted the proposition that they fight for Communism for no better reason than that it is bound to win by the force of historical laws.

We cannot, however, while making allowances for this ambiguity—which is fundamental to Marx's work—reinsert the concept of human rights into his theory, distilling the normative content from the hybrid doctrine that melts determinist prejudice with utopian fantasies into one indistinguishable whole. If Marxism were a purely historical description and prediction, it would not include the human rights doctrine, to be sure, but it

5. Karl Marx, *Capital*, vol. I, chapter 8, I.

would not actively oppose that doctrine either. The incompatibility between the Marxist doctrine and the concept of human rights comes through clearly when we see Marxism as both a disguised moralism—which it refused to admit—and an appeal for political action, which it explicitly wanted to be. To state that civil liberties and human rights principles are simply an ideological and institutional expression of the market economy that communism intends to abolish is not merely to press forward with a neutral "sociological" description, predicting the most likely outcome of current social conflicts. Rather, it is to affirm positively, encourage, appeal for, and contribute to a social order where civil liberties and human rights are abrogated. This is entirely in keeping with the notion of man as a social animal in its specifically Marxist variant. In a market economy, Marx argued, individuals are victims of the society in that their lives are prey to a contingent historical process that no one, separately or in alliance with others, can control; the society itself is alienated from "real men" and is governed by anonymous laws; individuality, as a consequence of its isolation, is lost. Communism, by restoring genuine community, by turning over to "associated producers" the control of social processes, would recreate the conditions of real individual development.

Marx did not imagine his new society as a sort of concentration camp—quite the contrary. Yet, a number of penetrating critics, even in his lifetime, without waiting for the achievements of "real socialism," noticed that if the Marxist social program ever came to be implemented, it would produce a highly despotic regime, making every human being a helpless property of the omnipotent state. Communism was supposed to be, according to Marx, a society in which the "negative freedom" or "bourgeois freedom"—the human rights guarantees—are pointless precisely because everyone willingly identifies with the community. Furthermore, since communism is principally the abolition of private property, once the bourgeoisie had been successfully expropriated, clearly neither the liberties nor the institutions protecting human rights in a bourgeois society would be needed.

It is true that many theorists, especially in the period of the Second International, who considered themselves full-fledged Marxists did not believe that socialism would destroy the rights embodied in the democratic institutions of "bourgeois society," and predicted that socialism, by extending democracy into economic relationships, would enlarge, rather than abolish, the scope of human rights. They took little account of the philosophical generalities in Marx's writings, interpreting his doctrine not as a moral appeal, but as a scientific analysis of capitalist society. Karl Kautsky and Rudolf Hilferding are only two of many who belonged to this company. It is arguable, however, that by suggesting this kind of selective reading, these men betrayed both the spirit and the letter of the canonical scriptures. Lenin, by comparison, was a much more faithful disciple of Marx. By defining the dictatorship of the proletariat as sheer, direct violence, obeying no laws and no rules, disdaining—as a matter of principle—all the institutions of parliamentary democracy, with its elections, freedom of speech, and all the rest, and proclaiming the abolition of the division of power, he followed Marx completely. By accepting—not just in fact, but in theory—the dictatorship of the party, stating unambiguously that the Soviet State would promise neither freedom nor democracy, announcing that cultural activity would be entirely subordinated to political tasks and that terror would be directly inscribed into the legal system, he showed his fidelity to Marx. By denouncing the "fables about ethics" and asserting that ethics was to be an instrument of the class struggle, by sneering at bourgeois inventions such as the distinction between aggressive and defensive wars or the principle that one should keep international agreements, by insisting that there are no permissible limits in political struggle—in all these, Lenin did not depart from Marxist principles. Neither did Trotsky when, with praiseworthy clarity, he stated that violence is the form par excellence of socialist power; that all human beings are to be considered as a reservoir of the labor force; that compulsory labor is a permanent principle of the new society; that no means ought to be discarded on moral grounds if they can serve the cause of Communist power; that Communists "were never concerned with the Kantian-priestly and vegetarian-Quaker prattle about the 'sacredness of human life'"; that moral questions are questions of political strategy and tactics; that it is nonsense to attribute any significance to a distinction between democratic and fascist regimes.

Steven Lukes argues that the only Marxists who consistently admit the validity of human rights are "revisionists who have discarded or abandoned those central tenets of the Marxist canon" that are incompatible with such a belief.[6] But in what sense can those who do believe in human rights still be seen as Marxists or consider themselves as such? While there may be many socialists who, without contradicting themselves, are committed to human rights principles, this is because there is no commonly accepted def-

6. Steven Lukes, "Can a Marxist Believe in Human Rights?" *Praxis* 1, no. 4 (January 1982).

inition of socialism; the idea itself, older than Marxism, has a number of varieties, some of them obviously incompatible with the Marxian variant. Nevertheless, it is true that some of the scientistically oriented Marxists mentioned above wanted to purify the doctrine of its normative elements, and, in doing so, distorted its sense. The neo-Kantian Marxists tried to supplement the allegedly value-free Marxist theory of society with Kantian ethics. Unlike the orthodox, to whom such a mixture was unimaginable, the neo-Kantians, though accepting that no normative ideas can be inferred from Marxist doctrine, found no logical difficulty in enriching it with the Kantian philosophy of practical reason.[7] I believe that both the scientistically oriented Marxists and the neo-Kantians were wrong. Marxism is no longer itself once we cut it down to its purely "descriptive" content and discard its normative background, which is hidden in the theory of class consciousness, of alienation, and of the future identity of individual and society. The Marxian critique of "negative freedom" and individual rights is a necessary conclusion from this theory.

Both variants of this half-Marxism proved to be historically abortive. The orthodox current of old, apart from its contribution to the Leninist variant, ceased to exist, and the social-democratic movement, which inherited a part of its legacy, was soon to lose contact with the Marxist tradition. Neo-Kantian Marxism died off with its proponents; attempts to revive some of its tenets in later revisionist movements proved to be short-lived. As a doctrinal corpus with all-explanatory pretensions, prophetic values, and prognostic guidelines, Marxism was virtually monopolized by the Leninist-Stalinist ideology and, without being essentially distorted, has become the legitimizing device of the totalitarian empire. It solved moral issues, not by dismissing them in favor of a value-neutral analysis, but by launching the vision of a new mankind, which would achieve its final liberation by making everything the property of the State, by proclaiming the irrelevance of "bourgeois freedom" and human rights.

The Soviets have assimilated into their jargon—reluctantly and under pressure from the West—some of the phraseology of human rights. Yet, this hardly suggests that they have embraced human rights theory; it is only a symptom of their ideological disarray. No Soviet leader today would dare to repeat Lenin's clear and precise judgments about democracy and freedom, nor are such judgments ever quoted in the Soviet press. That some

7. I discuss these questions in more detail in my *Main Currents of Marxism*, especially in volume 2, in the chapters of Austro-Marxists and on Kautsky, and in volume 3, in the chapter on Lukács.

Western phraseology was adopted—without, of course, altering the political realities or building any barriers that might limit the state despotism—indicates the force of the human rights idea. Yet it was adopted only in a strongly qualified version: when Soviet ideologists speak of human rights, they invariably stress that the chief human right is the right to work, and that this has been granted under the Soviet system only. What they fail to add is that this has been achieved by a system of compulsory labor that was established in principle at the very beginning of Sovietism. Thus the supreme right of man and his supreme freedom are materialized in the form of slavery. Nor do they dwell on the fact that this same freedom has been achieved under National Socialism and fascism.

This question, to be sure, cannot be lightly dismissed. The right to work emerged in the nineteenth century as a response to the helplessness, misery, and exploitation of workers. Even if we do not consider it a human right, feeling useful to other people is an undeniable aspect of human dignity. People who, as a result of social processes beyond their control, are unemployed or unemployable in great numbers, who feel redundant and useless, are injured not only in their welfare, but in their dignity as well. It is possible that absolutely full employment—the condition in which nobody ever looks for a job—is incompatible both with the market economy and with technical progress. For that matter, it is incompatible, too, with freedom from slave labor; perhaps it could be implemented only in a slave state. Experience tells us that the market economy is a necessary, although not sufficient, condition of political orders that are able to institutionalize and guarantee human and civil rights. Inevitable economic fluctuations that result in a certain amount of unemployment are tolerable so long as the unemployment *is* temporary. When economic fluctuations instead produce a large class of people who are doomed permanently to live on the charity of the State, and when such a class continues to grow, society is in danger, not only because of the increase in suffering, frustrations, and criminality, but because many people feel ready to renounce freedom for the security of employment. The dilemma is real and pressing. There are no reasons to believe that traditional liberal advice—to abandon state interventions in economic affairs since these function best when they are left alone—will prove efficacious. If democratic societies prove incapable of coping with mass unemployment, they are likely to encourage totalitarian trends, thereby putting into jeopardy the very institutional framework upon which the observance of human rights depends.

□

It is often stressed that the idea of human rights is of recent origin, and that this is enough to dismiss its claims to timeless validity. In its contemporary form, the doctrine is certainly new, though it is arguable that it is a modern version of the natural law theory, whose origins we can trace back at least to the Stoic philosophers and, of course, to the Judaic and Christian sources of European culture. There is no substantial difference between proclaiming "the right to life" and stating that natural law forbids killing. Much as the concept may have been elaborated in the philosophy of the Enlightenment in its conflict with Christianity, the notion of the immutable rights of individuals goes back to the Christian belief in the autonomous status and irreplaceable value of the human personality.[8]

Yet it was not the metaphysical character of the theory that prevented it from being incorporated into Marxist doctrine. And it was not the antimetaphysical spirit of Marxism that made it incompatible with the human rights principle. Rather, it was Marxism's fundamentally holistic approach to human life, the belief that progress can be measured only by the ability of mankind to control the conditions, both natural and social, of its life, and that, consequently, an individual's value is not related to his personal life, but to his being a component of the collective "whole." On the assumption that violence is the midwife of progress, one should naturally expect that the ultimate liberation of humanity would consist in the coercive reduction of individuals to inert tools of the State, thereby robbing them of their personality, and of their status as active subjects. This is what in fact all the regimes that base their legitimacy on Marxist ideology try to do; they are incapable *in principle,* not as a result of temporary deficiencies, of accepting the idea of human rights, for to accept human rights would indeed demolish their very foundation. What chance of ultimate success is there for this work of aiming at the extinction of personal life, reducing human beings to perfectly exchangeable units of productive processes? That is a separate question, which I leave aside in this essay. Still, it is possible to say that its success would result not only in the ruin of civilization, but in the ruin of humanity as we know it. My bet, however, is that it will not prove successful, that the human spirit will turn out to be refractory enough to resist totalitarian pressure.

8. On the Christian origin of modern "individualism," see Louis Dumont, "A Modern View of Our Origin: The Christian Beginnings of Modern Individualism," *Religion* 12 (1982).

Chapter Eighteen

Revolution—a Beautiful Sickness

We call revolution a mass movement which, by the use of force, breaks the continuity of the existing means through which power is legitimated. Revolutions are distinguished from coups d'état by the participation of a significant mass of people; the break in the continuity in the system of legitimation distinguishes them from legal constitutional changes which take place within the framework of the existing mechanism of power without infringing its legitimacy. A coup d'état can be an outcome or a component of the revolutionary process, or of course it can take place without a revolution, as is usually the case.

Such a definition, like all descriptions of social phenomena, is not precise enough to avoid doubts in some circumstances: it is often difficult to decide if we are dealing with revolution, or only with a coup d'état or with mass unrest. For the purposes of the present discussion, this definition is adequate.

We thereby avoid the perplexing problem of deciding which of the coups, rebellions, peasant uprisings, and religious wars of ancient and modern history deserve the name of *revolution*. Even though all earlier revolutionary movements produced their own ideological justification, it was not until 14 July that a universal paradigm of revolutionary ideology was created. Since that time *Revolution,* without further qualification, has become a slogan that distinguishes a separate class of doctrines and ideologies whose particular characteristic is the anticipation, not simply of a better social order, but of an ultimate State which once and for all will remove the sources of conflict, anxiety, struggle, and suffering from people's lives. Every difficult or apparently insoluble problem in social life, in international, class, or other con-

Translated from the Polish by Stefan Czerniawski from "Rewolucja jako piękna choroba," *Aneks,* no. 22, 1979; with revisions in English by the author; first published in German in *Merkur* 12 (1979). Copyright © 1979 by Ernst Klett Verlag, Stuttgart.

flicts, has, it becomes clear, one solution, which is the same for all problems: revolution—universal, all-encompassing, and irresistible.

The pre-existence of a revolutionary ideology is not a necessary, still less a sufficient, condition for an actual revolutionary process. Even in cases where that very process shapes the appropriate ideological forms, however, they have a natural tendency to produce this same anticipation of the ultimate State. This has the advantage that it can effectively mobilize the energy necessary for the paralysis of existing institutions, and it also removes all possible doubt about the means employed, which certainly cannot be evil if they are effective in achieving the ultimate State.

Revolution, as Lenin rightly observed, can take place only in situations in which the masses do not wish to live in the existing conditions *and* the rulers are not in a position to exercise power by existing methods. In other words, one condition for revolutionary processes is the (at least partial) paralysis of the mechanism of power brought about by circumstances independent of ideology and revolutionary movements. But even where both of these conditions are fulfilled, revolutions do not necessarily follow: we know of many abortive revolutions and many events that have led society to the brink of revolution but not over it. In this sense, all revolutions are accidental, in that they result from an unforeseen coincidence of different circumstances, and there is no 'law' on the strength of which any kind of social system must necessarily collapse as the result of revolutionary pressure. It is impossible to generally define conditions that inevitably generate revolutions. Losing a war, economic crises, accelerated demographic and technical change, and critical transformation of religious consciousness are all phenomena which could be conducive to revolutionary explosions, but which are not necessarily so. Some generalizations from historical observations are permissible, however, though these certainly may not be expressed in the form of "laws."

Burke's famous saying from *Reflections on the Revolution in France* (1790), "A state without the means of some change is without the means of its conservation," is sometimes quoted as a warning to oppressive or stagnating regimes: If you don't learn to improve things voluntarily, you will be destroyed in a revolutionary explosion. But this warning is not universally valid: on the contrary, as a technical guide for despots who wish to avoid upheaval and hold on to power it may be counterproductive and simply disastrous. A typical and by no means exceptional phenomenon is revolutionary disorder in oppressive systems at times of their relative "liberalization"; times of relaxation and moderation are—as has often been seen since

Toqueville's time—the most dangerous for a tyranny. Ruthless, brutal, and self-assured despotism may enjoy long impunity. Woe betide it, however, if it tries to humanize itself or to show the world a human face: instead of conciliating society with its wry smiles, it emboldens its critics and puts into motion a self-propelling mechanism of ever-more-audacious and ever-further-advanced claims, the pressure of which can eventually shatter it.

The processes that prepared for revolution in Russia certainly did not start in the epoch of stagnating oppression under Nicholas I; on the contrary, they began shortly afterwards when the regime initiated a period of reform, and were intensified with the gradual liberalization of the system of power (though the correspondence is obviously not exact). Similarly, it was not Stalinism in its most oppressive period that inspired the movements that began to corrode the totalitarian system; on the contrary, this was done by so-called de-Stalinization. The Hungarian revolution was a result of a de-Stalinizing relaxation, as were the social movements that brought Poland in 1956 and Czechoslovakia in 1968 to the edge of a revolutionary situation. The Iranian revolution can be seen as the culmination of the decline which the tyrannical authorities brought upon themselves by attempting on one hand to grow milder and on the other to lead the country on the path of accelerated technical and social progress.

But even from such observations, we can extract no "laws of history." The example of Spain shows that an autocratic system of government can, in favorable circumstances, gradually relax its oppression and ultimately transform itself into a democratic system without revolutionary upheavals. The probability of such an evolution, which is the most satisfactory for society, depends on a number of conditions which cannot, unfortunately, be created to order.

Political and police repression, however brutal, have never by themselves brought about revolutionary outbursts. Nor do they happen simply because of the poverty of the population. Universal poverty can, on the contrary, sometimes effectively defend tyrannical authorities from collapse, if the authorities are able to compel a substantial majority of the population to think of nothing beyond getting hold of a piece of bread.

But even from this it does not follow that a sympathetic adviser could simply recommend to despotic authorities: don't change anything, don't slacken oppression, don't try to ease poverty, don't weaken the police and the army, respond mercilessly to all disobedience, and so on. Such advice would be good only if the governmental machine effectively controlled all aspects of life in the country, if it could isolate itself completely from external influences and continue to stagnate indefinitely. In today's world, perfect stagnation and perfect isolation are unlikely. There are many circumstances which favor social crises and which the most farsighted tyrants cannot resist, demographic changes or cultural, technical, and economic influences from outside. All "modernization" is dangerous for despots, but they frequently have no choice and are compelled to undertake different sorts of modernization, inevitably running the risk that they will fall victim to it.

There exists, therefore, no theory by which a revolution may be predicted a long time in advance and which allows its probability, still less its outcome, to be determined. We may speak of a revolutionary process when we observe the rapid collapse of the institutional forms of collective life, as a result of which the instruments by which institutions regulated people's behavior—government, police, courts, representative bodies—cease to operate, and nobody controls the situation.

In many Third-World countries, the rulers like to talk of revolution as their own, stable, system of government; but this is empty rhetoric: it is partly connected with the positive aura which surrounds the word *revolution* in the jargon of various ideologies; it serves mainly, however, to legitimate a system of domination which is more or less autocratic. If the word *revolution* is to keep the sense given to it by historical experience, there is no such thing as a "revolutionary system of government." Revolution is the destruction of institutionalized forms of power: all new forms created by this process of disintegration are the ending of that process, not its continuation. The renewed stabilization of forms of authority, that is, the system which brings the revolution to an end, cannot by the nature of things be "revolutionary": if it calls itself that, it is generally in order to justify oppressive forms of government and the absence of social control over the authorities. All power systems emerging from revolutionary upheavals are, in the exact sense, counter-revolutionary, for each tries to stabilize its own forms of government and to tame the spontaneous processes that brought it into existence. *Revolutionary government* simply means a despotic government after a revolution; *revolutionary justice* and *revolutionary legality* are simply the absence of justice and legality; when a particular organ of the authorities proclaims that it applies "revolutionary justice," this means simply that it is subject to no law and kills, tortures, imprisons, and robs at its discretion all those whom it suspects, justly or unjustly, of disobedience. *Revolutionary courts* are nothing other than lynch law sanctioned by a government which owes its continuation to the fact that no law impedes it.

In such cases the adjective *revolutionary* loses all discernible meaning. It is possible to speak of revolutionary poetry or art, in the sense of poetry or art which awakens emotions favorable to revolution, that is, which contributes to the destruction of the existing institutions of power. However, when leaders call for revolutionary poetry or art they have nothing like that in mind; quite the opposite, they want poetry and art which help to stabilize their domination. As a result of this ambiguity, the adjective 'revolutionary' becomes so general that it can be applied to almost any word, as a means of taking away its normal sense while asserting that it is being retained and even "deepened." The ideologists of the student riots in the sixties spoke of "revolutionary science," that is, a science in which anything could be asserted, but nothing needed to be proved. If somebody claims to have created a "revolutionary chair," one may be sure that it is a chair on which it is impossible to sit. In many uses, the adjective *revolutionary* is as convenient as the adjective *dialectical* (*dialectical logic* is nothing but freedom from the principle of contradiction; to have a "dialectical majority" is to be in a minority; to win "in a dialectical sense" is the same as losing, and so on). Sometimes this adjective means nothing except vague approbation: members of the Temple's People sect not long ago collectively committed "revolutionary suicide" as a result of their leader's command: the suicide was genuine, but the adjective meant that it was also "right."

If we take the meaning that modern historical events have given to *revolution*, however, we observe that revolutions are not technical manipulations which anyone who is appropriately competent can "do," as a coup d'état can be "done." Revolutions, let us repeat, are spontaneous processes in the course of which the institutions of power disintegrate through the participation of the great masses of society. They are always the outcome of the coincidence of the most varied circumstances and we never have reason to believe the claim that they were absolutely unavoidable. Organized political and military activity can assist these processes and are also necessary to their conclusion (that is, to seize power and to stabilize a new system of government); they cannot, however, bring about revolution by themselves. Neither has terrorist activity ever resulted in revolution, and there is no reason to suppose that it will ever do so. For revolution—when foreign invasion is not mistaken for it, as often happens—is a sickness of society, the paralysis of its regulatory system, and it may be so characterized regardless of whether the regulatory system was despotic or democratic in nature. The recovery or rebuilding of the regulatory mechanisms marks the end of a revolution, and new mechanisms can be "revolutionary" only by virtue of their origin, not by virtue of their function, which would be a reversed use of the word.

Is there, however, any rule requiring that the mechanisms of power which emerge in the course of the revolutionary process must take despotic forms? This question was considered many times in connection with the dramatic disappointments of twentieth-century revolutions, and particularly the Russian revolution. It does not seem, however, that there is any answer that is unequivocally true in all circumstances. The October upheaval in Russia was not, as we know, directed against tsarism, which had been out of existence for eight months, but against the only government in Russian history which, though not elected, had the right to claim that it represented the majority of society, and which, although weak and not in control of the situation, had begun the process of building democratic institutions. That government emerged from the February revolution, from the disintegration of the ruling apparatus and the army. If the Bolsheviks achieved success and prevented the building of democracy in Russia, this was not only because they were better organized and were determined to take power by violence; it was also thanks to a series of fortunate (for them) accidents. In the course of a few years, they created institutions which, in their despotic features, significantly outstripped tsarist rule in its last decades.

On the other hand, if the events in Portugal in 1975 can be termed a revolution, they exemplify how, in a favorable external environment and with a sufficiently strong democratic movement, the revolutionary process may lead to the replacement of despotic mechanisms—already seriously weakened by internal corrosion—by representative ones. The Portuguese Communists clearly counted on being able, with Soviet help, to use the collapse of the Portuguese version of fascism for the establishment of their own dictatorship. This was not a completely vain hope, and could have been realized in more propitious international conditions.

We may say that if democratic mechanisms, though weak and badly functioning, are destroyed by the revolutionary sickness, there is no chance that they will be replaced by more effective democratic mechanisms (unless described as "revolutionary democratic institutions"). In despotic systems of government, the outcomes of revolutionary change may be various, depending on international conditions and on the strength of social movements interested not just in the seizure of power but in building representative democratic institutions.

In other words, the results of revolutionary upheavals depend partly on the relative strength of the different ideologies taking part on those upheavals. Ideologies which simply demand the establishment of a representative legal order and are ready to use the revolutionary breakdown for the destruction of oppressive forms of authority obviously increase the chance that one form of despotism will not be replaced by another, perhaps more savage, form. If, however, the dominant ideologies are utopian-revolutionary in the strict sense of the word, this means that "revolution" is seen as an apocalyptic solution to all people's problems, a complete beginning, a secular second coming, or the stirring of the cosmic Christmas tree from which the true star of Bethlehem fell to earth.

Revolutionary ideologies in this sense form a social phenomenon *sui generis*, a degenerate lay form of the religious messianism that has existed for a long time in at least three of the great religions of humanity: Judaism, Christianity, and Mahayana Buddhism (it has even been suggested—though not proven—that the idea of the second coming of Buddha to Earth emerged in southern India in the first century under the influence of Judaeo-Christian messianism). The idea of revolution as Apocalypse, as a route to the ultimate State, is radically different from the Enlightenment philosophy of progress. Belief in progress means hope for a better world, which will emerge from the present world as its continuation, by the growth of education, common sense, moral improvement, and technical development. *Progress* means continuity, the accumulation of achievements, improvement. Revolutionary messianism, on the contrary, feeds on the hope of a radical discontinuity in history, a break that opens the door to the New Time. The expectation of a New Time, of complete regeneration, is in fact the root of the revolutionary mentality; it is a belief that mankind can, as it were, free itself from all the burdens built up in its biological and social being over centuries, that it can wash away the sins of the past in the shock of a bloody revolutionary baptism, and begin everything anew from year one.

But how does this come about? Messianic hopes from the beginning of our era have counted on intervention from beyond the human world: the new calendar was to be initiated by a divine messenger, and the task of every person individually was penance and expectation. But it is a different story, if it is known that the Messiah is among us, incarnate in one sect, race, class, or party, which is the fortunate possessor of the truth. At this time the messianic technique must be ready. This technique can rely only on destruction, for, by definition, the New Time cannot be planned under conditions ruled by the devil. Apocalyptic action can accordingly rely only on total destruction.

Mirabeau has already managed to perceive that after every revolution, people immediately appear who proclaim the need for the next revolution, this time the final and conclusive one. In the nature of things, it cannot be otherwise. Every revolution needs social energies, which only broadly exaggerated expectations can mobilize, and in every revolution these hopes must be disproportionately great in relation to the outcome; every revolution thus unavoidably creates a great mass of disappointments. But after revolutions in which apocalyptic ideologies have played a significant role, after revolutions which can be described as dreams of the Eschaton, the disappointments are naturally enormous: they can, however, be survived if the messianic dream is not abandoned, and current facts are simply evaluated differently: This was not yet the "true" revolution; another one is needed which is certain to be the ultimate one. Similarly, millenaristic sects calculated the moment of the Second Coming to the day, and when the day passed without the great event, the sects reached the bitter conclusion that their calculations were mistaken, but they did not abandon the principle on which the expectation was based.

Hope in a New Time, an Absolute Beginning, or Total Youth is, it seems, a permanent and never completely extinguished form of human spiritual life. There is little reason to suppose that this hope could ever be removed from our culture, nor even that this would be desirable. It is a thirst for the annulment of the past. The revolutionary fantasies of modern times are the historical embodiment of this hope. Its original form is religious eschatology, where belief in a New Time, that is, salvation, included absolution from the faults, errors, and sins of the former age.

Hope in the New Time is resistant to rational arguments; in its typical form it is not a theory or an intellectual position, but a spiritual passion. Religious eschatology has no need of a rational basis; it relies not on forecasting and theory but on trust in a promise that was given to people at the beginning of time; that promise sustains their faith that the past can be as if erased in a moral sense, that the chain of evil and suffering can be radically broken.

Secular revolutionary eschatologies are versions of that same belief, distorted by two factors. They represent their hopes first as convictions resting on rational premises, which can be done only in bad faith. Secondly, because salvation has to be collective and because it must be brought about by means of special social techniques, the obliteration of the past must have a political rather than a moral character, which means that the Apocalypse consists in the destruction of culture, and in its perfect form is directed towards plunging all the inherited stock of culture into oblivion. The destruction of the past was not equally successful and consistent in all revolutions, and the ideological premises of this destruction were not expressed equally clearly in all of them. From the current perspective, the Russian revolution must pass for a relatively restrained and inconsequential version of the cultural apocalypse. A large proportion of the prerevolutionary intelligentsia were either exterminated or compelled to emigrate; the falsification of history became a daily routine; religious tradition fell victim to unrelenting repression; literature, philosophy and the arts were impoverished and stunted as a result of persecution, massacres and restrictions. Despite everything, the extermination and persecution were not sufficiently effective to break the continuity of culture completely. The radical idea of the complete destruction of inherited culture (*Prolekult*) was never the official policy of the authorities; it appeared that with even a slight loosening of political repression, Russia was able to produce new cultural energies, to demonstrate that it had not broken the ties with its past and had withstood the splendors of the New Time.

The Chinese apocalypse was significantly more radical, particularly in the period of the so-called cultural revolution. Not only were the destruction of the past, of inherited art, philosophy, religion, and science, and the destruction of schools and universities carried out much more consistently, but the family was also destroyed much more systematically and effectively as the social life form most resistant to nationalization. The revolutionary ideology of Maoism also expressed the tasks of the New Time significantly better and more distinctly: the complete erasure of cultural continuity and the molding of the New Man in a cultural desert. We cannot judge at this stage to what extent this work was a success and to what extent the Chinese have succeeded in preserving, despite terrible devastation, the capacity for spiritual regeneration; it seems, however, that there too the attempt to create a Complete Beginning has not been wholly successful.

The closest to the ideal—so far—has been the revolution in Cambodia (I mean the last liberation but one). Preparation for the New Time, the destruction of the old society, knew no limits. Towns, schools, the family, religion, all forms of social life, all resources of civilization lay in ruins: the new rulers rightly believed that the New Man, to be truly new, should not have the slightest connection with earlier cultural forms. In practice this meant that it was necessary to slaughter all literates and to shut up the remaining population as slaves in concentration camps. This task was successful to a significant extent: mass exterminations and systematic destruction turned the country into a wasteland; the foundations of the New Time were laid.

One thing could not be achieved, even in Cambodia, because the appropriate mechanism has not yet been developed: it was not possible to unteach people their language. A consistent destruction of history would also have required people to stop knowing their ancestral language, which itself carries the cultural tradition, imposes a certain structure of thought and thus limits the possibilities of creating the New Man, and it includes words and grammatical forms that the New Man should not know. The perfect revolution presupposes a perfect cultural desert; a method should thus be found of making people revert to a prelinguistic state.

The Youth of Mankind: troglodyte; anthropopithecus. Total liberation: a cage.

Apart from this still unsolved difficulty, it seems that the revolution in Cambodia has achieved the best result of all so far. On the basis of its history, it has been possible to define Total Revolution, the New Time, and the New Man significantly more precisely than at any earlier time: genocide, slavery, and bestiality. The apocalypse was almost perfected, the revolutionary idea was almost made flesh. The idea of returning to the Absolute Beginning, to beautiful youth, separated from its religious basis, materialized as best it could.

Chapter Nineteen

How to Be a Conservative-Liberal-Socialist

A Credo

Motto: "Please step forward to the rear!" This is an approximate translation of a request I once heard in a tram-car in Warsaw. I propose it as a slogan for the mighty International that will never exist.

A Conservative Believes:

1. That in human life there never have been and never will be improvements that are not paid for with deteriorations and evils; thus, in considering each project of reform and amelioration, its price has to be assessed. Put another way, innumerable evils are compatible (i.e., we can suffer them comprehensively and simultaneously); but many goods limit or cancel each other, and therefore we will never enjoy them fully at the same time. A society in which there is no equality and no liberty of any kind is perfectly possible, yet a social order combining total equality and freedom is not. The same applies to the compatibility of planning and the principle of autonomy, to security and technical progress. Put yet another way, there is no happy ending in human history.

2. That we do not know the extent to which various traditional forms of social life—family, rituals, nation, religious communities—are indispensable if life in a society is to be tolerable or even possible. There are no grounds for believing that when we destroy these forms, or brand them as irrational, we increase the chance of happiness, peace, security, or freedom. We have no certain knowledge of what might occur if, for example, the monogamous family was abrogated, or if the time-honored custom of burying the dead were to give way to the rational recycling of corpses for industrial purposes. But we would do well to expect the worst.

3. That the *idée fixe* of the Enlightenment—that envy, vanity, greed, and aggression are all caused by the deficiencies of social institutions and that they will be swept away once these institutions are reformed—is

Reprinted by permission of the publisher from *Encounter* (October 1978), with revisions by the author. Copyright © 1978 by Encounter, Ltd.

not only utterly incredible and contrary to all experience, but is highly dangerous. How on earth did all these institutions arise if they were so contrary to the true nature of man? To hope that we can institutionalize brotherhood, love, and altruism is already to have a reliable blueprint for despotism.

A Liberal Believes:

1. That the ancient idea that the purpose of the State is security still remains valid. It remains valid even if the notion of "security" is expanded to include not only the protection of persons and property by means of the law, but also various provisions of insurance: that people should not starve if they are jobless; that the poor should not be condemned to die through lack of medical help; that children should have free access to education—all these are also part of security. Yet security should never be confused with liberty. The State does not guarantee freedom by action and by regulating various areas of life, but by doing nothing. In fact security can be expanded only at the expense of liberty. In any event, to make people happy is not the function of the State.

2. That human communities are threatened not only by stagnation but also by degradation when they are so organized that there is no longer room for individual initiative and inventiveness. The collective suicide of mankind is conceivable, but a permanent human ant-heap is not, for the simple reason that we are not ants.

3. That it is highly improbable that a society in which all forms of competitiveness have been done away with would continue to have the necessary stimuli for creativity and progress. More equality is not an end in itself, but only a means. In other words, there is no point to the struggle for more equality if it results only in the leveling down of those who are better off, and not in the raising up of the underprivileged. Perfect equality is a self-defeating ideal.

A Socialist Believes:

1. That societies in which the pursuit of profit is the sole regulator of the productive system are threatened with as grievous—perhaps more grievous—catastrophes as are societies in which the profit motive has been entirely eliminated from the production-regulating forces. There are good reasons why freedom of economic activity should be limited for the sake of security, and why money should not automatically produce more money. But the limitation of freedom should be called precisely that, and should

not be called a higher form of freedom.

2. That it is absurd and hypocritical to conclude that, simply because a perfect, conflictless society is impossible, every existing form of inequality is inevitable and all ways of profit-making justified. The kind of conservative anthropological pessimism which led to the astonishing belief that a progressive income tax was an inhuman abomination is just as suspect as the kind of historical optimism on which the Gulag Archipelago was based.

3. That the tendency to subject the economy to important social controls should be encouraged, even though the price to be paid is an increase in bureaucracy. Such controls, however, must be exercised within representative democracy. Thus it is essential to plan institutions that counteract the menace to freedom which is produced by the growth of these very controls.

□

So far as I can see, this set of regulative ideas is not self-contradictory. And therefore it is possible to be a conservative-liberal-socialist. This is equivalent to saying that those three particular designations are no longer mutually exclusive options.

As for the great and powerful International which I mentioned at the outset—it will never exist, because it cannot promise people that they will be happy.

PART FOUR

On Scientific Theories

Chapter Twenty
Why an Ideology Is Always Right

In this paper I shall leave aside the various proposals about how the word *ideology* should be employed. Rather, I shall try to pick up its meaning as it looms up from everyday use and from journalistic (rather than sociological) habits and ask whether this use identifies a separate phenomenon. It is easily noted that in everyday speech the meaning of the word 'ideology' is restricted when compared to what most of sociological tradition, starting with Marx, would recommend. In common usage we do not normally apply the word to religious beliefs: we do not speak of, for example, "baptist ideology," and if "Islamic ideology" seems to us admissible, this is because we think of it as a peculiar political rather than religious entity. Nor does the word sound appropriate when it refers to particular doctrines or utopias having no significant social appeal. Philosophical creeds, when limited to specialists' circles, are not typically being spoken of as ideologies except when we wish to stress our disparaging opinion; to say, "Positivism is an ideology" suggests that, far from matching up to its scientific claims, positivist philosophy involves arbitrary value judgments.

The custom of ordinary language increasingly tends to reserve the word to systems of ideas displaying the following characteristics:

1. They express and articulate goals and principles of mass movements/political organisms or of movements aspiring to a mass following.

2. They provide these movements or organizations with justifications for their claims to power—already kept or longed for; more often than not the target is power that will be shared with no one else.

3. They assert and supply all the dynamic, aggressive, and violent aspects of these movements or organizations (including states) with doctrinal forms.

Reprinted by permission of the publisher from M. Cranston and P. Mair, eds., *Ideology and Politics* (Alphen aan den Rijn: Sijthoff Publishers, 1980), with revisions by the author.

4. They tend, with changing degrees of consistency, to achieve a complete or "global" character. In other words, they purport to offer solutions not only to particular social issues or particular grievances, but to all the important questions of human life, including religious or metaphysical ones; that is, they purport to be all-embracing *Weltanschauungen*.

Briefly, what common usage tends to imply most frequently is that the social function of ideologies is to furnish an existing power system (or aspirations to power) a legitimacy based on the possession of absolute and all-encompassing truth.

As such, the typical examples of ideologies so conceived are the doctrinal aspects of such movements as Communism (in all its variants), Nazism, Fascism, Pan-Arabism, Zionism, and various aggressive nationalist or racial activities, as well as imperial or imperialist ideas, whether or not they are based on an appeal to ethnic bonds. Conversely, the noun seems less fitting when associated with adjectives like 'liberal', 'pacifist' and 'conservative.'

Of course the question is not which meaning—broad or restricted—is more proper; any meaning can be suitable if it is reasonably well clarified. Rather the point is to ask whether the narrow meaning grasps a phenomenon that deserves separate attention not only in today's political terms, but also in the taxonomy of ideas. And if it does, it is proper to ask how far we can justify the frequent analogies with religious movements and ideas. This distinction seems to me of importance, and in my subsequent remarks I will try to explain why the popular opinion which either equates ideology with religion or sees the former as "substitute" for, or a "modern version" of the latter might be true only in a strongly qualified sense. However, I focus my attention on only one side of this distinction: on the "epistemological" aspect of ideology. While it is plausible to argue that ideologies produce some cognitive rules of their own or some manners of perception and that these rules to a certain extent are similar to those typical of religious life, nevertheless they are distinct in other aspects. Thus I will stress this distinction without denying the obvious fact that various religious movements have played or do play an eminently political function, and that many hybrid forms mix up traditional religious tenets with aggressive political aspirations.

What is common to both ideological and religious belief systems is that they both purport to impose an a priori meaning on all aspects of human life and on all contingent events, and that they are both built in such a way that no imaginable, let alone real, facts could refute the established doctrine. I refer here to the classic Popperian frame of interpretation. Religious and ideological doctrines are both immune to empirical falsifications, and they are able to absorb all the facts while surviving intact. If I strongly believe in the eye of Providence watching over all the details of my life, I do not need to fear that any event could throw doubt on the omnipresence of the divine wisdom. Whatever happens to me will fit into the framework: if fate favors me, it displays God's benevolence and is to be seen as a reward, an encouragement, or an act of grace. If it turns against my aspirations and frustrates my hopes, the same Providence is certainly at work: all the adversities have to be explained as punishment or warning; human life being unavoidably ambiguous, there is no moment in my life when I would not deserve to be both rewarded and chastised, when both mercy and justice would not be justly applied to me. Thus it is certain in advance that whatever happens, happens rightly and confirms God's infallible wisdom, the details of which in any case escape my limited understanding.

It seems at first glance that ideologies enjoy the same privilege of immunity to facts and the same proficiency in absorbing them, since the frame of meaning they give to human destiny is as unfalsifiable as the meaningful order of the world in the believer's perception. If I decide that the whole of history consists of acts of class struggle and that all human aspirations and actions are to be explained in terms of this struggle, then there is no way in which this principle could be conceivably refuted. Since everything in the empirical world is connected in one way or the other, once we state that class interests comprise all the aspects of social life, there is no need to stretch one's imagination excessively to find confirmation of the Marxist philosophy of history in every possible event. Once a certain society is defined as "capitalist" and thereby *ex definitione* ruled by the bourgeoisie, no conceivable actions of the government can fail to validate this verdict. If for any reason the life of the country is deteriorating in some aspects, the doctrine is borne out: the exploiters are oppressing the toiling masses in order to seek profit; if, on the contrary, everything is clearly improving, and workers' living standards increase, the docrine's truth is as well proven: the exploiters, terrified by the prospects of revolution, try to bribe the toiling masses in order to put them to sleep. If the government is liberal in sexual matters and tolerant of pornography, it clearly wants to divert the workers' attention from burning social issues and to channel the interests of the masses in a harmless direction; if, on the contrary, it is more or less puritanical and curbs pornography, it oppresses the movement toward liberation and prevents people from wasting energy which might otherwise be used to generate profit. Once you are classified as the devil, you cannot behave in any way that would fail to corroborate this assessment. Needless to say, once you decide that world history is defined by the struggle between Jews and Aryans, your interpretation will be as infallibly verified by all the facts as is the theory that whatever people do is 'ultimately' reducible to class interest, or the theory that all events, both natural and human-caused, reveal the divine guidance of the universe. The intellectual attraction of an ideology with universalistic pretensions is precisely that it is so easy. Once you learn it, which you can always do in no time and with no effort, everything is given sense and you are the happy owner of a key that unlocks all the secrets of the world.

This analogy, though, provides only half the story. Religious beliefs do not normally need to present themselves as rational hypotheses carrying explanatory value for empirical facts, as is required for scientific hypotheses. To be sure, attempts to rationalize religious beliefs and to convert faith into a sort of knowledge are not exceptional in the history of theology. Yet in the dominant form of religious self-understanding, there is no demand for such a legitimacy. The act of belonging to a community that identifies itself by the primordial revelation normally holds priority over the intellectual enlightenment that most religions claim to offer. The faith is interpreted as, and effectively is, a condition of a world view within which empirical facts appear as so many manifestations of the hidden spiritual meaning; in other words, the principle *credo ut intelligam* is usually included in the way in which the believers see their own act of believing. This is not the case with ideologies. These live on bad faith in that they pretend to offer an explanation of the world in the very acts of bigotry and fanaticism. They want the facts to confirm them in the same way that scientific hypotheses are confirmed, being thereby compelled to distort and conceal unfavorable facts. They are supposed to possess absolute truth and to be testable at the same time. While religions have often had recourse to lying, this is not an inherent part of their cognitive status, since their content is essentially unverifiable; ideologies, on the other hand, carry a built-in necessity of lying and cannot survive otherwise. Unlike religions, ideologies are not beyond science; they are positively antiscientific.

Thus the prowess of each in absorbing all the possible facts is different. Ideologies are not only bound to devise techniques of lying, but when the facts cannot be concealed, they also need a special psychological technique that prevents believers from seeing these facts, or shapes a peculiar form of double consciousness within which facts may be not only dismissed as irrelevant but also actually denied.

A friend of mine told me the story of his daughter, then three or four years old, racing with another girl in a park. The girl who ran slower always shouted loudly from her position of defeat, "I run faster, I run faster!" After a while the girl who was ahead burst into tears and rushed to her mother, crying, "I do not want her to run faster than me!" This is a simple example of how the human mind can be blinded to the most obvious facts when subject to noisy propaganda—even to the person's own disfavor. In short, wishful thinking is not the only mechanism of cognitive distortion. However, ideologies must have at their disposal a slightly more complicated mechanism that involves a specific concept of truth, and its task is to confuse or even to abolish the distinction between factual statements and assertions about the "essence" of things.

To be sure, an analogy with religious cognition might again be suggested at this point, yet once more it turns out to be misleading. In religious cognition the descriptive and normative contents are not separated; rather they are perceived in one single act of belief. And since God's authority confers validity to both, there is no reason why they should be valid in two different senses, as is the case with "secular" knowledge. Yet in ideologies, the distinction between normative and factual utterances is blurred in such a fashion that ostensibly descriptive judgments disguise normative rules which the believers are supposed to accept in their descriptive meanings.

Examples of how this confusion operates can be taken from many well-known sources. Communist ideology, however, or rather the ideology of the Communist State, is more suitable than any other, since it has achieved an unsurpassed degree of codification and displays an impressive consistency in its self-contradictory character.

Let us take a most unsophisticated example. When a priest says, "A Christian does not steal," he is simply saying that a Christian ought not to steal and that whoever steals is not a good Christian. In other words, he is offering a normative definition of a respectable Christian. Meanwhile, when we read in a Soviet catechism that "A Soviet man does not steal," the meaning of this saying is much richer. It might seem a common precept grammatically expressed, as is often the case, in the indicative mood. Yet it is not supposed to be simply precept. It tells us something about the essence of the Soviet man as he "really" is, as well as about real people who actually embody this essence. A believer is expected to take for granted not only that nonstealing is part of the "essence" of Soviet man as normatively defined, but also that Soviet people do not actually steal. The task of education consists in molding human minds in such a way that people are prevented from seeing what they do see, that is, universal stealing as an inherent and necessary element of everyday life, and that they really are ready to admit that theft, if it occurs at all, is an insignificant marginal phenomenon hardly worth mentioning. Thus the virtue of ideology is not only that it produces verbal hybrids that mix up facts, commandments, and assertions about the "essence," but also that it makes it possible to infer facts from commandments, to deduce what is from what ought to be, and that, if efficient, it produces people capable of performing precisely the miraculous transubstantiation involved in seeing facts as prescribed by norms.

Certainly we have now left behind the period when this ideology worked efficiently, and when people actually acquired this talent of believing a doctrine which each day was unmistakably and glaringly disproved in all its details by all the common facts of daily life. That ideology was able to achieve this perfection—even for a certain historical period—gives testimony to its independent power in social life.

Ilya Erenburg's "The Thaw" depicts a discussion meeting where people criticize a certain Soviet novel. One of the characters objects to the untruth of an extramarital love story in the novel, and seems to believe sincerely that the book is false in the sense of portraying un-Soviet conduct (a Soviet man does not have extramarital affairs) until, a moment later, after the meeting, he suddenly realizes that he himself is in exactly the same situation in his real life. This is precisely the moment of "thaw," the melting of the ideology. Once people become aware that the ideology they have been professing is contrary to obvious facts, it ceases to be an ideology. Rather, it is converted simply into a lie. While still repeated, taught, and obeyed under coercion, nevertheless an ideology that is perceived and known as mendacious has lost its natural ability to produce double consciousness.

Leninist-Stalinist Marxism expressly justified, at least to a certain extent, the curious epistemology of this apparently impossible phenomenon—sincere mendaciousness. Lukács, among others, was its codifier. The relevant part of his theory states that truth can be seen only from the particular standpoint of the progressive class, the proletariat; that the proletariat's superior wisdom is stored in the Communist party (and not, of course, in what any empirical proletariat thinks or believes); and that this wisdom emerges in acts of practical commitment rather than in "contemplative" investigation. Thus what produces truth is the political action of the Communist party. In other words, by definition, the party is never wrong, since it is the only mechanism generating the criteria of cognitive validity. Facts are helpless when confronted with the "totality" as perceived from this privileged standpoint (or rather praxis-point). Lukács even repeated in this connection, at least once, the Fichtean saying, "The worse to the facts," and he meant it.

This theory of knowledge, in which the all-engulfing "praxis" replaces and ousts all intellectual (and moral) criteria, was applied in a somewhat less sophisticated way in communist political consciousness. It became a psychological device which made it possible to obscure or even to abrogate the distinction between what is politically expedient to say and what is true in the ordinary sense. This distinction is admitted as a matter of course in political activities, and indeed in everyday life, and to cancel it appears quite an achievement. Yet communist ideology seems to have produced this result fairly efficiently, albeit only for a certain period. It turned out that strongly committed people were able to believe in lies they themselves had created or helped to create. It was possible that some political leaders fabricated politically useful dogmas, obviously contrary to their experience, and that they somehow believed them to be true.

It is no doubt a long way from the Marxian concept of ideology to the manner in which progressive and scientific ideology actually worked in the communist states. Long as it might have been, such a route is not very twisted however, and it can be retraced. In Marx's vocabulary, *ideology*, or false consciousness, was defined not by its falsity in the ordinary sense but by the fact that the believers were incapable of realizing that their thinking was determined by social, rather than logical, forces. In other words, both the producers and the consumers of ideological commodities fell prey to a delusion concerning the real motivations and causes of their beliefs. They imagined themselves as rational beings guided by intellectual criteria in accepting or rejecting various ingredients of their worldview, and meanwhile they unconsciously followed the vested interests of the class with which they identified themselves.

Liberation from ideological self-mystification consists, correspondingly, not in restoring the full vigor of intellectual criteria independent of social values—as such criteria are themselves figments of false consciousness—but in realizing the real motive forces behind one's own thinking. However this cannot be done within the consciousness of privileged classes since such consciousness is inevitably compelled to disguise itself from itself: people cannot produce universal, religious, metaphysical, social, or scientific ideas and at the same time be well aware of the fact that these ideas are just devices to perpetuate their privileges. Having no privileges to defend, the proletariat can not only get rid of all these self-deceiving instruments, but indeed it cannot successfully defend its own particular interest without having actually shed them.

In other words, Lukács did not need to tamper excessively with Marx's legacy to obtain his miraculous result: the truth of Marxism is not to be measured by "external" criteria as laid down by scientistic philosophy but by the fact that this doctrine expresses the movement of the proletariat, which alone is able to grasp the "totality" of the society (this ability in its turn being established on the basis of Marxist analysis). That the proletariat is possessor of truth *de iure naturali* we learn from Marxist theory, and that Marxist theory is true we know from the fact that it embodies the class consciousness of the proletariat. This admirable reasoning is applicable only if we add that the truth reveals itself not from the purely theoretical standpoint, but within political "praxis," which amounts to saying that political commitment generates truth. Since the consciousness of the proletariat, as we otherwise know from the Leninist doctrine, achieves its genuine shape only in the party ideology, the Communist Party reaches the enviable position of being par excellence the bearer of truth.

This, needless to say, is not the way in which politicians or simple believers express their ideological self-assurance; this is rather the implicit epistemological background to their almost spontaneous manner of mental behavior. In no other ideology, to my knowledge, has this ingenious contrivance been made so explicit and its rules set up with so much clarity by theorists as in the case of communist doctrine. The resultant inability to distinguish the truth in common sense from political expediency and the ability to discard all empirical facts as irrelevant to one's own cognitive superiority are both perfectly validated within this self-supporting ideology.

It should be added, nonetheless, that I have tried to describe the ideology in its perfect schizophrenic form as achieved within the Stalinist world. Since then we have observed an increasing deterioration of the ideological efficiency of communism. The basic material component might have remained untouched, as might the aspirations to administer the people's world perception. These aspirations cannot be satisfied, however, at least not in those European countries which are under communist power. However indispensable as a principle of legitimacy, the ideology is almost universally perceived as being simply mendacious; moreover the long habit of completely discarding empirical evidence and of assuming that anything, no matter how absurd, can be believed by ideologically trained people has made the ideology extremely clumsy and incapable of coping with the new situation. Meanwhile the ideology, which is simply imposed by coercion and which is clearly seen as a mere lie by the consumers, has lost the cognitive status of an ideology. In this qualified sense we may speak of the "end of ideology" in the communist world.

Chapter Twenty-one

The General Theory of Not-Gardening

A Major Contribution to Social Anthropology, Ontology, Moral Philosophy, Psychology, Sociology, Political Theory, and Many Other Fields of Scientific Investigation

Those who hate gardening need a theory. Not to garden without a theory is a shallow, unworthy way of life.

A theory must be convincing and scientific. Yet to various people, various theories are convincing and scientific. Therefore we need a number of theories.

The alternative to not-gardening without a theory is to garden. However, it is much easier to have a theory than actually to garden.

Marxist Theory

Capitalists try to corrupt the minds of the toiling masses and to poison them with their reactionary "values." They want to "convince" workers that gardening is a great "pleasure" and thereby to keep them busy in their leisure time and to prevent them from making the proletarian revolution. Besides, they want to make them believe that with their miserable plot of land they are really "owners" and not wage-earners, and so to win them over to the side of the owners in the class struggle. To garden is therefore to participate in the great plot aiming at the ideological deception of the masses. Do not garden! Q.E.D.

Psychoanalytical Theory

Fondness for gardening is a typically English quality. It is easy to see why this is so. England was the first country of the industrial revolution. The industrial revolution killed the natural environment. Nature is the symbol of Mother. By killing Nature, the English people committed matricide. They are subconsciously haunted by the feeling of guilt and they try to

Reprinted by permission of the publisher from the *Journal of the Anthropological Society of Oxford*, 16, no. 1 (Hilary Term, 1985).

expatiate their crime by cultivating and worshipping their small, pseudo-natural gardens. To garden is to take part in this gigantic self-deception which perpetuates the childish myth. You must not garden. Q.E.D.

Existentialist Theory

People garden in order to make nature human, to "civilize" it. This, however, is a desperate and futile attempt to transform being-in-itself into being-for-itself. This is not only ontologically impossible; it is a deceptive, morally inadmissible escape from reality, as the distinction between being-in-itself and being-for-itself cannot be abolished. To garden, or to imagine that one can "humanize" Nature, is to try to efface this distinction and hopelessly to deny one's own irreducibly human ontological status. To garden is to live in bad faith. Gardening is wrong. Q.E.D.

Structuralist Theory

In primitive societies life was divided into the pair of opposites work/leisure, which corresponded to the distinction field/house. People worked in the field and rested at home. In modern societies the axis of opposition has been reversed: people work in houses (factories, offices) and rest in the open (gardens, parks, forests, rivers, etc.). This distinction is crucial in maintaining the conceptual framework whereby people structure their lives. To garden is to confuse the distinction between house and field, between leisure and work; it is to blur, indeed to destroy, the oppositional structure which is the condition of thinking. Gardening is a blunder. Q.E.D.

Analytical Philosophy

In spite of many attempts, no satisfactory definition of *garden* and of *gardening* has been found; all existing definitions leave a large area of uncertainty about what belongs where. We simply do not know what exactly a garden and gardening are. To use these concepts is therefore intellectually irresponsible, and actually to garden would be even more so. Thou shalt not garden. Q.E.D.

Chapter Twenty-two

Fabula mundi and Cleopatra's Nose

Thesis: that no explanatory method exists in the study of the history of philosophy.

Was Schiller the first to remark, in his famous speech of 1789, that our image of the past is a projection of the present? I am not sure. Wherever responsibility for its first utterance lies, the idea itself, since then a thousand times repeated and rediscovered, has, thanks in great part to existential philosophy, become so trivialized that a certain amount of effort is required if one is not to succumb to it entirely. And yet to believe in it entirely is not only to grant, along with Schiller, that the significance of events in times past is measured by what we take to be their importance in forming our own world; that they take on meaning only when seen within the framework of a certain teleological order which we impose upon historical processes and which does not become apparent from a simple examination of facts. It is also to believe that what we call a *fact*, or an *event*, is no more than an arbitrary construction, and consequently that the distinction between truth and falsehood becomes blurred: any construction, any selection, any "structure" (for it is "structures" that define facts, not the other way around), is as valid and as good as any other. As a result, history, in the ordinary sense of the word—the primitive, common, pretheoretical sense—becomes either impossible or useless. Such a concept of history is extremely attractive: it frees us from the "fetish of facts" and from the obligation to learn, and leaves the facts to the poor craftsman of historical studies—the archaeologist, the paleographer, the librarian, the amateurs of numismatics, sphragistics, and genealogy.

However, a distinction suggests itself between the claim that the past can be understood only by a projection of the present and the theory whereby the significance of the present becomes apparent in the light of an artificially

Translated from the French by Agnieszka Kolakowska from *"Fabula mundi* et le nez de Cleopatre," *Revue Internationale de Philosophie* 3, nos. 1–2 (1975). Revised by the author in English.

constructed past. The first is a pragmatist view; the second, a Cartesian one. According to the first, it is the present that makes sense of the past, thereby also, inevitably, making it into a work of art; according to the second, it is the past—but an artificial past, a *fabula mundi*—that gives meaning to the present. If we accept the first claim, our knowledge of the past will be useful to us only insofar as it can be incorporated into a coherent whole.

If we accept the second, our knowledge of the past is of no value to us at all, for the point is not to understand the past but rather to construct a genesis that will explain the present state of things: whether that genesis is real or totally invented is of no consequence. All the theories of the natural state—some less consciously than others, and some quite consciously indeed—draw upon this artificial "historicity." There it is in Puffendorf's vision of the genesis of society; in Descarte's reconstruction of the genesis of the solar system; in Husserl's reconstruction of the genesis of geometry. It is a *fabula mundi*. And again, history in the ordinary sense of the word becomes, if not impossible, superfluous. And again we are freed from the fetish of facts.

A minimum of skepticism, it would seem, suffices to provide ample arguments in favor of the theory that the comprehensibility, indeed the very continuity, of historical processes comes about solely through "categories" previously adopted and established, and that there can be no logical validity in a move from "facts" (assuming that they exist) to a "global" description of the course of events. There is good reason to suppose that no kind of order can emerge from a simple cumulation of knowledge unless such an order has been previously constructed; purely empirical history, perfectly free from all arbitrary reconstruction, leaves us only with Cleopatra's nose[1]—a succession of events in which, although causality may be present, continuity is lacking, since no analysis of the "whole" can do away with the haphazardness of individual events or endow them with meaning.

Everything that applies to the history of nations, wars, revolutions, customs, and beliefs applies also, a fortiori, to the history of ideas and philosophy. The author of the remark about Cleopatra's nose was a kind of Cleopatra's nose himself: a philosophical and religious genius, a point of discontinuity, an unpredictable break in cultural history. After the event, everything can no doubt be explained away quite simply, and in ten different ways; Pascal and Euclid, Galileo and Sophocles, can all be equally well disposed of. There will always be a number of social "interests," or needs,

1. Pascal's famous dictum: if Cleopatra had had a shorter nose, the whole face of earth would have changed.

crying out for fulfillment and invariably finding satisfactory responses in the form of outstanding individuals and geniuses who perfectly fit the requirements. All that was needed, around 300 B.C. in Alexandria, was for someone to come along and write the *Elements,* just as, in the late fifties in seventeenth-century France, someone had to be found to write the *Pensées* (and without being able to finish them, at that); and lo and behold, along comes a volunteer to carry out the task. But how do we know that France needed a Pascal, or that the age of Ptolemy I was waiting for a Euclid? Simple: the proof that such a need really existed lies in the fact that both these men did indeed write what they did.

Accordingly, once we decide that everything is explicable, everything is indeed explicable. My late friend Lucien Goldmann displayed admirable ingenuity in linking up the smallest details of Pascal's *Pensées* with the plight of the French *noblesse de robe* after the Fronde. One would think that he could really write the *Pensées* without reading them, solely on the basis of the historical evidence concerning the class conflicts of the time. And it is here that the crucial point lies. For if there were a reliable method for a historical explanation of culture, we would also be able to use it as a tool for prediction. To be able to explain what has happened is also to be able to predict what has not yet happened, otherwise the word *explain* would not have the meaning normally attributed to it. To believe that we have at our disposal an effective method of explaining a philosophical idea in its entirety, whether it be psychoanalysis or historical materialism or any other explanatory theory in the history of ideas, is to believe that we can reconstruct it solely on the basis of our knowledge of the "factors" which we take to be the cause of its birth and mentally reproduce the same creative process, just as we reproduce an experiment in chemistry. That such a feat is unimaginable is proof, if proof is needed, of the impossibility of a historical explanation of philosophical ideas. It is proof, in other words, that no method of explanation exists.

What we properly call a method should be a sequence of operations which, when applied to the same subject, will give the same or approximately the same results. In the humanities, the identification and collation of sources apart, this is far from being the case. There are methods for establishing with a sufficient degree of certainty the monastery in which a given manuscript was copied or the town in which a given book was printed, but there is no method for explaining new philosophical facts through the psychological or sociological circumstances of their birth, no method that would reveal all the causes which contributed to the creation of the *Metaphysics* or the *Summa Theologica,* the *Ethics* or the *Meditations.* Neither psychoanalysis nor historical materialism nor any of their variants are methods in this sense, for apart from certain generalities, which are of little use, they give varying results when applied to the same subject. All that remains of such methods is contained in the most general guidelines to the effect, for instance, that the way people think is usually influenced by their social relations, the values accepted within their community, their upbringing, or their childhood traumas. Guidelines of this kind, however important, however trivial and true, will never attain a level at which they might aspire to the name of methods.

This is not because of their transitory faults but because of the limitations inherent in any study of cultural phenomena. What we seek when we try to explain one particular creative act in the history of culture is not among those things that can be quantitatively expressed in a historical study, such as demography, prices, production, the size of a book edition, the number of people who saw a certain theatre production, the frequency of certain words, or even the popularity of certain ideals and beliefs; all this is not what we are after. While we might vaguely guess at the forces operating behind that one particular act, the distribution of those forces remains unknown to us. As a result neither explanation nor prediction is possible. But if this is so, it is not because our knowledge is "still" imperfect, but because it is not absolute; in other words, it will always be the same in this respect as it is now. For not only are we unable to calculate those forces, we cannot even frame a question about their distribution in an intelligible way; we find it impossible to imagine that they might one day be reduced to a single quantitative scale. Whoever claims to be able to explain particular phenomena in the history of music, or of the novel, can prove this claim only by writing a novel or a piece of music which does not yet exist but which will be created tomorrow by someone else. And we may safely assume that if ever such a genius does present himself, he will be no other than God omniscient.

These arguments might seem trivial; their conclusion, however, is not quite so trivial, and may be expressed in the proposition put forward at the beginning of this essay—namely, that no explanatory method exists in the study of cultural history.

We are thus led back to the concept of chance. This, it is needless to repeat, is not a concept that explains anything, but its merit lies in the fact that it does not claim to explain anything. It is not a form of explanation, but a well-founded renunciation.

A possible objection might take this form: "We do not presume to explain every last detail, but we can partially explain a large number of facts." This does not hold much water. I am not claiming that nothing can be explained, or that there are no causal connections—far from it. But that is not the point. Many events may be reasonably explained, and the popularity of certain philosophical or religious ideas may often be "reduced" to social circumstances. But the historical development of philosophy is riddled with countless breaking-off points, and each creative act, each creative individual, is such a point. These breaks of continuity, or mutations, these Cleopatra's noses, are like the movements of Epicurus's atoms: at certain points the atoms diverge from the straight line, so that their positions at any given moment cannot be random; yet their course is not predictable. It is useless to say that philosophers don't appear out of nowhere or exist in a void, that they are subject to the influence of their social surroundings and cultural heritage, and so forth. Platitudes of this sort add no more weight to our explanations than the claim that the *clinamen* of the Epicurean atom is situated in a particular place, and not everywhere. This is indeed the case, and yet neither this place nor the atom's previous course can explain its deviation; consequently the overall result at any given moment is the work of chance.

Someone was first to say "cogito," first to utter the words, "Corpus omne perseverat in statu quiescendi," or, "Le premier qui ayant enclos un terrain . . . ," or again, "Der Mensch ist etwas was überwunden sein muss." Whoever would claim that someone had to utter those words should be told, "You will never be able to prove that someone had to do so." How easy indeed to fall prey to the illusion of the past's necessity. The past is irrevocable, and thereby inevitable for us, and we find it difficult to imagine that it might not have been so at a time when it was not yet the past. Because a European culture in which Descartes, Newton, Rousseau, or Nietzsche died in their childhood does not exist—because they are all, to some extent, part of each one of us—their nonexistence is no less inconceivable to us than our own; and no one, without contradicting himself, can imagine his own total absence. This inability of ours to conceive of ourselves as nonexistent emerges when we rationalize it as the belief that the past, that past which we know and which contributed to make us what we are, was always as inevitable as it is today—a belief which rejects chance and is loath to admit that things "might have been different." Here, then, is the reason we strive to unearth trends, rhythms, and regularities in the history of philosophy; and here, by the same token, we find our justification for the claim that one philosopher is the "precursor" of another, as if the sense of a human life could be teleologically determined by something that was yet to come, as if the culture of an age were waiting for someone to appear, striving towards a certain point of culmination, a culmination ultimately embodied in a person of genius: to wit, Fontenelle's "At last Descartes appeared." But a culture does not really develop in this way. Aquinas's *Contra Gentiles* did not lie dormant, as a potentiality, in Aristotle's *Metaphysics*, awaiting its actuality; the works of Marx led no latent existence in Hegel's *Phenomenology;* no Plotinus lurked, germinating, among the pages of Plato, nor did Plotinus carry within his own bosom the invisible embryo of Maimonides. The structure of time is not symmetrical; consequently no one is a precursor, although we are all epigones.

But, having adopted the point of view imposed by the theory of Cleopatra's nose, can we follow it through consistently? There is ample room for doubt. Would Pascal himself have conceded, by analogy with his aphorisms about Cromwell and Cleopatra, that if St. Paul had died before his conversion, the entire history of the world would have taken a different turn? He would surely have recoiled from the suggestion that Christianity, like the Roman wars and the English revolution, belongs to the realm of chance and as such might never have been born. For he believed that, alongside secular history, there is Holy History; and Holy History defies chance by definition. But there is not one among us historians of philosophy who does not have his own little holy history, to wit a certain idea of historical continuity peculiar to him and definable in its rhythm, sense, and direction. If he did not, the historian of philosophy in the modern sense, as opposed to a mere recorder of events, such as Diogenes Laertius, could not exist. History interrupted at every turn by accidents that the intellect is powerless to bring to submission, conceived as a desperate series of explosions bursting forth from a void—such a vision, even if empirically true, is unacceptable, and reason has good cause to rebel against it. We need these little holy histories of ours, for they allow us to erect an ordered structure from a garbage-heap of discontinuous events. Robbed of all continuity and direction, history would be useless; but our culture, in order to exist, must render it useful, must carve out its own identity from its past and assimilate that past, appropriate it as a past endowed with meaning and a continuous identity, so that it resembles the subjective past of a human being.

Thus we have reasons for constructing our own *fabulae mundi* and denying the significance of Cleopatra's nose, or at least reducing its status to that of an "occasional cause." From this we may draw a single, modest moral: We must always retain and remember the distinction between a fact and the *fabula* that engulfs it; we must never permit the thought that facts might be abolished and swept away in some kind of supreme synthesis; we must, in short, call facts and *fabulae* by their true names. And we may further conclude that each *fabula* must bear the traditional caution: *quod tamen potest esse aliter.*

Chapter Twenty-three

Emperor Kennedy Legend
A New Anthropological Debate

This 6684th annual meeting of the Academy of Science provoked a heated controversy. The main paper presented at the meeting dealt with a little-known legend of an Emperor called Kennedy who is said to have ruled two large countries in the remote past B.G.C. (Before the Great Calamity). Dr. Rama, the author of the paper, confronted and scrupulously analyzed all the sources available. This is not, to be sure, a large collection by comparison with, say, the amount of material we have on another ruler, Alphonse XIII, who is said to have governed another country, called Espagna, some time earlier or later, yet Dr. Rama proved that more can be extracted from the existing sources than scholars previously believed.

As is known, after the Great Calamity which occurred in the years 0–72 (approx.) when about two-thirds of the inhabitable land was engulfed by waters and the remainder almost destroyed by huge explosions of unknown origin, only eight books from the preceding period were preserved in full. They are

> John Williams, *Creative Gardening*, Omaha, Nebraska. (Whether Omaha, Nebraska is one or two persons is still a matter of dispute).
>
> Alice Besson, *La vie d'une idiote racontée par elle-même*, Roman. (The book seems to have been produced in a country or locality called Gallimard.)
>
> Laszlo Varga, *Bridge for Beginners*, translated from Hungarian by Peter Harsch, Llandudno, 1966.
>
> Dirk Hoegeveldt, *De arte divinatoria Romanorum*, Lugduni Bat., 1657.
>
> *Annuario telefonico di Ferrara.*

Reprinted by permission of the publisher from *Salmagundi* no. 72 (Fall 1986).

Arno Miller, *Neue Tendenzen in amerikanischen Sozialwissenschaften,* Hoser Verlag Erlangen, 1979.

Dinah Ellberg, *All My Lovers.*

The eighth book is omitted, as it was written in an entirely unknown script apart from one mysterious word, *Nagoya* printed on the second to the last page; according to the best authorities it was probably a magic incantation designed to frighten off the evil spirits coming from a foreign land. None of the books, for that matter, has been deciphered fully, but some fragments, smaller or larger, do exist now in satisfying translations. It must be mentioned that the numbers in books probably refer to years; since nothing is known, however, about the method according to which time was calculated in the B.G.C. era or when their years began, it is impossible properly to date the events. Moreover, it is not known whether people used to calculate time forward or backwards; it is quite possible, many scholars argue, that they marked years by a number corresponding to the lapse of time still remaining to the Great Calamity, so that, for example, the year 1657 was actually three hundred years later, and not earlier, than the year 1957.

The Emperor Kennedy Legend is mentioned only in one of the books just listed, which suggested to some scholars that it had not been widely spread or considered important among the savages. However, in almost two dozen books preserved in fragments, as well as in over a hundred and twenty journals that have been recovered so far, thirteen of them almost intact (among them *Chemical Engineering, Trybuna Ludu, Crosswords for Children*—the latter practically unintelligible—*Il Messaggero,* and *Vuelta*), the legend appears several times, and Dr. Rama, after having thoroughly examined the entire material, provided for the first time a coherent interpretation. The main components of the myth, according to his study, are as follows:

1. President (a title of obscure origin, obviously equivalent to "Emperor") Kennedy ruled simultaneously two big countries called respectively America and USA.

2. He came from a legendary island called Ireland, located in the North; whether this island was identical with another one called Iceland and mentioned in another source has not yet been definitively established; perhaps just a typographic error made two countries of one.

3. He was rich.

4. He fought the rulers of three other kingdoms called Russia, Soviet Union, and Cuba. He defeated them, so it seems, but then was himself

defeated in a battle which took place in the Bay of Pigs. Yet he remained the emperor of both his countries.

5. One of the hostile countries called Berlin (almost certainly another name for Russia) built a huge wall to prevent the Emperor's army from invading it, but the Emperor boldly insulted the enemies from this very wall.

6. He has two brothers; the older was killed before and the younger after the Emperor's death.

7. The Emperor himself was struck by his enemies and died.

8. His widow Jacqueline subsequently married a "millionaire."

Dr. Rama discovered one more, previously unknown item of information of great importance. In half a page preserved from the journal *Ici Paris*, the Emperor is called "un grand coureur des jupes." The only plausible translation of this expression is that he often used "to run in skirts." Since it is documented that skirts were exclusively female garments, it appears clear that the Emperor was an androgynous figure, embodying both male and female characteristics. Dr. Rama corrected as well the mistaken interpretation of the word *millionaire* which until recently was uncritically translated as "rich man." He found a previously neglected comment in a preserved fragment of the *Miami Star* which says, "What is a million nowadays? Peanuts." As the peanut was a very small kind of nut, a *millionaire*, far from being a rich man, is a poor man, a man who owns very little, just a few peanuts. This fits well in Dr. Rama's interpretation.

Dr. Rama happens to be a disciple of the famous scholar Mr. Lévi-Strauss, who produces a special kind of pants used both by male and female humans and who therefore argues that everything can be seen as a structure made of a pair of opposites, so that each term of the pair is meaningless without the other; indeed, if you cut off one leg of pants the remaining leg is meaningless. Dr. Rama, employing this hermeneutic device, offered the following interpretation of the legend.

Emperor Kennedy's myth was an attempt to reconcile, in mythological imagination, basic irreconcilable contradictions of human life. First, there is the opposition of dreams and reality. In one source, America—one of two countries he ruled—is called "the dream of mankind," whereas another source speaks of the "harsh reality of USA," which clearly suggests that USA was considered real. Dream and reality were thus combined in his figure. Secondly, we have the opposition North-South: he came from the North but he ruled the South, as it appears from a remark found in a preserved fragment of a paper which states unambiguously that the "South is in the grip of Kennedy's magic." Since in this period South was hot and North was cold, both conditions being unpleasant, albeit for different reasons, the emperor's figure, it appears, was expected to abolish, by magical means, the bad sides of both North and South.

Scholars have worried a lot about how to explain the mythological sense of the wars which the Emperor had fought, but here, too, Dr. Rama came up with an ingenius interpretation. We remember that the Emperor embodied both male and female characteristics. It seems that he encouraged his subjects to become males (according to the just quoted *Ici Paris*, he made many people "cocus," which means "coq," that is, roosters). In most mythologies the rooster is a phallic symbol, but the defeat, as mentioned, was inflicted on him by pigs, and pigs, too, were a symbol of masculinity ("those male chauvinist pigs"—we read in a fragment preserved from a brochure, "The Unspeakable Martyrdom of American Women"). Thus, a complicated male-female dialectics emerges from the legend: the male-female figure produces males, is defeated by males, and eventually killed, presumably by a woman or on women's order; this last fact has been established by the confrontation of two sources: in one of a few pages preserved from a booklet, "True Facts about the Soviet Union," we read that the "happiness of Soviet women is beyond description," whereas another source—a page from a journal mysteriously called *The Times*—speaks of the "utmost misery of Soviet men"; and so we see that, at least in one of the main hostile countries, women were happy and men unhappy, which suggests that this country was a kind of gynecocracy.

We conclude therefore that the emperor's attempt to overcome the male-female opposition was attacked from both sides—male and female—and ended with the ultimate catastrophe. The legend is to prove that the male-female synthesis is impossible.

The last pair of opposites on which the legend has been built is rich-poor. The emperor was rich but, a source says, he was "a champion of the poor." Clearly, he symbolized an attempt to abrogate the linguistic contrast between wealth and poverty. The fact that he was defeated and that his wife became poor (a wife of a "millionaire") proves that his effort to bring into harmony those two terms of opposition ended in failure.

The deep, pessimistic meaning of the myth is this: the basic contradictions of human life cannot be abolished; any attempt to make them consistent is futile.

Dr. Rama's interpretation, though applauded by many scholars, was by no means universally accepted. The strongest attack was launched by Dr.

Gama, a follower of the famous Dr. Sigmund Fraud who was the founder of another (so-called analo-psychic) school of hermeneutics. Dr. Gama questioned virtually all the points in Dr. Rama's interpretation and the entire framework of Mr. Lévi-Strauss's pants-doctrine. Dr. Fraud's theory says that the only thing people want to do all the time is to copulate, but in order to survive, they compel each other to do other things as well, which makes them unhappy; as a result of this unhappiness some write poems, others commit suicide, still others become political leaders, and so on. "I admit," Dr. Gama said, "that Dr. Rama found some interesting facts which throw new light on the legend; his fantastic interpretation, however, is utterly untenable; new facts confirm clearly, once again, that only the Fraudian theory is capable of explaining the story. The true meaning is indeed transparent to any unprejudiced mind.

"The pig, far from being a symbol of masculinity, symbolized an effeminate male, a *castrato;* it is known that people in those times castrated male pigs which they used subsequently as food. The expression, *those male chauvinist pigs,* far from bearing out Mr. Rama's speculation, fits perfectly in the Fraudian doctrine; the expression is an insult, to be sure, but it means castrated males, males unable to produce offspring. The word *chauvinist* is not yet properly explained, but most likely it is a cognate to *chauve,* meaning 'bald, hairless,' and baldness was another sign of emasculation, whereas hairs stood for male prowess (this can be seen from a sentence in one of the books preserved intact: 'This hairy beast tried to rape me'). The interpretation is thus clear: the emperor was defeated in the land of *castrati* ('pigs') and then he had to run in skirts not because he was an androgynous figure, as Dr. Rama would have it, but because he was clearly half-male; in other words he was almost certainly castrated. He tried indeed to restore masculinity to other males—presumably castrated as well—but he failed. If in one of the hostile countries women were in fact happy and men unhappy, this was probably because in this mythological land men were castrated. Having gotten rid of the source of their penis envy, the women were happy. What other explanation is more plausible? Consequently, the legend is an expression of the universal human fear of castration, and the failure of the emperor symbolizes the fact that castration is irreversible. Once again the theory of Dr. Fraud was confirmed."

This was not the end of the meeting, though. Another scholar, Dr. Ngama, attacked both previous interpretations. Professor Ngama is a disciple of the great Dr. Calamarx; the latter's theory states that there are poor people and rich people, and they fight against each other. In the course of their struggle they invent various mythologies; the mythologies of the rich were to convince everybody that the rich should remain rich and the poor must stay poor, whereas the mythologies of the poor stood for the opposite. In the future—Dr. Calamarx proved—the poor would slaughter all the rich, and everybody would be *very*, very happy ever after. "It should be obvious to anybody in his sane mind," Professor Ngama argued, "that, scientifically speaking, both 'theories' produced in this meeting are not only false but reactionary as well. Mr. Rama's pseudo-theory amounts to stating that the alleged 'structures' he concocted are perennial, in other words that wealthy people will always be wealthy, and paupers must remain paupers. As to Mr. Gama's pseudo-theory, it states that, instead of fighting against injustice, poor people should only worry about the possible loss of their sexual prowess. Meanwhile, the real meaning of the legend is quite clear. That the emperor himself was rich is irrelevant to the story, as all the emperors in the past have been rich—only in the universal happiness of the future will the emperors be poor. What is relevant is that the emperor was 'a champion of the poor,' as even my adversaries had to admit. One must therefore conclude that his enemies were champions of the rich, because all struggles are ultimately reducible to the conflict between rich and poor. All known elements of the myth clearly confirm this interpretation. The emperor was defeated by pigs, but pigs, far from being this or that sexual symbol, as the theories of my adversaries purport to show, were symbolic representations of wealth. Indeed, both speakers preferred to overlook a leaflet signed by the Absolutely Revolutionary Invincible World Liberation Movement of Toiling Masses, which clearly says, 'Kill those wealthy pigs!' This noble emperor, champion of the poor, was treacherously murdered by his foes, but Mr. Rama himself proved that his widow subsequently married a poor man. The message of the legend is this: one great warrior for the cause of the poor has been killed, but the struggle goes on. The legend obviously belongs to the folklore of poor people and the truth of Dr. Calamarx's invincible theory has been once again vindicated."

Faced with three conflicting theories, the Academy had to find the truth, as usual, by voting. After four ballots which yielded no clear majority, most fellows in the fifth voting finally opted for Dr. Gama's explanation and so, the truth of Dr. Sigmund Fraud's theory was definitively and scientifically established. Dr. Gama was delighted, while the two defeated scholars, whose errors had been thus exposed, wept bitterly. To defend a wrong anthropological theory may be punishable by death.

Education to Hatred, Education to Dignity

This honorable award places me among people in whose company, naturally, I am proud to be, and yet, at the same time, I am affected
by a certain uneasiness. Among these people are personalities to whom we
must be especially grateful for their spiritual guidance: Albert Schweitzer,
Martin Buber, Karl Jaspers, Sarvepalli Radharkrishnan, Janusz Korczak—
to mention only a few of those deceased. Our gratitude is directed toward
them in particular, because they taught us how to remain aloof from hatred
without escaping from conflict and how to dispense with the language of
hatred. And it is the subject of hatred that I wish to address in a few words.

Even though there is no current political subject I wish to broach, being
Polish and being honored so much by German friends, I cannot refrain
from considering and expressing my belief that it is worthwhile to further
the cause of German-Polish reconciliation at every opportunity, and not
only in a negative sense, that is, to clear away the magnitude of historically
accumulated hatred between our nations. I do not consider old-fashioned
the notion of Central Europe as an area that belongs together culturally; I
dare to believe that the revival of such a cultural area, free of domination, is
possible as well as desirable; indeed, it may even be critical to the fate of
Europe. This I am considering, too, when I make some general remarks
about the phenomenon of hatred.

That a world without hatred is desirable is hardly a productive statement
since scarcely anybody would disagree. Unfortunately, that in itself shows
that this saying alone, without any further explanation, would be of minimal value. But it by no means passes for obvious that such a world will only
become possible, if at all, through a struggle that is free of hatred: in other
words, it will be the more likely to come into being, the less hatred enters

Translated from the German by Wolfgang Freis from *Börsenblatt für den Deutschen
Buchhandel* (Frankfurter Ausgabe, 1977). Revised by the author in English. Originally a speech delivered in Frankfurt on 16 October 1977 on the occasion of receiv-
ing the peace prize of German publishers.

into today's conflicts. After all, almost all forms of hate propaganda appear as means to establish the brotherly world community, and the hatred of evil (or whatever is labeled evil) makes those who hate automatically saintly, as if it were an example of the logical law of double negation: He who hates him, who hates what is holy, is holy himself. It even sounds ridiculous to say that hatred, regardless of its target, produces evil. Anyone recalling Spinoza's simple words, "hatred can never be good," or repeating St. Paul's brief precept of Romans 12:21, "Overcome evil with good," risks being laughed at as a naive preacher or even earning the hatred as an enemy of a better world.

In this context, I shall repeat principles that we may consider distillations not only of the best but the most indispensable and the most invariable of the moral teachings of many great religious prophets and many great philosophers:

> There is no right to hatred, regardless of the circumstances.
>
> It is absurd to say that somebody deserves hatred.
>
> We are capable of living without hatred.
>
> To renounce hatred in no way means to renounce struggle.
>
> Right turns into wrong if it asserts itself by hatred; or—which amounts to the same—it is self-destructive to employ hatred for the sake of justice.

These are thoughts long known, some of which are obviously value judgments, whereas others relate to empirical facts. But it is possible to produce moral as well as factual arguments against them. These may be summed up in three leading ideas: first, hatred is natural and thus unavoidable; second, hatred is effective in any struggle, thus also in the struggle for justice; third, hatred may be justified morally, since there are hateful people and things.

These arguments demand a response.

Surely it is possible that hatred is natural in the same sense as are all other elementary passions. But if this is supposed to mean that nobody would be able to live without hatred, the assertion certainly is wrong empirically; as few as those may be who do not let hatred guide them, they have existed and do exist in our world. In case this assertion suggests, however, that the majority of us, yes, even the overwhelming majority, are too weak to free ourselves from hatred, the assertion may be true, yet this is irrelevant to the moral assessment of hatred, and it does not invalidate at all the precept of living without hatred. All moral precepts are unnatural to a certain extent; they would indeed be superfluous if their function were fulfilled altogether by instincts. Since it is certain, on the other hand, that we are able to control our natural passions, the fact that so many of us live in evil does not make any one individual less evil. We would certainly be in a worse position if we agreed with Luther's notion that God lays down commandments we are not capable of complying with—that God is simply demanding from us unachievable feats. As soon as we ascertain that moral precepts basically exceed our capabilities, all moral distinctions between human beings must almost disappear, regardless of how much we may count on God's mercy.

Against Luther's despair I would like to set Kant's principle: if we know what we *ought* to do according to moral precepts, we also know that we are *able* to do it; indeed, only from the fact that we ought to do it do we learn that we can do it, even though we do not know necessarily whether or not we shall accomplish our obligation in the moment of trial. We do not know for certain if a world without hatred is possible after all, or if there are natural causes that make it impossible. But even if we do not take seriously the anticipation of such a world—if we are convinced that hatred will never be eradicated from the world—this still does not justify our own hatred seething within us. Evil must be part of the world, but woe to him who bears it: this admonition is one of the strongest bricks in the building of Christian civilization. Without it, that is, without the conviction that the statistics of evil do not excuse the evil within *myself*, the notion of responsibility would be vain and superfluous.

Hence, if it is undeniable that hatred begets hatred, this is but a fact of nature, not a fatality that we can resist any more than we can prevent a released body from dropping to the ground instead of rising up. If anyone asked, "Is it reasonable to expect that the victims of Himmler or Beria should not hate their executioners, that people who are being tortured, humiliated, robbed of their freedom, their dignity, and their elementary rights, should be free of hatred for their torturers and oppressors, that all of them should be able to imitate Jesus Christ?" I would answer, "No, we cannot expect anything like it." Still, the question remains whether we have a *right* to hatred even under such inhuman and atrocious circumstances; whether our hatred, as natural and expected as it may be, is morally legitimate; in short, whether there are people who deserve hatred.

It appears, strictly speaking, that hatred can be deserved no more than love. Neither one can be deduced from justice. Something may be deserved only by the power of a law; but no law can demand, impose, or force love; consequently, neither can it demand hatred. Both are given gratuitously, without legal reason.

But one may ask if there are not people, things, movements, and systems that justly deserve complete destruction, and if hatred is not synonymous with striving after total destruction? I would answer that there are certainly human establishments, institutions, customs, endeavors, movements, political systems, beliefs, perhaps even people, who deserve destruction. Hatred, however, is not the same as the desire for destruction (to say nothing of the conviction that something deserves destruction). Our hatred is directed at human beings and human groups—at nations, races, classes, parties, at rich or poor, at black or white—and not at such abstracts as political systems or ideas. *Odium peccati,* hatred of sin, is a metaphor: we can only hate the sinners, and among them, perhaps, ourselves. Hatred is more than striving for destruction; like love, it includes a kind of infinity, that is, insatiability. It does not simply strive for destruction, but for never-ending suffering, to become Satan; and it is the nature of the devil never to be able to reach satiation in the work of destruction.

Herewith we also answer in part the second question: Can hatred ever be effective for a good cause, can it be holy, in this sense? If we ask a complementary question, it becomes apparent that an unequivocal no suggests itself as an answer: Why do all totalitarian systems always need hatred as an irreplaceable tool? They need it not just to maintain a desired readiness for mobilization and not even principally to channel human despair, hopelessness, and accumulated aggression toward others and thus forge them into their own weapons. No, the desire for hatred is explained by the fact that it inwardly destroys those who hate. It makes them morally helpless against the State; hatred resembles self-destruction, or spiritual suicide, and thus it uproots solidarity among the haters. The expression "blind hatred" is pleonastic; there is no other. Since hatred occupies, at least in its complete form, the entire human spiritual sphere in that it is also similar to love, it could appear as a means to integrate personality. But the opposite is the case, which points on the one hand to the asymmetry of love and hate, and on the other hand to the reason why no totalitarian state can renounce education to hatred. Hatred's pure negativity, which paralyzes all human communication, also destroys the inner unity of personality, and hence it is irreplaceable as a means to disarm the human soul.

Our inner integration is the result of consorting with others, of trust and friendship; it is not the result of the self-focused, monadically isolated void of the ego. The all-consuming energy of hatred renders any interchange impossible; and thus it disintegrates me spiritually, even before I am able to disintegrate my enemy. In this sense, one may say that to live in hatred is to live in death, and that hatred, which continuously dominates the mind, becomes doubly degenerated self-necrophilic passion. Totalitarian systems and movements of any orientation need hatred less against external enemies and threats than against their own society, and less to maintain willingness for struggle than to inwardly deplete and make spiritually helpless those whom they educate and summon to hatred, rendering them incapable of resistance. The continuous yet silent message of totalitarianism asserts, "You are perfect, they are perfectly depraved. You would have lived in paradise long since, if the malice of your enemies had not prevented it." The function of this education is less to create solidarity among the haters than to produce a self-complacency in its pupils and to render them morally and intellectually impotent. The self-complacency of hatred bestows upon me the feeling that I am the happy possessor of absolute values. Thus, hatred finally culminates in a grotesque self-idolization, which is—as in fallen angels—only the reverse side of despair.

If we really do love, we are uncritical toward the object of our love. If we really do hate, we are uncritical toward ourselves as well as the object of our hatred; for to be critical means to be able to differentiate, and hatred renders us incapable of any differentiation. It pits our total and unqualified rightness against the total, absolute, and incurable baseness of others.

This, then, is the secret weapon of totalitarianism: to poison the entire mental fabric of human beings with hatred, and thus to rob them of their dignity. As a result of my destructive rage, I am destroyed myself; in my self-complacency, in my innocence, my dignity is lost; my personal cohesion as well as communication and solidarity with others are lost. Hating includes nothing like solidarity; haters do not become friends because they share a detested enemy. Except for moments of direct fighting, they remain alien or hostile to each other, too. Hardly any societies seethe with more clandestine and open hatred and envy than those that attempt to base their unity on hatred and promise to institutionalize brotherhood. And to say that hatred must be repaid with hatred is to say that in order to win in a just struggle, one must first lose the reasons for the legitimacy of this struggle.

It is by no means plausible that we are powerless in fighting without hate; strength in fighting is generated much less from our own hatred than from the cowardice of the enemy. Our cowardice is our own worst enemy; to abandon hatred and fanaticism does not at all mean to withdraw from struggle. It may be true that many of us cannot rid ourselves of cowardice except by means of fanaticism and self-inflicted blindness. But if we therefore conclude that we must mobilize hatred to be successful in a struggle, we immediately jeopardize the validity of the struggle itself.

Education to democracy is education to dignity, and that presupposes two things: a readiness to fight combined with freedom from hatred. Freedom from hatred that is achieved only by escaping from conflicts is a fictitious virtue, like the chastity of eunuchs. Common to all human conflicts, however, is a natural self-impelling and self-accumulating mechanism. Nothing is more commonplace than a conflict that is insignificant by itself escalating to deadly hostility, since the manner in which it is dealt with generates new and more intense conflicts. Reconciliation and willingness to compromise without cowardice, without opportunism, and without conceding what one considers the heart of the matter—that certainly is an art not given freely to anybody as a natural gift. But the fate of the democratic order of the world depends on our ability to master this art.

Two main principles of education are set against each other. Schematically, they may be labeled the Calvinistic and the Jesuit forms of education. I do not insist on the historical exactitude of these terms, which today certainly sound anachronistic. The point is to single out two opposing theories of human nature, each of which suggests its own specific educational rule. Calvinist doctrine proceeds from the assumption that our nature is hopelessly depraved and that redemption depends completely on freely given, undeserved, and—to the human eye—irrationally granted grace; education cannot raise the damned from the abyss any more than it can bring down those predestined for glory. As a consequence, the function of education actually is not to help human beings on the road to salvation but rather to diminish by coercion the number of deeds that offend God—for the sake of God, not of human beings. The rigidity of the irrevocable double predestination makes educational efforts either futile or redundant. The complete depravity of our nature makes it satanic and odious. The need to keep strict reins on external sinfulness tolerates all means.

Jesuit philosophy, on the other hand, assumes not only that nobody on earth is absolutely and hopelessly depraved, but also that all natural instincts and energies contain some good and may be led to good, so that supernatural help will always find something to catch hold of. Although this principle—as well as any other maxim conducive to life—may be, and indeed has been, abused, it includes, I believe, an essentially benevolent attitude toward human beings. It encourages us as much as possible not to abandon the hope of reaching an understanding with other humans; it prevents us from being convinced with certainty that somebody can personify pure evil; thus it weakens the willingness to hate.

The phenomenon of hatred has three dimensions: moral, political, and religious. I intended only to emphasize my opinion that the moral and political sides of hatred do not contradict each other; that is, there is no circumstance under which hatred, although morally condemned, may be recommended as politically conducive to preparing the way for a world free of hatred: the means justify the end. However, religious tradition, at least in our cultural space, calls for more than simple abandonment of hatred: We ought to bestow good on our persecutors, and pray for our enemies. Must such a demand, which violates natural instincts, count as universally binding? Only the greatest banality can be given as an answer: It is certain that only very few are, or ever will be, equal to the task; but the fabric of our civilization rests on the shoulders of these few, and we owe them the little we are capable of doing.

Hatred-charged and conflicting demands and resentments in all regions of the human world—those that recall a *hortus deliciarum* as well as those that rather resemble a penal colony—appear to threaten us at any moment with an all-consuming explosion; on the other hand, indifference or escape from tensions promises only a mild, gradual, and almost imperceptible apocalypse; we are searching for an alchemical formula for the fire of purgatory, a fire that cleanses and carries pain only with hope. No one can boast to have discovered the formula, but we have a vague presentiment that we shall not seek it in vain if we endeavor to unearth it in our philosophic and religious traditions. Proceeding on uncertain and swampy ground, going astray, retreating, here and there circling, we have few reliable points of orientation at our disposal, which may be reduced to a few simple, long-known commands and prohibitions, including the following: Be willing to struggle without hatred; cultivate a reconciliatory spirit without concessions in the essentials.

In a world filled with hatred, vindictiveness, and envy, which to us—less through the poverty of nature than our gargantuan voracity—appears narrower and narrower, hatred is one of those evils, it seems plausible to say, that will not be driven out by any institutional action. In that case, we may assume without exposing ourselves to ridicule that each one of us can contribute to limiting hatred in society by restricting it within ourselves; thus each one of us can achieve for himself the uncertain and fragile anticipation of a more endurable life on our Ship of Fools.